# BEER, BLOOD & CORNMEAL
### Seven Years of Incredibly Strange Wrestling

# BEER BLOOD & CORNMEAL

## SEVEN YEARS OF INCREDIBLY STRANGE WRESTLING

### BOB CALHOUN

Copyright © Bob Calhoun, 2008

Published by ECW PRESS
2120 Queen Street East, Suite 200, Toronto, Ontario, Canada M4E 1E2

LIBRARY AND ARCHIVES OF CANADA CATALOGUING IN PUBLICATION

Calhoun, Bob
Beer, blood & cornmeal / Bob Calhoun.

ISBN 978-1-55022-827-4

1. Incredibly Strange Wrestling. 2. Calhoun, Bob. 3. Punk rock music.
4. Garage rock music. 5. Wrestlers—California—San Francisco—Biography.
6. Journalists—California—Biography. I. Title.

GV1195.C34 2008          796.812092          C2007-907095-7

Editor: Michael Holmes
Cover Design: David Gee
Text Design and Typesetting: Melissa Kaita
Photos are by Roger Franklin unless otherwise noted.
Production and Photo Section: Rachel Brooks
Printing: Webcom


DISTRIBUTION
Canada: Jaguar Book Group, 100 Armstrong Avenue, Georgetown, Ontario, L7G 5S4
United States: IPG, 814 North Franklin Street, Chicago, Illinois 60610

PRINTED AND BOUND IN CANADA

ECW PRESS
ecwpress.com

*To Jackie, my mother,*
*for picking me out of a lineup.*

# CONTENTS

Author's Note **1**

Foreword **3**

**1**   Moving In with the Sasquatch **7**

**2**   The Incredibly Strange Rejects Who
     Stopped Living and Became Mixed-Up Wrestlers **13**

**3**   The Three Mile Baby **35**

**4**   The Fat Kid **55**

**5**   Stinky's Peep Show **75**

**6**   Celebrity Gang Bang **95**

**7**   The Force Field **117**

**8**   Leg Biting Riot! **135**

**9**   The Poontangler and the Devil Chicken **149**

**10**  Ashida Kim, The Ninja **169**

**11**  Christians to the Lions **189**

**12**  The Big-time Politics of Small-time Wrestling **199**

**13**  Uncle N.A.M.B.L.A. **217**

**14**  Hot Man on Man Action **235**

**15**  Warped **261**

**16**  Liquid Gold **279**

**17**  Homomania **305**

**18**  Moving In with the Sasquatch (Slight Return) **321**

**19**  Amsterdamage **333**

**20**  Epilogue **357**

Acknowledgements **363**

Selected Bibliography **365**

# AUTHOR'S NOTE

THE LUNATIC LUCHADORES of Incredibly Strange Wrestling plied their craft under the anonymity afforded them by the masks that almost all of them wore. As I wrote this book, I decided to respect the sense of the unknown that was carefully maintained by promoter Audra Morse (often to the derision of the "smart" wrestling community) and thus used pseudonyms for the majority of the people discussed here. Like the denizens of some kind of s&m scene, those who used to grapple their way through our disturbing one act plays may not want their current co-workers or, hell, spouses to know about the kind of depravity that they unleashed in the squared circle. Where possible, I refer to ISW characters by only their wrestling names whether I was writing about them in the ring or outside of it. Chango Loco, for example, is always referred to as Chango Loco. With wrestlers who portrayed more than one character, as was so often the case, pseudonyms are used for their real selves to protect their privacy while maintaining continuity of narrative. Two people played Macho Sasquatcho and those two also donned other costumes and wrestled as other characters as well. In the case of Audra Morse and others involved with the show who freely gave their real identities to the press during the ISW run covered in this book, I use real names.

As for me? I've officially fessed up to being Uncle N.A.M.B.L.A. and groping poor Lil' Timmy for the amusement of drunk Samoans who really wanted to kick my ass.

— Bob Calhoun

# FOREWORD

MY FAVORITE LOW-BUDGET musical film is *The Incredibly Strange Creatures Who Stopped Living and Became Mixed-Up Zombies* by Ray Dennis Steckler, its director, scriptwriter and major male star. So when I started work on my "ground-breaking" *Incredibly Strange Films* book back in 1982, my first goal was to select a title. I knew that anything perceived as "low culture" was already disrespected and disdained. Therefore I wanted to avoid words with a built-in pejorative aura, such as "B Movie," "Schlock," "Weird," "Bad" ... the list goes on and on.

In the full scope of the book's project — to chart the entire territory of lesser-known cinema ignored by academia and official film magazines — I felt I was dealing with independently created "art" that transcended contemporary "critical" standards of judgment, and crossed borders between genres. Just because a film looks low-budget because it *is* low-budget doesn't mean it can't contain transcendent, absolutely marvelous moments of cinematic "epiphany" and humor — say, classic scenes of writing, acting and direction from an idiosyncratic "genius." The term "incredibly strange" seemed to bespeak an entire area of culture, so after titling the book project *Incredibly Strange Films*, I went on to produce two volumes titled *Incredibly Strange Music, Vol. One and Two*. I had plans to produce *Incredibly Strange Comics, Incredibly Strange Painters, Incredibly Strange Architecture, Incredibly Strange Travel Destinations*, and an *Incredibly Strange People* series . . . but life got in the way.

Nevertheless, I registered the domain name Incrediblystrange. com hoping the website could be a magnet enticing thousands of people to contribute, much like Wikipedia. And maybe it still can happen. (The important "thing" is that the website be monitored for the quality and integrity of its information content.)

So what does this have to do with this book? Around 1995, when I first heard about Incredibly Strange Wrestling, I felt that familiar feeling of hackles rising when one's "territory" is being threatened. But of course, I hadn't invented the adjectival pairing of "incredibly strange" — Ray Dennis Steckler had. And I hadn't gotten his okay when I titled my film book; I just told him the title and he went, "That's great!" So in 1997, when I finally met two members of Incredibly Strange Wrestling, it wasn't in our shared hometown of San Francisco (out of some perverted sense of pride de pique I had avoided seeing the act, although friends had raved to me about it), but in Olympia, Washington, where I had been invited to speak at the Olympia Film Festival, showing, appropriately, a 16mm print of the *Incredibly Strange Creatures Who Stopped Living and Became Mixed-Up Zombies*. The two Incredibly Strange Wrestling members who came up to meet me were Audra Morse and wrestler Chango Loco. Often, when you meet somebody, the first lines out of your mouth determine whether you will make a friend out of the person, and Audra immediately charmed me by bowing down repeatedly extending her arms (as in "making obeisance") and chanting, "We are not worthy! We are not worthy!" Who could resist *that?* If it happened to you, you'd probably like that person for the rest of your life. . . .

In the early '80s, before Incredibly Strange Wrestling was "born," I had already spent dozens of hours renting and watching "incredibly strange" Mexican wrestling films, otherwise known as "lucha libre" (which roughly translates as "free wrestling" or "free fighting") from various video rental stores along 24th Street in San Francisco's Mission District. The street is a haven for Hispanic culture, offering candles, Plexiglas pyramids, posters and countless other iconic artifacts and graphics adopted by hipsters from San Francisco to New Orleans. (A concise but substantial introduction to lucha libre can currently be found on the website www.fwakanimation.com.au/luchalibrelinks.html.)

Now, if this were a "classic introduction" to a book, it would provide a historical context, a section on methodology, a biography and bibliography (and in this case, a filmography and magazine-ography), as well as a summary of the chapters contained within. Even though ideas, factual history and chronological detail are very important, in my mind a book is a failure if it is not also *entertaining*. And when a book is very entertaining (as you'll find in this volume), one can overlook the liberal use of then-current vernacular speech, as well as stylistic quixoticisms. That is the price of reading some kind of actual "truth" committed to paper by a non-academic, non-careerist writer who has actually *lived* the life he is writing about. That writer is Bob Calhoun, who wrestled under the moniker of Count Dante.

We are fortunate that this picaresque saga of one 6'3", 300-pound musician-hulk's experience with the Performance Art entity known as Incredibly Strange Wrestling (ISW) exists at all. During the group's chameleon-like history, and especially during the spectacular comedic pratfalls that caused audiences to roar with laughter, numerous actual physical injuries occurred. Very few historical accounts have captured the improvised behind-the-scenes emergency triage measures inspired by sudden necessity — all because "the show must go on"... no matter where you are in the world, and no matter how few resources you have.

Behind this book's Sturm und Drang emerges an invisible portrait of the group's animating cohesive force-matrix, the "mom" known as Audra Morse. Her position is less than enviable. Imagine the continuous challenge of having to recruit new members, arrange housing, transportation, costumes, props, gigs and tours for a barely professional amateur entertainment troupe of genuinely wild and crazy characters — what a relentless, stress-packed life! From the underground that props up the above-ground world of wwf and other nationally syndicated wrestling venues, Incredibly Strange Wrestling encompassed "real" wrestlers, culturally clashing with veterans of the punk rock of isw. Inevitable conflicts between the two are sometimes funny and sometimes tragic. Since the early 14th century in Europe, and much earlier in countries like India and China, how many unknown stories have there been behind every little touring magic show, mom-and-pop carnival, circus sideshow, and commedia dell'arte (also known as extemporal comedy)? Unfortunately, very few of these stories have yet been recorded.

Nobody in history has ever wanted to work a boring day job — everyone has had fantasies of being an entertainer on the silver stage, going from town to town having unpredictable adventures. As one of the characters in this book says, "You really should be a pro wrestler. It's a great life. You get to go to different towns and fuck different women." So it's no surprise at the end of this autobiography when, despite having survived more than a decade of numerous physical and psychological traumas, our slightly untrustworthy narrator, Bob Calhoun, says, "Each time [I get a call from someone mentioning] starting a new wrestling show, I can't help but run logistics in my head. I start thinking about calling up wrestlers and scaring up a ring and a venue. Every time, Count Dante is just a little bit closer to getting back in the business. . . ."

— V. Vale, www.researchpubs.com
and publisher of the *RE/Search*
"Incredibly Strange" series of books

# 1

# MOVING IN WITH THE SASQUATCH

WRESTLERS GO CRAZY. That's what they do.

You have to be a little crazy to get into the ring in the first place. That goes without saying. Sure it's fake, phony, staged, whatever. That's beside the point. If you get up on that top rope and fall the wrong way or you jump expecting someone to catch you and they aren't there, you can end up in a wheelchair sucking plankton through a tube and shitting in a bag for the rest of your life. That's always a possibility. It's always there in the back of your mind.

But that's not the real reason that wrestlers go crazy. Wrestlers navigate between their mundane realities and a fantasy world of ass-kicking and bloodletting. For some, that fantasy world where they can solve all of their problems by wrapping a steel folding chair around another man's skull is just too appealing. Those wrestlers become the characters that they play in the ring when they're just standing in line at the Dairy Queen waiting for a chocolate dipped cone or withdrawing a few twenties from the ATM.

It makes some kind of sense for a freak like the Macho Man to morph into his in-ring persona. He made millions of dollars off the wrestling game. He's wrestled in front of thousands of people and television audiences of millions more. "Macho Man" Randy Savage doesn't have a day job. He doesn't have to be anybody else but the Macho Man. That's why he can walk around with his muscles flexed to the point where it looks like every vein in his body is about to explode. That's why he can speak as though every syllable he utters somehow causes him internal bleeding, or at least constipation. That's what people want out of him. That kind of behavior gets him product endorsements. Being a spandex-wearing nut job 24/7 helps him step into a Slim Jim ad and collect the residuals.

What was really fucking nuts was when the guys from Incredibly Strange Wrestling started to leave their real selves behind in favor of becoming their purposely ridiculous alter egos. We were rated the worst wrestling promotion year after year by *The Wrestling Observer Newsletter* until Time Warner's wcw was able to wrest that distinction from us by spending millions of dollars producing some of the worst television imaginable. A guy in a chicken suit and El Homo Loco were our biggest stars. We had a Scientologist boy band and a Mexican Viking. People threw tortillas at us. The promoters actually passed them out before the show and encouraged the boozehounds, party girls and retro hipsters that pressed themselves up against the ring to fling them at the wrestlers. Nobody was supposed to take this shit seriously.

What's more, we all had day jobs. We weren't exactly never-beens or also-rans. Incredibly Strange Wrestling was the hottest show in San Francisco during those years when the 20th century collided into the 21st. We started out in the South of Market club scene and ended up selling out the Fillmore more times than many rock stars. We toured the U.S. and Europe and landed ourselves on TV and in newspapers.

Your typical ISW show combined two sets of surreal satire

dressed up as masked Mexican wrestling with raucous post punk sets by bands like the Super Suckers, NOFX, the Dickies, and the Queers. The Donnas once opened for ISW when they were still just fresh-faced schoolgirls from the ritzy suburbs of Palo Alto. After they finished their set of bubblegum arena rock, they had to suffer the indignity of sharing the backstage with a bunch of half-dressed flabby wrestlers. The wrestlers had to strain to avoid leering at so much musical jailbait. At our height, Billie Joe Armstrong of Green Day and James Hetfield of Metallica could be seen shouting at ringside; Jello Biafra of the Dead Kennedys often played the part of a bad guy manager and Fred Durst of Limp Bizkit once even begged to get into our wrestling ring.

We made more money than we ever should have from the wrestling show, but we never could have scratched out a living from it in expensive San Francisco even if we ate at the taco truck every day for the rest of our lives. We all had to be our boring-assed normal selves most of the time. Our livelihoods depended on it. But therein lies the appeal of going utterly bonkers and strutting around Haight Ashbury with your mask on and cursing out street kids like you're a mutant hybrid of Stone Cold Steve Austin and Rey Mysterio Jr.

As Count Dante, I was the deadliest man alive. I owned a mansion and a yacht. I had a kung fu rock and roll success seminar. I could disable any attacker in less than thirty seconds with my killer karate grip. Count Dante didn't default on his student loans or have John Rocker of Rocker Studios confiscate his band equipment for failing to pay the rent for five months in a row. Count Dante never had to leave half his dick at the door so he could shelve library books for eight bucks an hour. But I knew when to leave the Count in the ring or on the rock and roll stage where his penchant for leopard print kimonos and fiery oratory were appropriate. At least I thought I did.

The rest of the wrestlers had their day jobs too. The Cruiser was a web designer and animator but he had no problems diving off a twenty-foot ladder into a vat of canned chocolate pudding when you put him in front of 1,300 paying customers. El Homo Loco worked at a biotech firm. Super Pulga was a schoolteacher and El Pollo Diablo, the eight-foot-tall cock from hell, ran a mailroom at a document delivery company.

Nobody was supposed to take this shit seriously, but they did.

I should have known that it was a bad idea to move in with the Sasquatch. Anyone who dresses in a filthy, sweat-stained Chewbacca suit and demands that people break fluorescent light tubes over his head wouldn't strike most people as stable roommate material.

In his shopworn $99 Halloween costume, Macho Sasquatcho was the Incredibly Strange Wrestling champion. Fans chanted his name when he entered the ring and they cheered wildly when he landed on an opponent's chest with a thunderous leg drop. Macho Sasquatcho started in the early retro punk dive bar days. He fell from grace and was barred from the promotion for over a year, but then came back to wrestle in front of capacity crowds at the Fillmore and barnstormed North America on the Vans Warped Tour during the summer of 2001. Getting tossed through tables or slammed with steel chairs was par for the course. Broken bones and bruises were the risks we took and the price that we paid for the veneer of victory and cult celebrity status.

But the Sasquatch never knew when to leave his violent fantasies in the ring. He started wearing his Wookiee suit and his plastic and pleather championship belt around town for no reason whatsoever. It wasn't to promote an upcoming show or to go to some kind of theme party. He even wore the two-piece ensemble while he slalomed down the Colorado ski slopes on a family vacation.

At first this kind of lunacy was humorous, hilarious in the way that only lunacy can be. Everyone in ISW had a good laugh over it. But after a while even some of the other wrestlers (not exactly the most sensible lot to begin with) started to voice their concern.

"Dante, please don't let the Sasquatch keep the belt," one wrestler pleaded. "It changes him."

Macho Sasquatcho's real name was Tom Corgan. He was a bulgy-eyed man in his early thirties with pasty white skin from staying inside just a bit too much. He walked with a permanent bow-legged waddle from six years of Incredibly Strange Wrestling shows without the benefit of medical coverage. During his matches, he often took spills off the ring apron that practically broke his ankles. Too many times, he came off the top rope and twisted his knee as he attempted some spectacular move in order to attain that much coveted "crowd pop." After beating the shit out of himself to the delight of a concert hall packed with garbage tossing drunks, Tom went home and self-medicated with bong rips and Budweiser and limped around until the pain subsided. From head to toe the cartilage in his joints had lost all of its flexibility sometime after wrestling more than 100 matches in 45 days during the 2001 Vans Warped Tour, which was probably his life's greatest achievement.

Tom's hairline was starting to recede Richard Nixon–style, but once he started doubling as the unmasked neo-nazi heel known as the Oi Boy he took to shaving himself completely bald. During the first set of an Incredibly Strange Wrestling show, he came out to audience applause in that Chewie costume, and during the second set, he gained their ire with a racist tirade as his skinhead character. This duality became alarmingly ingrained in Tom's everyday personality.

Despite his often-bizarre behavior such as ruining parties by bodyslamming unwitting revelers into birthday cakes, Tom was always there for me. He stood by me through all of the silly squabbles and nasty fights that were the behind-the-scenes norm for the wrestling show that had given us both a smattering of local celebrity. He was in my corner. He was my go-to guy. When I was out of work and could barely make rent, he flowed me free slices from the South of Market pizza place where he was employed. It might not have been much, but those gourmet pesto slices really helped me stretch a paycheck. He always helped me move and I helped him move, and he moved apartments a lot between 1997 and 2002. "You really know who your friends are by who shows up to help you move," he said more than once.

But I had seen wrestlers start to really lose it before. The signs were all there with Tom, but they were never that easy to spot. Wrestlers were kind of nuts by definition so the only time you could tell that they had really gone off the deep end was when it was already too late.

I still knew that I should have done everything within my power to keep from moving in with the Sasquatch, but that's just what I did. In December 2002, my girlfriend and I moved in with Tom Corgan. We didn't last two weeks.

# 2

## THE INCREDIBLY STRANGE REJECTS WHO STOPPED LIVING AND BECAME MIXED-UP WRESTLERS

IT WAS THE MID-1990S. The city wasn't what it used to be. Punk was dead. The scene was done. You would hear this over and over again from crusty old scenesters, bitter barmaids or burnt-out homeless hippies.

The city wasn't what it was when Buck Naked was still alive. Buck came out on stage wearing nothing but a cowboy hat, an acoustic guitar and a plunger over his crotch. He strummed demented country tunes long before y'allternative became just another fashion statement. Buck worked at the Paradise Lounge. That was the place to play. Early one morning in 1992, Buck decided to walk his dog in Golden Gate Park after coming home from the bar. Buck got into it with a crazy cab driver who was feeding pigeons out of an oversized bucket of birdseed. The argument got more heated. The cabbie pulled a handgun out of his pail of feed and shot Buck three times. The cabbie spent nearly $1,000 a month on birdseed and he really hated dogs.

Buck Naked's ghost loomed large over San Francisco's music scene. The scene was pussy-assed horseshit compared to the days when the Mummies wrapped their bodies from head to toe in linen bandages and drove to their gigs in a tricked out hearse. They arrived to shows at Redwood City Pizza joints or Fresno Knights of Columbus halls looking like low-budget Imhoteps. They played garage rock in the 1980s when nobody wanted to hear garage rock. They played Silvertones when most guitarists still wanted pink glitter B.C. Rich Biches. Back then guitar snobs called Silvertones and Mosrites "old" or "pieces of junk." Nobody had stumbled upon the phrase "vintage" yet.

The scene ended right after the Dead Kennedys played Jim Jones' Peoples Temple before it was converted into a post office. The scene had a wooden stake driven through its heart the last time that Flipper played the Farm. The scene fucking blew chunks when Journey let that white pants wearing, big nosed fuckwad Steve Perry join the fucking band. The scene was so much cooler when you could drop acid with Hendrix, shoot up with Janis and cop a feel on Grace Slick back when she was hot in a proto MySpace art girl kind of way.

The scene was never going to be as cool as it used to be. We missed the boat. I knew this. But the scene, even in its perpetual decline, was the only one we had. It wasn't like I was going to move back to Menlo Park any time soon.

Back in Menlo Park, I constantly got pulled over in my 1968 blue Chevy for "suspicion of being Hispanic." They saw my dark hair and brown eyes sitting behind the wheel of that Bel Air and they just knew I had to be Mexican. I'm a white trash, Irish Catholic Euro mutt, but racial profiling pigs consistently claimed that my perfectly working headlights and tail lights were out. They wrote me fix-it tickets that I didn't even have to go to Grand Auto over.

I also couldn't get laid to save my life in Menlo Park. I remember bothering the slightly eccentric-looking girls who worked at bookstores and coffee houses to no avail. Sometimes my heart fluttered and sank when I saw a pink haired gal get off the train at posh Atherton. I wondered where she lived and why she was there, but there was never a place to meet her or anyone like her, except for San Francisco.

I started spending five or six nights a week bar-hopping in the city and risking a DUI every time that I made the forty-minute commute back to the cop ridden danger zone of quiet San Mateo County. Sometimes I saw the opening band at a club on Haight Street and then drove across town to SOMA to catch the headliner. It's amazing just how many bands you can tolerate when you're in your twenties. I was like a sponge soaking up distorted guitar fuzz. I was compelled to spend all of my time in cramped and dingy punk rock dives straining to hear vocals through bad PA systems. I swilled beer, stayed up late and went to after show parties in narrow Victorian flats where a bunch of black haired hipsters were crammed into hallways adorned with beautiful ornate molding that was mostly covered up by rock band stickers, Xeroxed fliers and posters that were carefully chosen for their comic irony.

That was back when I rushed to see whatever lo-fi noise outfit was being touted by the newsweeklies on any given Friday. There was an odd aura of significance to seeing something that was at once popular without really being mainstream. It was a balancing act that all of us who fled to San Francisco for one reason or another seemed to pride ourselves in walking. More than anything, I wanted to be in one of those cult bands that could pack the halls without the aid of music videos and product endorsement deals. I longed to be somewhat, but not overly, famous if such a thing was even possible.

Around 1996, I started living in my practice space at Rocker Studios on Third Street, which was kind of like a punk rock YMCA. It even had a working shower and other musicians lived there too. A punk trio named the Bar Feeders all lived together in makeshift bunk beds like a scruffy, skater Three Stooges. Marco Via Lobos, who was always self-recording his band's next album never to finish it, was the kooky caretaker and Craig was the aging glam metaler still chasing his rock and roll dreams. There was also Jesse whom I had mistakenly called Kirk for so long that it practically became the only name he answered to. He was a drum-playing Gulf War I vet who lived with his mom and always talked about going to the Northwest to find some kind of family inheritance that had been stolen from him. No one was going anywhere, but we were all a community living in a kind of clubhouse.

It didn't take all that long before you could sleep while some drummer down the hall worked off his meth high by practicing paradiddles for hours on end starting at 3 A.M. Every Sunday, all of the residents of Rocker went to the Portrero Hill indie-rock club the Bottom of the Hill for their three buck all you can eat barbeque where we caught even more bands and guzzled $2.25 Pabst Blue Ribbons because it was all most of us could afford.

After a little more than a couple months went by, I moved into a shoebox studio apartment at 475 Third Street. My new home had crooked floors that were warped from decades of seismic activity and chipped tiles that were probably elegant when the building was a hotel in the 1930s. The place stank from the Indian guy down the hall who has always beating his wife and burning his curry. The crackheads on the street corner were also my neighbors when they could all pull their SSI checks together for a month's rent. But I was in San Francisco to start a band, play clubs, maybe even live the dream and get a beat-up old van, spending months on end rocking tiny little dives and crashing on floors as I toured the country. Performing, playing bass guitar and being an all-out weirdo mattered more to me than where I was living.

Around this time, I started a band called Count Dante and the Black Dragon Fighting Society. The name was taken from a crazy martial arts master with a badly penned-in afro that placed a barrage of ads for his "World's Deadliest Fighting Secrets" booklet in the *Luke Cage: Hero for Hire* and *Incredible Hulk* comics that I pulled off the spindle racks at the local Quik Stop when I was a kid.

Originally, Count Dante was only going to be the name of my band. Like everyone else we were all going to wear bowling shirts as we cranked out really loud power riffs through vintage amps. But wearing street clothes and standing on stage was just too boring. The Eagles did a reunion tour, charging 100 bucks a pop and just looked like crap. For 100 bucks, I at least want to see Don Henley in a goddamned spacesuit! I decided I wanted to be in the kind of local cult band that people actually showed up to see and I believed the key was to push things farther — weirder than most people were willing to.

I became Count Dante, or at least a relatively chunky version of him. I had my friend Zane's mom Ruby make me custom sequined and animal print karate kimonos. Ruby was the punk rock mom with dyed pink hair. She had been a Bay Area rock and roll backstage force since Jimi Hendrix gave her acid at the Monterey Pop Festival. She was a waitress at the Mabuhay Gardens in North Beach during its hardcore punk heyday, but she always loved rockabilly in all of its forms as long as it was played well or was at least funny.

She took me to see the Dead Kennedys at this punk collective called the Farm when I was only fourteen and she knew everyone from El Vez to Jello Biafra to Sammy Hagar. I honestly believed that having her make my outfits was a surefire path to San Francisco stardom. The only problem with making it in San Francisco was that it was hard to make it anywhere else. San Francisco was international but idiosyncratic.

For the sake of even more authenticity, I spent two hours over a boiling pot dying a beginner's white belt into a karate master's black belt. I made my band members, Ed and Andy, wear regular karate or judo gis as well and started referring to them as "The Black Dragon Fighting Society" because that was the organization that the original Count Dante claimed to front. Since there were only two of them, it wasn't a very large society.

I ran out on the stage, did punches and kicks, and claimed to be the deadliest man alive the way that the real Count had. In my hands Dante became a motivational speaker as well. I delivered what I called "The World's Only Kung Fu Rock and Roll Success Seminar," and my stream of consciousness infomercial spiel became as much a part of our set as guitar solos and drum fills. In between songs I told the meager crowds that I would show them how to "gain the mount on success through the deadly eye gouging and bone breaking techniques of the Orient."

"I will show you how to have success in the job market, the stock market, the board room and the bedroom," I continued with an over-the-top delivery copped from Muhammad Ali then reinterpreted through the karate Elvis, Tony Robbins and Tom Vu for good measure. We played '70s rock at punked out tempos and our songs had names like "Redwood City Rock City" and "Beware the WonderBra."

We managed to get some gigs at the lower end Haight Street and Mission District dives that almost anybody should have been able to play at, but even that took some doing. The rock bottom clubs in the San Francisco music scene had their standards and criteria. To play on a Wednesday night you still had to know people. You had to work it. Booking took a bit of time on a barstool talking up the bartenders who almost always doubled as bookers. It was also a good idea to get to know the bands that you wanted to play with. You couldn't just sit in your apartment and mail out demo tapes, make follow-up calls and expect people to give a shit about your power trio.

The few people who caught our act seemed to be baffled by it more than anything else. Maybe it was the angry vocal style mixed with funny lyrics that caused the confusion. I didn't wear a sign saying, "joke band" on my forehead. People couldn't tell if I was serious or just plain nuts. I could have made things easier on myself if I had just canned what originality I had and started playing oh so ironic three chord punk covers of Carl Douglas' "Kung Fu Fighting" or Rod Stewart's "Do Ya Think I'm Sexy?" Like that familiar wedding DJ still spinning the Commodores' "Brick House," that sort of thing would really get the crowd moving, but it wasn't for me. It would have been like selling out and giving up. It wouldn't have been about music, or about performing or fucking with people. I may have been ripping off my name and building my identity on the back of some obscure kung fu/comic book huckster, but I still believed in writing my own songs, taking that mishmash of borrowed elements and putting my mark on them.

Throwing in the towel and becoming just another kooky cover band would have been like signing up for some infernal poseur popularity contest judged by a cosmic panel made up of Quentin Tarantino, Florence Henderson and Rerun from *What's Happening!!* I had that screw loose where I couldn't have done that and been happy about it no matter how many cute girls with black skirts, little backpacks and horn-rimmed glasses showed up to our gigs.

We were getting a steady string of shows at the Nightbreak on Haight Street, but they were mostly on Wednesday nights. The Nightbreak wasn't a complete dead end for us though. It was kind of the last rock club that was worth a damn left standing in the Haight-Ashbury, which is really pitiful when you consider the neighborhood's history.

The I-Beam, the legendary Haight Street haven of punk and new wave in the 1980s, had closed its doors in the early 1990s, leaving only its sign behind to taunt musicians and club goers with the memories of what it once had been. The sign's continued existence also kept alive the rumors that the club would one day reopen and usher in some kind of noisy new era. It never did.

The Nightbreak had these free shows called "Sushi Sundays" where unknown bands could play and theoretically build followings. They actually had this Japanese guy who set up his sushi cart in a corner and made some surprisingly good California rolls. He brought in all of his own ingredients and unloaded them out of the trunk of his car in a bunch of ice chests. It kind of made me feel better to know that he was handling all of the food himself because the thought of raw fish being stored in the filthy backroom of the Nightbreak wasn't all that appetizing.

Decent bands with a draw still played the Nightbreak because the club owners would actually put a couple hundred bucks together for guarantees. There was this eclectic metal/funk/surf band called M.I.R.V. (named after a Nixon era missile defense system) with a comedic stage show and funny lyrics that still gigged at the Nightbreak. I really wanted a shot at opening for them. As silly as it seems today, that was a pretty big deal to me back then. Still, those Wednesday nights combined with a couple of free Sundays weren't really moving me up the ladder. Playing the opening slots for the bigger bands was the ticket to building that elusive thing known as "a following."

Fast Mike was this short, scrawny scenester who was our biggest booster back then. He booked the Nightbreak's midweek slots (but not the coveted weekends) and he was the one who kept booking us there. He also liked to have me rant and rave on the spoken word shows that he and Matty Fuckface put together. Fast Mike was one of those precious guys who got it. He looked like he should play drums for the Ramones and he was religiously devoted to this 1980s New York psychedelic punk outfit called the Fuzztones that used to turn up occasionally on the USA Network's long since defunct Saturday night video show *Night Flight*.

Living off student loans and doing as little as possible, I spent my afternoons at the Nightbreak sloshing oat-laden hippie microbrews and choking down stale "oriental bar snack" poured out of plastic sacks from Costco. One afternoon Fast Mike gave me the hard sell about hooking up with Incredibly Strange Wrestling.

"Look, man," he said, "with those karate suits and those speeches of yours, you've just gotta join Incredibly Strange Wrestling. You'd be perfect at it. Look, I'll give you Audra's phone number. You've got to give her call."

I nodded in Mike's direction, but the prospect of bugging Audra made me more than a little hesitant to take that number. Audra Morse was a large and imposing woman with a pretty face and nothing but attitude. She could break down punk rock veterans with an expletive-laced tirade and "You asshole!" seemed to be her favorite salutation. Although she rarely took a drag off a cigarette, she spoke with the husky, smoky voice that you'd expect from the promoter of both Incredibly Strange Wrestling and Stinky's Peep Show ("The Home of the Large & Lovely Go-Go Girls"). I had bothered Audra before about booking my band, but my efforts only annoyed her and actually seemed to set me back. I left the Nightbreak that day without getting her phone number.

But Fast Mike was shockingly persistent. He ran me down on Haight Street one afternoon while he was posting fliers and he took the time to scrawl Audra's digits across the back of one of his handbills. I took it and folded it up into my pocket, but I didn't forget about it.

I had seen Incredibly Strange Wrestling. I knew what it was all about. I was a little bit skeptical, but Fast Mike was right. It was the show that I needed to play. It was a perfect fit and maybe wrestling a few matches and making some speeches that got the crowd riled up was the way to create a buzz for my band and everything else that I aspired to do. Hundreds of people were already packing South of Market clubs to see this retrobilly, masked Mexican wrestling spectacle of sleaze. It was the best way possible to get the Count Dante name out there.

Incredibly Strange Wrestling got its start in 1995 when Crazy Robin, the owner of the Paradise Lounge, decided that he needed a concert hall where the floor space wasn't constricted by the Paradise's support beams, bracing walls and balconies. He bought the transmission repair shop next door to his club and named it the Transmission Theater as an odd homage to the building's past.

Audra booked the Paradise back then although she was barely old enough to drink in it. Despite being fresh-faced and in her early twenties, she could still bark out orders with the best of them and she convinced Robin to break in the Transmission with an after-hours wrestling show put on by her and the rockabilly bastard Johnny Legend.

Johnny Legend sported a beard that stretched all the way down to his navel, making him look like ZZ Top's burnt-out junkie cousin. He had fronted rockabilly revival bands since the early 1970s, but more important he was a pro wrestling and monster movie nut without equal. When he was a kid he hung around the Olympic Auditorium in L.A. just waiting for the chance to meet the hated heel Freddie Blassie. Legend started a Blassie fan club in the early 1960s — a time when most fans thought that pro wrestling was real and no one dared to lionize the bad guys. Legend's adolescent devotion to his trash-talking idol paid off, as he and Blassie became the best of friends.

In 1975, Legend wrote the music and lyrics for a pair of Freddie Blassie novelty tunes called "Pencil Neck Geek" and "Blassie — King of Men." By the 1980s, Legend hooked up with the equally wrestling-obsessed Andy Kaufman and introduced the reality-bending performance artist turned reluctant sitcom star to Blassie. The trio collaborated on Kaufman's art film spoof *My Breakfast with Blassie*, in which Legend earned a director's credit for holding the camcorder steady while Freddie spewed a string of off-color remarks and Kaufman discussed fake snot gross-out gags. Legend even has a brief cameo as a turban wearing guru alongside Jim Carrey in the disappointing Kaufman biopic *Man on the Moon*.

If the concept of Incredibly Strange Wrestling with its hodgepodge of rockabilly, lucha libre and monster movie gimmicks was anyone's brainchild, then it had to be Legend's. In the 1980s Legend even wrote articles for the splatter mag *Fangoria* where he tried to sell gore obsessed thirteen-year-olds on the idea of Mexican monster wrestling movies from the 1960s and '70s. These south of the border cinematic gems combined lucha with spy stories and dime store gothic horror where protagonists such as El Santo and Mil Mascaras were always just a monkey-flip away from defeating the legions of Satan.

The "Incredibly Strange" part of the show's name was most likely cribbed from the Ray Dennis Steckler zero-budget zombie flick *The Incredibly Strange Creatures Who Stopped Living and Became Mixed-Up Zombies*. Billed as "the first monster musical," its dialectic of badly recorded rock and roll numbers, disjointed dance sequences and papier-mâché undead even looked like an early isw show.

Another possible source for the "Incredibly Strange" label was V. Vale's RE/Search guide *Incredibly Strange Films*, which spotlighted the exploitation films that were Legend's stock in trade and made them cool to new wavers, goths and the skate punks who actually took the time to read *Maximumrocknroll* from cover to cover. When punk rock hit San Francisco's North Beach in 1977, Vale became its scribe with his self-published *Search & Destroy* zine, which lay the intellectual framework for the scene that isw later sprang from. His film book, with its striking black and white cover image of a gigantic floating skull looming towards a buxom blonde babe, features an interview with Steckler and other innovative exploitation filmmakers as well as essays on Santo, sexploitation and Edward D. Wood, Jr. But whichever source inspired isw's name, it showed the unmistakable hand of Legend. Realistically though, both Vale and Legend were siphoning off the brand that Steckler inadvertently created with the overly long title of his 1964 monster mash, and both would gladly admit this.

Although everyone in Los Angeles loved Legend, no one seemed to want to work with him. It took Audra in San Francisco to get the ball rolling on the wrestling freak show. To do this, she relied on a coterie of tattooed neo-greasers who were either barroom bouncers that she worked with at the Paradise or players in the SF psychobilly scene. August "Augie" Ragone was the mouth of the group, "Hellbilly" Barry came up with most of the characters and costumes, and Brett Kibele was Audra's right-hand man. They all propped up their hair with pails full of pomade, but they never held up liquor stores or ransacked small towns like the celluloid juvenile delinquents that they modeled themselves after. In reality, each owned as many monster toys and action figures (all carefully preserved in their original bubble wrap) as any ten *Star Wars* geeks together. If Legend was part of the second generation of rockabilly dude, and the Stray Cats were the third, then these guys were the fourth.

For what little organization there was, Augie, Barry and Brett were all organization men and they also donned masks and doubled as wrestlers. Audra often tried to pass them off as Mexican lucha libre stars but their pasty white skin and the flaming dice and nautical star tattoos that lined their arms and legs clearly told audiences otherwise. Lingering doubts that anyone had as to these grapplers' national origin were quickly put to rest whenever they took the microphone and unleashed a torrent of Nor Cal accented expletives in clear if not perfect English.

Brett wrestled as Borracho Gigante (The Big Drunk) and his only discernable wrestling move was to bust a big can of beer over his opponent's head. Barry was by far the most creative of that early corps and he was the only one who possessed a shred of in-ring training and acrobatic ability. Augie's characters usually took their names from the old monster movies that were his obsession.

The inaugural ISW show took place in late March 1995. It was an invite-only/after-hours affair held in the then soon-to-be-opened Transmission Theatre right after Johnny Legend's set at the adjoining Paradise Lounge. I didn't go to that first show, but I was aware of it. My costume maker, Ruby, was sent an invitation because Legend was always proposing marriage to her. She never went for it because Legend wouldn't shave off that crumb-catching beard of his.

Ruby told me about the show and even gave me the secret password to get into the wrestling matches, but I was tied up that night at this Korean-owned Scottish pub called the Edinburgh Castle — of all things opening for *Trainspotting* author Irvine Welsh with my spoken word act. It was probably a better move for me to keep the gig with Welsh. My lambasting monologue about the surgeon general, disembowelment and decapitations seemed to go over pretty well with the packed house at the Castle and, for whatever it was worth, it even earned me some ink in a newsweekly in Scotland.

I was still driven to make it to that first isw show, however. I even attempted to convince Welsh and his Eurotrash cronies to come along with me in my rusted out '68 Chevy but they were far too preoccupied with scoring E, getting all touchy feely and jumping around to Celtic Soloflex music so it was a no-go.

Years later, I saw that first show while sifting through hours of old isw vhs footage for that ever elusive video release that we'd always been struggling to put together. For that show, they didn't have a wrestling ring or anything that was remotely close to one. All of the matches were held on a dirty tarp draped over some broken down wood pallets. The first match consisted of a couple of bouncers wearing masks demonstrating simple high school wrestling take downs that they probably hadn't used since their very last scholastic Greco-Roman meet.

In those early morning hours the main event pitted Audra herself in a mask that looked like heavy metal icon King Diamond's face makeup against some uncoordinated chick that she barely even knew. Audience members jumped on the riser at random intervals and tried to attach themselves to the wrestlers for no reason whatsoever as plastic cups, ice and beer bottles flew in every direction. The wrestling, if you could call it that, was godawful and overall the show was an incoherent wreck. But through the boozy recollections of that initial audience, a legendary success was born and there was a ton of demand for a follow-up.

The first isw show that I attended was their second effort. By this time the Transmission Theatre had officially opened for business and Audra and company had managed to get their hands on an honest-to-God wrestling ring complete with ring ropes, ring posts and turnbuckles — the whole nine yards. There was a small stage set up behind the ring where the bands played. They projected clips of old El Santo movies and black and white wrestling matches onto one of the side walls to remind people of the aesthetic that they were going for. There were no stools, chairs or arena seating of any kind; the crowd was forced to mill about as two full bars poured the beer and the booze. There was something unsettling about that because fake fighting and alcohol should have added up to one hell of a riot.

The wrestling was greatly improved as well as Audra was forced to spring for some Tijuana luchadores who could pull off all of the high-flying moves that were promised by her promotional hype. She also made use of what were obviously local, independent wrestlers. Independent wrestlers or indie workers meant either has-beens cast off by the WWE or WCW (like the Honky Tonk Man or Jake "The Snake" Roberts) who were still trying to pick up a paycheck off their former big league glory or else they were the kids who had shelled out thousands of dollars to those dubious pro-wrestling schools in the hopes of making it into the majors. Audra hired the latter variety.

But using these guys always posed a problem for the promotion. Sure, the match quality increased by leaps and bounds over using enthusiastic but untrained monster geeks and hipsters, but indie workers by their very nature were a conservative lot and the vast majority of them always tried to make Incredibly Strange Wrestling as generic as possible.

That second ISW show opened with a match between a roly-poly blond guy and a longhaired Chicano in one of those kung fu gis that made him look like a Chinese waiter. It was really the kind of match that could have been on the bill at any low-budget pro wrestling card on a Saturday afternoon at your local high school gym. There was nothing either incredible or strange about it, but it was just the prelim.

More competent but uneventful matches followed until a wrestler called the Abortionist entered the ring. He wore surgical scrubs bathed in blood and brandished a baby doll head skewered on a gnarled coat hanger. He was fighting for a woman's right to choose. This is what I was paying for when I put down my money to see something called "Incredibly Strange Wrestling." His opponent for the evening was a masked Christian wrestler who constantly cheated to win as the Abortionist was positioned as the good guy! It was San Francisco after all and finally I was seeing something that wouldn't play at the Kern County Rec Center. The Christian won the match by clouting the Abortionist over the head with a big, shiny cross while the ref's back was turned. The fans at the half-full nightclub booed wildly. That match was everything that Incredibly Strange Wrestling aspired to. It was everything that it should be.

The card quickly degenerated. As with the first show, Johnny Legend and his band provided a portion of the evening's musical entertainment with their usual covers of the theme songs to American International '50s exploitation flicks such as *High School Caesar* and *I Was a Teenage Werewolf*. Legend wore a sequined jacket that was given to him by Freddie Blassie — at least three sizes too big for the emaciated rockabilly frontman.

Another awful, pro-wrestling inspired punk band called Foreign Object also played and they spent most of their set insulting this statuesque transsexual ring girl, which did save us from having to hear them strain to play their instruments. "Hey honey, we had hotdogs for dinner," Foreign Object's sweaty frontman said repeatedly until the statement had lost any of its Andrew "Dice" Clay–like shock value. When the spat between the lone shemale and the rude and crude rock band started to get physical, Legend (never one who struck me as the voice of reason) got on the mic and tried to calm the situation down. As the thinning but die-hard crowd at the Transmission had had way too much to drink by this point, things started to get ugly. I took this as my cue to leave.

Despite the awe-inspiring appearance by the Abortionist and his bloody coat hanger, I would be lying if I said that I was hooked on ISW after seeing that show. It wasn't a defining moment in my life where I was reduced to some kind of stalking fan boy who had to attend every last ISW card, wait for it to end, and then beg anyone who would listen for my shot in the ring. There were plenty of those guys, but I wasn't one of them — at least not at first. Sure, it should have dawned on me that ISW was a perfect fit for my "talents" being a 300-plus pound loudmouth (well, maybe back in my svelte days I only cut 290 pounds), but it didn't. I was glad that I went, but it honestly felt like the kind of thing that you shell out for once or twice just to tell everyone that you did it.

Even with the show's lack of production values, or maybe because of them, ISW kept gaining momentum behind a cast of crude characters that lived up to the show's lofty name. The Abortionist was soon joined by his arch nemesis Cletus the Fetus. There was also the Ku Klux Klown who made his ambitious entrance wearing full Grand Cyclops garb and clutching a burning cross only to tear off his sheet after stepping through the ring ropes to reveal a twisted, sharp toothed circus clown underneath. The Klown often teamed up with a wrestler named Harley Racist to battle a Hasidic Jewish tag team led by Yom Ripper.

The most disgusting member of an overall revolting cast was the wrestler with the somewhat generic name of J. R. Benson. He somehow always got knocked unconscious during his matches and had to be revived by his valet. In her first attempt, the valet tried rubbing her panties in his face. When that failed, she squatted down over his head and actually urinated all over him. Needless to say, this did the trick and he was able to continue his match without being disqualified, but I'd really hate to be the unlucky opponent who had to do a collar and elbow tie-up with him while his face was dripping with skank piss. I think that I'd have rather taken a loss due to referee count-out on that one.

There were also a few wrestlers inspired by less than classic monster movies such as the Aztec Mummy, which was one of early ISW's better costumes. Not coincidentally, Johnny Legend distributed VHS copies of the 1964 Mexican monster-wrestling epic *Wrestling Women Vs. the Aztec Mummy*. With its caped grappling gals exchanging holds with an ancient terror from Tenochitlán, the film not only served as a blueprint for the linen wrapped ISW wrestler, but for the whole show. Sadly, for his video version of that movie, Legend committed a psychotronic act of sacrilege and replaced its original musical score with some sub par surf and rockabilly instrumentals to the disappointment and outrage of Mexican mummy movie purists the world over.

Joining the Aztec Mummy was the Amazing Caltiki, who got his name from a 1959 Italian produced monster romp called *Caltiki the Immortal Monster*. The film was co-directed by Italian horror great Mario Bava and concerned an amorphous flesh-eating blob brought to life by a Mayan curse. The wrestling Caltiki wasn't quite so inspired as his namesake; he was just another rockabilly blowhard wearing an imported lucha mask.

Even as late as 1996, the World Wide Web as we know it today with its nearly omnipotent Google searches, intrusive pop-up ads and easily accessible online dating services, was still waiting around the corner. The Internet and its then clunky Yahoo! interface were just something that you may have had the chance to look at while loafing at your temp job. Most people still weren't hooked up in their homes back then, and everyone still checked the local newspaper or called the multiplex for movie showtimes.

But wrestling fans were surprisingly early adapters of technology. ISW with its array of politically incorrect character names, burning crosses and golden showers received a bit of a buzz in pro wrestling Usenet groups and online bulletin boards. Most of this interest among the die-hards was spurred by the diligent reporting of David Meltzer in his one-half industry insider sheet and one-half gossip rag "The Wrestling Observer Newsletter."

"The Observer," as it is affectionately called in wrestling fandom circles, is comprised of 12–18 double columned pages of eyestrain inducing eight-point type that goes into excruciating detail on every facet of the professional wrestling business. In the days before Vince McMahon came clean about the showbiz nature of what he then labeled "sports entertainment," Meltzer was the only one reporting on what really went on in pro wrestling's backrooms. This kind of honest journalism earned him the ire of many promoters and wrestlers — as well as a list of devoted subscribers.

The newsletter contained deeper analysis of television ratings than you could even find in *Broadcasting and Cable* combined with exhaustive criticism of the success or failure of certain storylines. Storylines were referred to as "booking" in wrestling parlance and Meltzer ceaselessly delved into whether or not the booking of a particular feud (often referred to as "programs" or "angles") made sense from a proper dramatic perspective. When storylines went nowhere or were out-and-out dropped with no explanation (an all too common occurrence even in the wrestling big leagues like the WWE and definitely in the waning days of Time-Warner's WCW), Meltzer let the world know that "the booking doesn't make sense," or "they didn't build up to it." You couldn't find more intricate writing on the mechanics of drama and storytelling in the literature stacks of a university library.

Reading "The Observer," you couldn't help but wonder where

David Meltzer would be if he had channeled his impressive attention to detail into Middle East studies or sociology instead of the
trials and tribulations of spandex wearing musclemen.

Once names like the Ku Klux Klown, Cletus the Fetus and
Harley Racist started cropping up in "The Observer," there was a
small clamor for videotapes of the shows by curiosity seekers and
wrestling completists. The audacious but amateur nature of ISW also
set off many turgid BBS debates on whether or not the show was in
fact pro wrestling. Oddly, these discussions mirrored arguments in
the art world over the merits of Andy Warhol's repeated images of
*Campbell's Soup Cans*.

With Incredibly Strange Wrestling's honest combo of rock and
wrestling and that all important psychobilly street cred, the music
world was also quick to notice the new oddball form of punk entertainment. The promoters of the 1995 Lollapalooza tour contacted
Johnny Legend and asked him if his new wrestling group could
perform on some West Coast tour dates.

Lollapalooza was an eclectic alternative music road show that
brought the kinds of alternative, goth, punk and industrial bands
that used to only play clubs and theaters to major outdoor arenas.
During the 1980s, performers like Henry Rollins or the Butthole
Surfers were content to play the bigger range of punk rock clubs.
With Lollapalooza, they performed in front of hundreds or thousands of high school kids wearing ripped up fishnet stockings and
store-bought Dead Kennedys T-shirts as all of that fair skin (on
stage and in the audience) sizzled under the bright summer sun.

By 1995, Lollapalooza was in its fifth year and already an insti-
tution that had even been spoofed on *The Simpsons*. With only a
couple of shows under its belt, ISW was going to be another freak-
show on its fair way, joining the unsigned band stage, the recycling
awareness table and the body piercing booths.

The tour that year was headlined by Sonic Youth and also included
Courtney Love's Hole whose *Live Through This* album was critically

acclaimed, highly successful and indispensable for angry young women with natty platinum blonde hair. isw's first Lollapalooza show was on the Fourth of July at the Gorge Amphitheatre near Seattle. Camera crews from MTV and E! Entertainment Television were on hand as Audra, in her masked wrestling persona, called out Courtney Love to a no-holds-barred death match. Love, the grieving widow turned gutter slut icon declined the challenge, saving all of her wrestling for much later in L.A. County courtrooms.

Thirty thousand concertgoers attended the Lollapalooza show that day, leading David Meltzer to mistakenly report that the isw show had "the largest paid crowd to witness pro wrestling in North America in 1995."

While that may have been the number of people who put down their money to see Hole and Sonic Youth, that wasn't how many of them actually paid attention to isw. A pesky newsgroup poster going by the name of Clint Larson wrote that, "There were more people playing the Sega Saturn than watching [the wrestling]."

Another Usenet fan named Michael Cox who also attended the show reported: "I was there, and the wrestling took place at the third stage (called The Lab) tucked into one corner by the food tents (and far, far away from the main stage.) Five hundred people might have been watching at any given time, if they were lucky."

Still, all fan boy sniping aside, Lollapalooza was a start for isw and potentially a big one. Besides, most indie wrestling promoters would give their eye teeth to have as many as 500 fans watch their matches — most small-time wrestling cards were lucky to draw just 100 people paid or unpaid. Lollapalooza landed isw on MTV as well as in the pages of the *Seattle Post-Intelligencer* and the *San Francisco Chronicle*.

Legend and Audra co-promoted a few more Lollapalooza programs, but their collaborative relationship fell apart almost as quickly as it had started. The kinds of lowlifes that Legend had wrestling for him proved to be too creepy even for Audra. The rigors of getting into a cramped work van and touring with them forced her to sever ties with the bearded rock and roller who had created the show that she considered herself part owner of.

When you consider that *Celebrity Death Match, South Park, Jackass* and the cable TV pro wrestling wars were all on the near horizon in 1995, the exposure from Lollapalooza should have at least resulted in a cable TV developmental deal for ISW. Instead those tour dates nearly destroyed the show and resulted in a Trotsky–Stalin-like schism between Legend and Audra with both of them promoting their own shows under the Incredibly Strange Wrestling banner. Legend took L.A. and Audra ruled in San Francisco as both sides claimed legitimacy. It was a typical creative divorce where ownership of a piece of intellectual property isn't exactly easy to prove or establish. Legend created the show but Audra was the one who made it happen.

Audra's San Francisco shows were far better than Legend's Hollywood productions; the Southern California product never improved much past those early ISW efforts. Although Johnny Legend was soon relegated to only promoting his matches at the annual *Fangoria* horror movie conventions in Pomona, Audra, with her greater ambitions, was more damaged by the breakup. Hollywood, with its TV networks and movie studios, would always be out of her reach. The Southern Californian scenesters in the know regarded Audra as the one who ripped off the lovable Legend. She could never put together a wrestling show in that city's nightclubs using the ISW name, where being seen by hip starlets, Hollywood brat packers, movie moguls and TV producers was not just a possibility but a likelihood.

As Johnny Whiteside in the *LA Weekly* put it as late as 2000, forevermore Audra was the leader of "the Frisco troupe of turkey necks who flat-out hijacked local madman Johnny Legend's 'Incredibly Strange Wrestling' concept and format."

# 3

# THE THREE MILE BABY

THE FIRST TIME I called Audra was a miserable failure. I punched in the number that Fast Mike had scribbled on the back of that flier and got Audra's answering machine. I left a message that sounded more like I was applying for a job at a bank than a red blooded bruiser trying to muscle his way onto a wrestling card.

"Hello Audra," I said in a calm, measured tone. "I got your number from Fast Mike at the Nightbreak. My name is Bob Calhoun, but I perform a kung fu spectacular under the name of Count Dante and Fast Mike assures me that I would be perfect for Incredibly Strange Wrestling…."

I meandered on like that, eventually leaving my home number. Needless to say, I didn't exactly impress her. Weeks went by without a callback.

At first I didn't give a shit about ISW, but as time went by without hearing anything, I started to feel like my one big break was slipping through my fingers. I called her back and summoned the full fury of my feuding wrestler voice.

"THIS IS COUNT DANTE," I bellowed into her answering machine. "I AM A MASTER OF MARTIAL ARTS! A MASTER OF KUNG-FU AND A MASTER OF BRAZILIAN JIU JITSU AND I AM HERE TO TEST MY SKILLS IN THE BRUTAL ROCK AND ROLL BLOODSPORT THAT IS INCREDIBLY STRANGE WRESTLING! I CAN WRESTLE! I CAN TALK AND I CAN ROCK! I CAN DO IT ALL! MY NUMBER IS 555-2925! THAT NUMBER ONCE AGAIN IS 555-2925! CALL ME NOW!"

Audra called me back about two hours later.

"This is Audra from Incredibly Strange Wrestling," she said. Her voice was gravelly yet somehow feminine. "I'm looking for . . . Count Dante."

She paused before saying my name as if for dramatic effect, but you could almost hear her rolling her eyes on the other end of the line.

"This is Count Dante," I said, struggling to sound stern and macho without yelling in her ear.

Audra cut quickly to the point and asked if I could wrestle.

"Well, I train in Brazilian Jiu-Jitsu," I replied making the most of my meager martial arts credentials.

"Well, that's not wrestling," she shot back.

"Oh, but it is," I said pleading my case. "Jiu-jitsu, like judo, is a grappling art. It isn't about punches and kicks like kung fu or karate. It's made up of wrestling moves like take downs, armbars, and chokeholds. In wrestling you go to a pin, but in jiu-jitsu we go to a submission. The mechanics are the same though. We still learn how to throw people and how to take falls."

Now really, Audra was right about this. Jiu-jitsu may have been grappling but it sure wasn't pro wrestling. There is nothing really like pro wrestling. It is neither fish nor fowl. While the art form does have some relation to the fighting disciplines that it mimics, its similarities are merely superficial. The object of judo, jiu-jitsu, boxing or collegiate wrestling is to beat your opponent. The object of big-time wrestling is to create the illusion of a fight. Other fighting arts are competitive while professional wrestling is cooperative. Pro wrestling utilizes a wide array of moves and signals that I knew nothing about. Audra was much more exposed to pro wrestling than I was, but while she knew that jiu-jitsu "wasn't wrestling," she wasn't exactly sure how it wasn't. It was a case of the blind leading the blind.

Audra was still listening. This gave me an opening to further my pitch: "Plus I already have the wardrobe. I have a closet full of sequined karate gis. You know kimonos, robes. I have a leopard spotted one; a red, white and blue one with red sequins; and some others."

Audra seemed more impressed by my ring attire than by my grappling experience. I told her that my kimonos were sewn by Ruby. She knew who Ruby was. Even in San Francisco, a woman in her forties with hot pink hair who showed up to see every psychobilly band that came through town tended to stand out. By working the clubs, Audra had seen a lot of Ruby. I'm not sure if that hurt or helped me, but Audra relented from her tough girl persona long enough to tell me to drop by the afternoon of the next ISW show at the Transmission.

That show fell on Friday, February 14, 1997 — Valentine's Day. I had been living in the city for a couple of years by that point and all I had to show for it was a band mired in the futility of playing Wednesday midnight gigs. My dreams of coming to San Francisco and becoming some kind of king of the weirdos or a low-level rock star weren't panning out and I wasn't having that much luck with the ladies either. The usual extent of my romantic life consisted of striking out with bespectacled art girls with tiny backpacks at trendy bars. Needless to say, I wasn't doing anything else that Valentine's Day.

What I did have going for me though was a really cool 1966 Oldsmobile Starfire with power windows and bucket seats. Its copious amount of chrome shone and the body was painted with that sparkly rust acrylic that was called '57 Chevy Bronze. It had sleek lines and looked like a sports car only so much bigger that I could fit my bass amp in the trunk without anyone knowing it was in there. Its only drawback was that I sometimes had to circle the block more than five or six times to find a scarce piece of San Francisco curbside big enough to park it legally.

I wasn't going to show up to the Transmission that day as just another bowling shirt wearing nobody. I needed to make as big a splash as possible so I wore the gaudiest gi that Ruby had made for me. It was a star spangled kimono with red sequined trim and a short Elvis cape that was held on by strips of Velcro. I found a parking space by this "straight friendly" gay bar called the Stud. It was San Francisco. The city was full of freaks so nobody even gave me a second look as I made my way two blocks up Harrison Street from my car to the Transmission. I burst into the still closed nightclub looking like a crazed karate super patriot but everyone was too busy to notice.

The Transmission Theatre was a hub of activity as various neo-greasers climbed through the rafters above the ring adjusting the lighting for the night's show. I recognized most of them as bouncers and barbacks from the Paradise Lounge from the hours that I'd spent trying to get shows there. Brett Kibele stood in the ring adjusting the tension on the ring ropes with an oversized monkey wrench while some other roadies and stagehands erected a platform in the far corner of the venue for the bands to play on.

Diffused sunlight shone through the Transmission's oversized garage doors. This only made the place seem darker than usual. All it illuminated were the dingy wooden countertops and the grease stained concrete floor. An odor permeated the air that combined the scent of spilt whiskey with all of the gallons of red transmission fluid that had long since seeped into the cracks in the flooring.

Audra stood over by the main bar, clipboard in hand, and dealt with the ceaseless minutiae of putting on a show that encompassed several rock bands and two overly stuffed sets of wrestling.

This was the first time that ISW expanded its domain from just the Transmission to the adjoining Paradise so Audra had to deal with three extra bands on top of everything else.

There was a crowd of people milling about Audra as she leaned up against a chrome barstool. Guitarists wanted to know what time they had to soundcheck, wrestlers wanted to know who they were up against and just about everyone needed to claim a handful of drink tickets or put people on the guest list.

"I don't have fucking drink tickets yet!" Audra screamed as if the whole city block needed to hear her. "You are all going to have to fucking wait! The show doesn't start for six goddamned hours! I will let you all know when I need names for the guestlist, until then calm the fuck down!"

"You all have something better you could be doing than bothering me," she added at a somewhat reduced volume. She made a slicing gesture with her flattened hand as if to visually communicate that the matter was closed. Following that barrage, I decided that it probably wasn't a good time to approach her.

I stood around the middle of the floor with some other wannabe wrestlers who were hoping to get their shot. One of them was Tom Corgan. Like the rest of us, he was in much better shape back then when he was still in his mid-twenties. His gait hadn't developed that permanent waddle from those subsequent years of squared circle violence. His hairline was only receding and he still had plenty of strands on top. Tom was years away from the consistent head shaving that left him in the guise of the skinheaded Oi Boy whether he was wrestling or not.

It was before the Sasquatch, before the Oi Boy, before any of it. We were both just guys jockeying for a spot on the wrestling card, trying to get our little piece of local fame. We were the misfits who were made fun of in high school. We were the nutcases who couldn't get promoted at our jobs. In the fringes, the back alleys and nightclubs we could be stars by putting on one act morality plays with one fall and a ten-minute time limit. But right at that moment, on Valentine's Day 1997, both Tom and I were outsiders looking in and he needed me as much as I needed him.

Corgan and I had met before at this standard-issue sports bar that was down the street from my apartment. He was drinking a pint of beer then and working on a large platter of chicken wings soaked with Tabasco sauce. One of us must have been wearing some Gracie Jiu-Jitsu paraphernalia because we struck up a conversation about the finer points of Brazilian grappling arts. Brazilian Jiu-Jitsu was all the rage in martial arts in the mid-1990s and was by far the most homoerotic fighting style ever developed. So much of it relied on this defensive position called "the guard," which entailed lying on your back, wrapping your legs around your opponent's midsection, thus stunting his attack. While this method was effective and you could incapacitate your opponent with an armbar or chokehold from this seemingly compromised position, to the random onlooker it really just looked like a bunch of guys in white pajamas lying around dry humping each other.

Tom trained at Crazy Carlei Gracie's school in North Beach. Carlei was a loose cannon uncle of the more famous Royce and Rickson Gracie. Carlei lost a bitter trademark lawsuit to the business-minded Rorion (the Gracie brother who was the mastermind behind the early Ultimate Fighting Championships). After being sued out of business by his own nephew, Carlei earned a further bit of local notoriety when he beat the shit out of a San Francisco parking official. Poor Carlei had gotten one parking ticket too many and took it out on the poor sap driving that little ticket cart. Everyone who has owned a car within San Francisco city limits has had rich fantasies about assaulting those wannabe cops with their little chalk tire markers. Carlei had just enough of that volatile mixture of balls and stupidity to actually go out and do it.

I trained in the Mission District at the much mellower Academy of Fighting Arts whose motto was "Kenpo, Jiu-Jitsu and Cold Beer."

It wasn't the most intense dojo in the world but the senseis did keep a mini fridge filled with beer in the school's office. The school was run by a mullet wearing knife dealer named Duane and a lawyer named Tony Head who helped Rorion sue the pants off Carlei. Both men had earned their blue belts from Rorion and were given the go ahead to open a Bay Area Gracie Training Association.

After spending a year parading around San Francisco in a leopard print karate gi claiming to be "the deadliest man alive," I'd decided that maybe I should go out and actually learn a martial art in case someone decided to challenge me. After watching those early UFCs where Royce cut through so many unwitting kung fu and karate men using an esoteric array of chokeholds and takedowns I decided that Gracie Jiu-Jitsu was the style to learn. For all I knew back then, the real Count Dante himself could have still been alive and well and coming to kick my ass. I had to do something to protect myself.

However the Academy of Fighting Arts was hardly a hangout for tough guys. The one year that I went into a tournament our whole team had our asses handed to us in short order. While other schools actually trained in the hours leading up the competition, our team chose to smoke pot, guzzle beers and go see a Van Halen tribute band. We were the Bad News Bears of the Gracie Jiu-Jitsu world. In that tournament, I defaulted into a championship fight in my weight division so I was awarded a second place medal for just showing up.

Corgan learned a far more aggressive version of Gracie Jiu-Jitsu from Carlei than I had at my brew-swilling fighting academy. The tournament medals that he had won were the honest results of winning fights. But that didn't matter. He knew the same takedowns and chokeholds that I did. I was convinced that we could work out a match. However, any hopes of stringing together a series of Gracie Jiu-Jitsu moves into something resembling an entertaining pro wrestling match were soon dashed when a pair of wrestling wannabes looking for a time slot got into the ring to practice their moves.

They were two short guys from Boston. One called himself the Missionary Man and his costume consisted of a shabby black sweat suit with a white stripe painted on the collar with Liquid Paper to resemble a Catholic priest's tunic and the other one was a nondescript masked punk rock character called Kid Anarchy. They proceeded to put on a dazzling array of wrestling moves. They did suplexes, superplexes and off the top rope splashes. They climbed the ropes as quickly as they leapt off them.

"Holy shit," Tom exclaimed, "they just pulled off a fucking Frankensteiner!" The Frankensteiner was a really fast leg scissors take down from the top rope. The move was named after this severely juiced up 1980s tag team called the Steiner Brothers. In lucha libre circles the move is most often referred to as the Huracán rana.

Missionary Man and Kid Anarchy didn't have the chemically induced bulging biceps of the Steiners. They were little guys but we were all floored by their acrobatic display nonetheless. ISW did bill itself as Mexican lucha libre and the fans were promised this kind of fast-paced, high-flying ring action. It was then that I started to grasp what professional wrestling was, and that what it was could break my fucking neck.

There was no way that I could pull off any kind of top rope maneuvers without either killing myself or my opponent. All of a sudden a boxing match where I only got my brains bashed in or a judo tournament where I ended up dislocating both shoulders seemed far less frightening to me than pro wrestling. But I was Count Dante and I had an imagined reputation to live up to. I couldn't just pussy out and leave that day with my tail tucked in between my legs. I had passed the point of no return and couldn't bring myself to just back out.

"Maybe we should fight for real," I suggested to Tom. "Maybe we should just go in there and beat the shit out of each other."

Whether it was real or fake, Tom Corgan lived for fighting in all of its forms, and he understood just how and why jiu-jitsu "wasn't wrestling" far more than either Audra or I did. "No, no man, we don't have to go there," he answered. In a rare moment, he was the voice of rationality.

"Look, you've got the outfit here," he said. "Why don't you just manage me? We can even work on some angle and build up a match for the next show and I could show you some moves by then and we could work something out."

I knew I had the voice and I had the clothes. I was confident of that much. Also, ISW was sorely lacking for any kind of storylines or angles at that time. Most of the matches were planned in much the same way that Tom and I had just planned ours — on the fly only hours before showtime. There was really no way to develop the plot threads intrinsic to truly captivating pro wrestling under such conditions.

We brought our idea to Audra and she was actually enthusiastic about it. "Good," she said, "We need some fucking managers."

That was it. I was in.

In 1997, Corgan's wrestling character was the radiation scarred mutant offspring of America's worst nuclear meltdown. His name was the Three Mile Baby and his raison d'etre was Tom's own mutilated hand. He had lost his thumb years before while repairing his motorcycle. All that remained of it was a slight nub and a mound of scar tissue. In the backwards logic of professional wrestling this also made him a master of the claw hold although one wondered how he was able to gain any leverage with such a cranium grip while missing his opposable digit. That didn't matter though. It was up to me and Tom's other opponents to do what pro wrestlers refer to as "selling the move," which meant writhing around in the most intense mock agony (with arms flailing wildly so the whole audience could see) at the slightest application of the dreaded hold.

Tom's Three Mile Baby ring wear was not nearly as inspired as that worn by the Sasquatch or even the Oi Boy. The centerpiece of Tom's costume was a store-bought La Parka mask. La Parka was probably the most beloved luchadore ever to make it onto American television because he wore a skull mask and always brought a chair into the ring. Fans knew that sooner or later, someone was going to end up with that chair wrapped around his dome. That made La Parka a real crowd pleaser.

Even without the chair, La Parka did have the best Mexican wrestling mask, so Corgan had chosen wisely. Just about everyone in ISW back then wore somebody else's mask so there was no real shame in it despite all of Audra's speeches to the indie press about her wrestlers being "authentic Mexican superheroes." In a strange way, I always thought that ISW's flagrant use of what was clearly someone else's intellectual property kind of got Mexico back for that country's love of blatant copyright violations.

Corgan did have plans for further developing the Three Mile Baby, however. Those plans involved adult diapers and squirting fake baby shit on the audience. He was the Three Mile *Baby* after all. He might as well go all the way with it. Sadly, his dreams of flinging baby crap on drunken spectators never materialized.

That Valentine's Day show was going to mark Tom's second appearance in ISW. He worked at the late-night pizza-by-the-slice joint across the street from the Transmission. The first time he heard about the wrestling show he had to be a part of it, so he confiscated a couple of pies from his work and took them across the street to try to bargain his way into the ring. His plan worked a little bit too well.

Corgan's opponent for his inaugural bout was ISW champion El Gran Fangorio who wrestled on the local indie circuit under the name Shane Dynasty. Shane was a product of All Pro Wrestling in Hayward, California. He was well steeped in the petty sadisms and constant one-upmanship that plagues all of small-time wrestling and is especially encouraged in APW.

Shane's mentor to the wrestling business if not its ring was APW owner Roland Alexander. Alexander got more than his allotted fifteen minutes of fame when he was one of the subjects of Barry Blaustein's pro wrestling documentary *Beyond the Mat*. Throughout that film the rotund and unshaven Roland generally resembled someone who just got through cleaning his bathroom. He even goes into a business meeting with the WWE's Vince McMahon wearing a dirty T-shirt and sweatpants.

Roland started out in professional wrestling as a fan boy in the offices of 1960s and '70s Bay Area wrestling promoter Roy Shire who mostly promoted battle-royals out of San Francisco's Cow Palace. Shire had a reputation for being a harsh taskmaster, running a tight but dour locker room. "He didn't allow any of the wrestlers to play cards or joke around back there," Hollywood grappling legend Gene LeBell later told me. That business style was passed onto the impressionable Alexander. Like so many of those old school wrestling promoters, Shire required that the business be protected at all costs: you didn't let anyone know that pro wrestling was fake. You beat the tar out of anyone who said that it was.

This kind of hazing was later reserved for new students of Roland's academy in the name of teaching them "humility." Most of it served no purpose as far as making the new charges better performers in the ring. Its real purpose was to assuage the egos of the more experienced students who had already parted with enough money learning how to run the ropes to have gone to Stanford Law School instead. An even more brutal version of this discipline was dished out to the Tom Corgans of the world who dared to get into the ring with a "real pro wrestler" without "paying their dues," which really just meant without giving barrels of cash to Alexander and others like him. In the 1990s that old phrase "protecting the business" took on a whole new meaning.

Corgan's only hint of real training came when he was writing a story for his college newspaper on Max Sharkey's famous pro wrestling training camp in Minnesota. Rick Rude, Ric Flair, the Road Warriors and Jesse "The Body" Ventura had all made their way through Sharkey's school at one time or another and Corgan finagled a couple of free days of training out of the place by claiming that he needed it for background for his story. When Tom was at Sharkey's school, Sean Waltman was one of the students there. Waltman later gained WWE fame under the name of X-Pac but today he is making the rounds through cyberspace via a stomach-churning sex video with the very masculine former lady wrestler Chyna. After the end of her professional wrestling career, Chyna has clung to the fraying threads of her celebrity as a drug-addled participant on the VH1 reality show *The Surreal Life*.

Tom never returned to Sharkey's school, never put down any money and never received more than those two days of training. The rest of his experience came from taking falls on a backyard trampoline when he was a teenager and drunkenly cutting up his forehead with a hidden razor blade to be more like Abdullah the Butcher. In the eyes of someone like Shane Dynasty/El Gran Fangorio, this made Tom Corgan more than worthy of abuse.

Corgan was an amateur but he was also an artist. He had a storyline for his match with Shane that went beyond the usual "two guys get in the ring and they just hate each other" scenario. Tom's plan involved having the ref break them every time Shane pushed him into a corner. This would have been standard operating procedure for any regular wrestling promotion, but Incredibly Strange Wrestling was different, as its name indicated. The standard ISW ref strolled around the ring with a beer in one hand and a cigarette in the other. They ignored the match that they were supposedly officiating in favor of flirting with off-duty strippers at ringside. It was a good little gag. It became ISW's trademark.

With his wrestling boots on, Shane stood a few inches taller than Tom and possessed a strong if not muscular physique. As Gran Fangorio, he wore a mask decorated by sharp, jagged teeth that may have actually been his own creation instead of just being pulled off a Styrofoam head at a Mission District La Raza store.

From the bout's opening bell, the lackadaisical ISW ref never lifted a finger to pull the two wrestlers apart. The inexperienced Corgan didn't know what to do when the centerpiece of his match was denied him. He froze with a panic that must have been visible even through his skeletal lucha mask. Shane wasted no time in delivering what could only be characterized as a severe beating. He distributed vicious combinations of punches, open handed slaps and stiff clotheslines. Tom just stood there and took it not knowing what else to do.

Shane repeatedly hit Tom across the back with a steel chair and delivered a top-rope dropkick. Every ounce of Shane's 240-pound frame landed squarely on the back of Tom's head. That blow could have easily killed Tom or put him in a wheelchair. He was knocked unconscious for several seconds leaving Dynasty with nothing to do but take the pin and win the match. The beating was about to resume after the pinfall, but Corgan came to and threw a flurry of body shots into Shane's stomach out of sheer desperation. That sudden burst of defense caused Shane to take a powder through the ring ropes and into the backroom.

Tom managed to obtain some shaky video footage of that match and he showed it to everyone in his inner circle over and over again. For him, surviving that beating was akin to earning some kind of frat house initiation badge. Most normal people would have never returned to ISW again after absorbing such abuse but Corgan wasn't a normal person.

He was hooked.

As the crowd poured into the Transmission and the show was about to begin, the backroom was crowded, a hub of frantic activity. The guitarist and bassist of the opening band checked their tunings while their drummer tapped out beats with his sticks on any available flat surface. Wrestlers of all shapes, sizes and levels of experience milled about and nervously went over the matches that had only been put together hours before.

The Transmission was a nightclub and not a sports complex, so its backroom didn't have the lockers, benches and showers that were afforded by a regular gymnasium. Like the rest of the venue, the backroom had a cracked, concrete floor. It was filled with busted up tables, rickety stools and zigzagging stacks of wood palettes. Wrestlers sat on piles of wood while they laced up their boots. The power chord crunch of the opening band drifted into the room and provided an overwhelming layer of background noise.

Authentic luchadores whom Audra had imported up from Mexico donned their colorful costumes and tightened their masks while talking amongst themselves in rapid-fire Spanish. Shane Dynasty and a clique of other indie workers stood off in the corner of the room behind the beer kegs. Just about everyone else involved with the show was a friend of Audra's in one way or another.

A group of Mission District Chicanos who used to work with Audra at this defunct nightspot called the Trocadero Transfer formed the backbone of the under-card. There was Jose, Boris and Chango Loco. Jose and Boris were good-natured roughnecks who were mostly in isw to guzzle beer and hit on tipsy rockabilly babes. Between them, they had a cast of interchangeable characters that included the stethoscope wearing Doctor Loco, the nunchaku-wielding Karate Azteka and the serape wearing Chupa Suave (roughly translated it meant "Soft Suck"). In each show they wrestled multiple times and doubled as the disinterested referees.

Chango Loco was different. He was hipper, more urban, and more intense. His body was covered with colorful tattoos. His earlobes and other soft tissue regions were decoratively pierced by more than their fair share of wood and metal. He thoroughly embraced the modern primitive chic that was all the rage in San Francisco in the mid-1990s and he had played drums for junk rock bands like the White Trash Debutantes.

But most important, he was outwardly devoted to his religion of Santeria and he incorporated all of its sacraments and rituals into his wrestling character. He had a penchant for grand ring entrances where he spit balls of fire out of his mouth while he pushed his way through the audience. Through his dangerous stagecraft, he tried to transform himself into the orisha Chango that was his wrestling namesake. An orisha is a Santerian demigod or spirit guide (or an aspect of one overall god). Chango in particular was a warrior king who commanded fire, thunder and warfare. ISW's Chango Loco believed that the god Chango was a very real force that guided his destiny. Although the fire had a religious dimension for Chango Loco, he also understood the Gene Simmons appeal that it had for the nostalgia crazed hipsters that made up ISW's core audience.

Chango Loco definitely had his fans but the mantle of ISW's biggest star had already been attained by the tutu and tights wearing El Homo Loco. Homo Loco was the brainchild of the very gay but not quite flaming John Pierre. John Pierre had an extra nipple on his chest that he liked to show off backstage. He often reminded everyone who was listening that Pierre meant rock or rock hard in French while John was another word for restroom. "With a name like John Pierre, my Southern Baptist parents should have known that I was going to turn out gay," he often proclaimed. If a straight woman who hangs out with nothing but gay men is derisively referred to as a "fag hag," then a gay man who exclusively surrounds himself with straight women (except during pride week) should also have a name. Whatever name that may be, John Pierre was it.

In the ring El Homo Loco was a natural physical comedian. Just the manner in which he pranced around elicited belly laughs from the audience. His entire wrestling offense involved dry humping his opponent into submission. This was San Francisco after all, and El Homo Loco was the queer archetypical character that audience members had all subconsciously longed to see when they had decided to attend something called Incredibly Strange Wrestling.

The only payment that most of us were to receive for slamming each other around the ring came in the form of iced-down bottles of Corona and a couple of kegs of swill beer that the Transmission's bouncers wheeled into the backroom at various points in the evening. Audra had one hard and fast rule: you couldn't drink any beers until after your match and if you got caught sampling the keg before you went on, then your match was scratched altogether. Luckily, Tom's match was the second one up so it wasn't like I had very long to wait before collecting on my alcoholic payoff. Audra often bragged to the press about being able to bribe her local luchas with beer, adding to the show's lowbrow charm.

Corgan was going to wrestle a short, wiry, tatted up mod named Jefferson Monroe who wrestled as the Missing Link. Monroe could handle leaping off the ring ropes and had trained in a mélange of assorted styles of kung fu. Tom was excited because he could easily catch Jeff from a top rope dive and planned to make use of such a maneuver to bring their bout to a close. My job was to simply come out and bark advice at the Three Mile Baby from ringside. Following the Baby's hard fought victory, I was to grab the mic and proclaim my intent to become his manager, boasting of the benefits that the Three Mile Baby would reap from such an arrangement.

This was really just wrestling booking 101 and the purpose of this minor plot twist was to build up to a match where Count Dante battled the Three Mile Baby for the right to manage him on the next show. Of course this portrayed handling the Three Mile Baby's business affairs as some sort of prize worth risking one's neck for, which was pretty absurd when you stop and think about it.

The Three Mile Baby, the Missing Link and I all huddled behind a dusty curtain and waited for the tuxedoed wrestling announcer to call our names. It was impossible to resist the temptation to peek through that curtain just to see what the crowd looked like, but whenever someone stuck their head through, Audra was quick to yell at them for breaking up whatever illusions the show could muster.

The five to seven minutes allotted to the opening match seemed like hours while we waited. Finally, Kid Anarchy and the Missionary Man had finished with their attempt to put on a four-star classic for their ISW debut. Moments later we heard the whiskey soaked voice of the wrestling emcee announce the combatants for the next match: "*And now making his way into the ring for our very next bout, weighing in at 200 pounds the Three Mile Baby!*"

He announced the Missing Link with the same kind of panache. I didn't receive a formal introduction because I was playing the part of an interloper on the proceedings and wouldn't be making my entrance until the contest had already commenced.

I heard the shaking of the ring from the Three Mile Baby and the Missing Link running the ropes and used the crash of a couple of body slams as my cue to enter the Transmission's main room.

As I parted that curtain and strolled the short distance from the backroom I could see that the audience was packed right up against the ring, no barricades or security ropes to separate them from the action. The crowd seemed to expand and contract like a living organism as bunches of people made their way to get drinks from the Transmission's two bars and others filled the spaces that had been abandoned. Some intoxicated young women were tightly pressed up against the ring apron. They backhanded and elbowed the people behind them to keep from being crushed by the sheer weight of the crowd. Once they had regained their balance after a wave of human turbulence, they resumed cursing at the wrestlers.

The match went by like a blur. I shouted and yelled words of advice and encouragement to the Three Mile Baby when he was winning and feigned excruciating disappointment when he was on the receiving end of the Missing Link's attack. Finally the Three Mile Baby won with a power slam that worked its way into his claw hold. The ref lazily counted to three while puffing on a Lucky Strike.

I heard the clanging of the bell that signaled the end of the fight. It was now my chance to get on the microphone and address the biggest, rowdiest crowd that I had ever been in front of.

"I am Count Dante, the deadliest man alive," I exclaimed while holding the mic in my right hand and subconsciously waving my left arm up and down as if to punctuate each proclamation. "I have beaten the masters of jiu-jitsu, kenpo, kung fu and wrestling in NO HOLDS BARRED DEATH MATCHES! I have used my kung fu skills to conquer industry and amass a fortune and I, Count Dante, will show you, the Three Mile Baby, my secrets to ultimate success! I will put champion gold around the Three Mile Baby's waist!"

The crowd went nuts and seemed to cheer every word I said. I was a big guy with a big voice and I was wearing a ridiculous stars and stripes karate suit. Speeches (often called promos) had always been a major part of American professional wrestling. That crowd loved lucha libre. They loved the gymnastics, the costumes and the surrealism that it conveyed, but they also wanted that kind of over-wrought oratory laced with incalculable machismo. I could deliver that. In fact, I was damned good at it.

The Three Mile Baby was not unmoved by my speech but he was still skeptical of my offer. He ripped the microphone from my hand and announced that I had to wrestle him for the privilege of managing him. We didn't get bogged down in the particulars. Another pair of wrestlers waited behind that curtain itching to go on, but I would be lying to say that I was concerned about them at that moment. I was riding a high like I had never achieved before.

As I made my way to the backroom, people in the crowd reached out to touch me just like they'd reached out to Hulk Hogan on cable TV. Pro wrestling occupies a strange zone between reality and fantasy and I had just crossed over into it.

We burst into the backroom and headed straight for that tub of Coronas. Everyone was positive and the air in that room was nothing but congratulatory.

"You look like a wrestler," Corgan said enthusiastically. "No, no, I mean it. You look like a fucking wrestler. That's why they responded to you. That audience sees you and they think Dusty or Andre or something. A big fat guy. You are what they think of when they think of wrestlers!"

I had a bottle opener on me, which quickly made me the most popular man in the room even with the jaded indie workers. A broad shouldered cowboy wrestler with a mustache who looked like he came straight out of 1975 or earlier kept on asking me to open bottles for him.

"You're my best friend in this room," he said with a laugh, but then he looked me up and down and almost conferred what Corgan had just gotten through telling me. "You really should be a pro wrestler," the cowboy said. "It's a great life. You get to go to different towns and fuck different women."

At that moment I thought that that grappling cowpoke had taken too many shots to the head. At the very least it seemed like he must have been overstating his case, but damned if he wasn't right. One rocker chick latched onto me and proclaimed that I was her new boyfriend while other women shot interested glances my way. Chicks never looked twice at me after my band played. But a minute and a half of intensive macho bluster earned me a make out session in among those wooden planks that filled the backroom. Who knew what would happen when I actually wrestled a match?

I was hooked.

# 4

# THE
# FAT KID

I WAS THE FAT KID. I got picked on, beat up and bullied. It's not the most original story, but it's true. It's who I was, who I am and what happened to me. I can remember in the first grade a gang of kids slamming my face into a metal drainage grate in the middle of the playground for no reason other than I was fat. They didn't know me at all. They probably didn't even know my name. I sure didn't know theirs, but they beat the crap out of me anyway all because I was soft around the middle.

Looking back on it, this older kid who gave me the most grief on the tanbark was kind of chubby himself. Maybe he was on the receiving end of all of those Indian burns and fat lips for his first two years of school and when he got a little bit bigger, he decided to take it all out on me. The other kids never made fun of him for his flabby gut, but they sure gathered around and laughed at me while he kicked my ass around the foursquare and tetherball courts. God, school really sucked.

As for that bigger kid, one day my older sister took me to school and kicked his ass in the parking lot of Roosevelt Grammar School in Redwood City, California. Getting his ass kicked by a girl was pretty humiliating for him even if the girl in question was a good six or seven years older than he was. He never bothered me again. It was the nicest thing my sister ever did for me.

My sister was a brown belt in kenpo karate at the time and I really wanted to take lessons. If any kid needed them it was me. But my mother, an honest to God Okie from Muskogee no less, was way overprotective of me. She wouldn't let me take the kids' classes. This probably turned out to be a good thing because, decades later, my sister's karate instructor was convicted on child molestation charges. The pervo sensei was into little girls and not little boys but I still don't see this as a positive atmosphere to learn spinning back kicks in. My mother was right but for all the wrong reasons.

While my sister was earning her black belt, karate tournaments were not at all an uncommon family outing. On the way to one particular tournament, my mother told me that they had announced that Elvis Presley himself was going to show up and judge some matches and maybe even get on the mat. This was '70s Elvis, with a big gut all his own and sideburns that were so exaggerated they threatened to take over his entire face.

I was a kid from a single parent family, so I spent way too much time in front of the television set watching whatever old movies the UHF bandwidth had to offer. My idea of the perfect male role model was some kind of cross between the movie Elvis and the scientist from a 1950s giant bug flick. If only the King could have used his hip shaking, rock and rolling ways for science instead of just fixing cars and getting in and out of jams! Couldn't MGM have just produced one movie where Elvis figured out how to destroy some kind of radioactive monster or used his keen intellect and Southern charms to thwart a hostile invasion from another planet?

Even without combating creatures borne of a twisted world of science gone mad, my six-year-old brain could think of nothing more earth-shaking and cataclysmic than witnessing The King of Rock and Roll at the karate tournament in San Jose. If Elvis could be there, then maybe even David Carradine of TV's *Kung Fu* would show up too. One of my last memories of my mother and father still being together was staying up late and watching an episode of *Kung Fu* with the old man.

Through my fertile imagination I conjured up mental images of Elvis taking on ten black belts and laying waste to them all with his masterful thrust kicks one after the other. One of the hapless karate jobbers could even be my sister's loser boyfriend. Maybe Elvis would even take on David Carradine! I couldn't begin to guess who would win such a contest between two so evenly matched martial artists. But I was asking for way too much there. Elvis was more than enough.

We arrived at whatever high school gym or civic center where the tournament was being held and took our seats amidst the tiers of wooden, bolted-on bleachers. The event began and various karate men and women took to the mats to compete in point sparring matches and kata exhibitions. I looked around the sprawling mats and over by the judges' tables trying to catch a glimpse of Elvis Presley. Was he going to wear one of those gi-like jump suits like he wore in the *Aloha from Hawaii — Live Via Satellite* TV special? Would the judges allow all of those rhinestones to be worn in an officially sanctioned competition?

But the announcement came only minutes into the event: "Due to a clause in his contract barring him from making public appearances on the same day that he is performing in concert, Elvis Presley will not be appearing at this karate tournament."

I was beyond disappointed. I was crushed.

Less than a year later, a blitz of radio and TV ads for an upcoming Elvis concert at the Cow Palace hit the airwaves. I begged my mom to take me. She loved Elvis and always had. I thought that she wouldn't be able to resist the King in concert. Who could deny those radio spots with that deep and authoritative announcer's voice processed through heavy amounts of slap-back echo? It was even more compelling than the TV commercials for the re-release of *The 7th Voyage of Sinbad!*

But we were very poor after the divorce and my mom probably couldn't part with the twelve bucks a ticket that it would have cost to see the King at a concrete and steel indoor arena on the outskirts of San Francisco. "We'll see him the next time he comes to town," my mother assured me.

Less than a year later, Elvis was dead.

I probably never imagined this as a kid, but I have now spent a good portion of my adult life striving to become what I'd pictured if Elvis had showed up to the karate tournament.

I was going to have to wait more than another two months until the ISW show that followed up my auspicious managerial debut. The show was going to be at the Transmission on April 25, 1997. On one hand, I could barely wait. Two months seemed like forever and a day, but on the other hand I knew that I needed as much time as possible before that next show because I was going to have to wrestle this time around. Even after the Missionary Man and Kid Anarchy pulled off that Frankensteiner, I honestly believed that Tom and I could get through a few minutes of ring action by stringing together a few armbars and really good judo throws and take downs. Ignorance is bliss.

One of the drawbacks to wrestling with ISW was that neither Audra nor Brett nor anyone else provided us with anything resembling a ring to practice in. We somehow had to just divine the finer points of pro wrestling through osmosis or some other unseen process, then go out in front of a hall crowded with 800 or more people and entertain them in this very physical and even dangerous way. This was especially precarious considering that Audra encouraged a lucha libre–inspired style of ring work with all of its high-risk, off the top rope maneuvers. How could we learn to jump off those ropes without killing ourselves or the people that we were wrestling when we didn't have any ropes to practice on?

Despite the dumb-headedness of all of those wrestling schools where the indie workers came from, they all did at least provide an honest to God ring to practice in. Even though the instructors at those schools were mostly sadistic pricks, they could actually teach you how to take falls and run the ropes. Those schools were never a complete scam despite the masses of arbitrary bullshit that they felt compelled to heap upon their tuition paying pupils. Call me crazy, but I never saw how scrubbing Roland Alexander's toilets made you a better pro wrestler, but I guess it worked for some people.

At one time or another, all of us in ISW contemplated signing up for one of those wrestling schools, but the thousands of dollars that they wanted up front was usually a pretty strong deterrent to taking lessons. In my case, tales of Corgan's first match with Dynasty had instilled a healthy fear of indie workers in me. On top of it all my wrestling school reticence wasn't helped by the fact that Dynasty was one of the cooler indie workers. If he was one of the more level-headed of his kind, I would hate to deal with the rest of them.

A handful of Alexander's APW wrestlers who also worked a few ISW matches did go on to bigger and better things as far as major league pro wrestling was concerned. Mike Modest, who wrestled in ISW as one half of the race-baiting tag team called the Border Patrol, was Alexander's teacher's pet and got that unsuccessful World Wrestling Entertainment audition in *Beyond the Mat*. He didn't make the cut as far as Vince was concerned but did make it into Ted Turner's World Championship Wrestling during that promotion's dying days.

Modest was always regarded as a top-notch technical wrestler in the mold of the Canadian Crippler Chris Benoit by that handful of devotees who religiously followed both the Northern Californian indie scene and anything that ever took place in a Japanese wrestling ring. When Modest got his televised shot at wcw, however, he botched a spot and dropped his opponent on his head. All of wcw's aging and immobile stars like Kevin Nash jumped on that mishap and Modest never wrestled in a wcw ring again.

One of Modest's opponents in that isw Border Patrol match was Mexicano Blanco, who went on to Extreme Championship Wrestling and later wwe as the nearly indestructible, rubber-boned Spike Dudley. He was a former English-Lit major with an emphasis in Shakespearian studies, but as a wrestler he excelled in falling from heights of twenty feet or more, bleeding profusely, wrestling in rings filled with barbed wire or broken glass and getting 8-bit Nintendos slammed over his head. Most recently, he wrestled for tna.

Probably the most memorable isw appearance by a wrestler who went onto the wwe also turned out to be the most tragic. Mike Lockwood wrestled in isw as "The Leprechaun" Erin O'Grady, but he later gained some measure of televised fame as the comedic "Crash" Holly on *Raw* and *Smackdown!* The flair for comedy that served him so well in the big-time was plainly evident the one or two times he wrestled for isw. I drunkenly remember him from my first show. As Erin O'Grady he wore a green, sequined leprechaun suit and brandished a bottle of Bushmills. "Do you want me fucking whiskey?" he badgered the crowd in the worst Irish brogue of all time. "Do you really want me fucking whiskey?!" He then took a big swig of the amber liquor, held it in his mouth for a second, looking like he was ready to pop, then sprayed it all over the fans in the front rows. "There's your fucking whiskey!!!"

Lockwood gained a cult following soon after he started appearing with the wwe in 1998. On July 1, 2003, the wwe let him go citing that the organization did not have "further plans for his character." By November of that same year, Lockwood was dead.

The medical examiner in Florida ruled it a suicide from an overdose of painkillers, but his mother Barbara still believes that it was an accident. "Mike had too much to live for," she told *USA Today* in 2004.

Wrestlers tend to die. They tend to die a lot. According to *USA Today*, sixty-five active pro wrestlers died between 1997 and 2004 — twenty-five of them from heart attacks. Wrestlers are twelve times more likely to die from heart attacks than other Americans between the ages of twenty-five to forty-four. They are twenty times more likely to die before forty than pro football players.

The steroids, the painkillers, the incomprehensible schedule and the increased physical demands brought on by the audience's ceaseless hunger for harder falls and ever-increasing bloodletting are mostly to blame for this. But, for whatever reason, wrestlers seem most vulnerable when their ring careers appear to be over. Lockwood, the British Bulldog, "Ravishing" Rick Rude and Mike Hegstrand (Road Warrior Hawk) all died while confronting the thought of life outside of wrestling's limelight. Most of them either passed away from the handfuls of pain pills needed to deal with the enduring agonies brought on by years of bodily abuse or by juicing up on another cycle of 'roids in the hopes that packing on more muscle would win their old jobs back — or by a combination of the two.

I now live in Lockwood's hometown of Pacifica, California, which is a coastal suburb of San Francisco. When people here find out that I was somehow involved in pro wrestling, their eyes often light up and they talk to me about Lockwood unaware that he is no longer with us. Even in the Bay Area, the death was barely picked up by the media with the exception of the small circulation *Pacifica Tribune*. I didn't know Lockwood, having only seen him that one time in ISW, but I still never know how to break the news to them that that all too rare combination of class clown and high school star athlete stopped living when he was only thirty-two years old.

It was only a little over two weeks before my second ISW show that I got a call from the Missionary Man who told me that he was having a meeting over at his apartment to go over the matches for the upcoming show. He had only wrestled that one match for Audra and he was already organizing meetings. For a sweatpants-wearing geek who was showing up, hat in hand, trying to get a break with the rest of us nobodies, he appeared to have risen to the top pretty quickly. What did he have that I didn't have? Was it that Frankensteiner? I guessed it had to be. It was the only possible explanation. That one spectacular move loomed pretty large.

He told me to be sure to bring my workout clothes because we were all going to go down to the gym in his apartment complex to go over some moves after the meeting. I asked him if my jiu-jitsu gi would be okay and he assured me that it would be.

Corgan and I had already planned out our match and set it up at the last show so we didn't really need to figure out who was going to wrestle who, but that mat time with other wrestlers around was much needed — at least for me.

In the park across the street from my apartment building Tom and I took the time to mime out some of the most pivotal points of our match. There we were, acting as if some spindly, unkempt trees were ring posts as we ran back and forth like idiots to simulate the act of running the ropes. The band of street people who made their homes in the alleyways adjacent to that park looked on at what must have appeared to be the craziest white people they'd ever seen in a city chock full of crazy white people.

"Remember, when I whip you into the ropes and you run back and forth," Tom instructed, "you are a prisoner of momentum." That was one of the biggest physical precepts of all of pro wrestling — being a prisoner of momentum and running back and forth like a goofball. For the ISW of the time however, that picnic-in-the-park practice session was the pinnacle of advanced planning.

The Missionary Man lived in this large, multi-storey, multi-towered apartment complex in San Francisco's Tenderloin District. The Tenderloin was best known for its fine selection of female and transvestite streetwalkers, homeless shopping cart pushers, rancid Lebanese-run pizza joints, ramshackle Asian massage parlors, Korean touchy-feely bars and high-class strip joints that cost a fortune to get into. Amidst all of that sleaze and squalor were the Great American Music Hall and the Edinburgh Castle. While I saw everything at the Great American from the Jesus Lizard to the Plimsouls, the Castle, despite all of its poetry readings and literary nights, was still besieged by a steady stream of indigent scam artists looking to palm the paying customers' whiskey shots right off the bar.

Understandably, Missionary Man's building employed a round-the-clock security guard and I not only had to be buzzed into the lobby, I had to print my name on a sign-in sheet just as if I were requesting proper clearance to enter a major research lab at Genetech or IBM. The middle-aged, African-American security man gave me a look that somehow told me that I was not the first wrestler to be buzzed in that night.

With its 1980s construction, plain white walls and squishy, monotone carpeting, the Missionary Man's apartment building seemed out of place in a San Francisco dominated by its Victorian flats with crown molding and hardwood floors. The fact that the building had a gym inside made it seem like it belonged someplace like New York even more.

When I stepped out of the elevator and made my way down the hall I could hear the blustery commotion from the meeting. Coming to the Missionary Man's door, I decided to just let myself in. I was immediately confronted by a small apartment filled with wall-to-wall wrestlers.

An unmasked Chango Loco stood off to the side of the living room with his arms folded over his puffed up chest as he contemptuously surveyed the other wrestlers. He had the look of a West Point educated colonel saddled with a brigade of unfit conscripts. Craig Martins, who had gotten his big ISW break by winning a dream date with El Homo Loco on the previous show, was busily chatting with Jose about the staggering amount of times WTBS seemed to show the Ray Harryhausen flick *Clash of the Titans*.

"Turner must love that fucking movie," Jose indignantly said while shaking his head in disbelief.

Kid Anarchy was propped in a far corner of the room on a makeshift bed with not one, but both of his arms held permanently outstretched by thick, plaster casts that ran all the way up to his shoulders. He and the Missionary Man had done an ISW related publicity stunt at some hipster art show that involved doing some moves off a ladder right in the middle of the crowd. Just as Kid Anarchy climbed triumphantly to the top rung, a drunken fuckhead from the audience pulled the ladder out from under him and sent the acrobatic wrestler to the hardwood floor below. Anarchy stretched out his hands to keep from landing on his skull and shattered major bones in both of his arms in the process. Not missing a beat, the Missionary Man went for the pin anyway as Anarchy's arms flopped around painfully at angles that they were never meant to bend at.

Anarchy seemed to take this all in good stride however and promised that, while he obviously wouldn't be healed in time for the April show, he would be up and running for the card after that. He and Missionary Man were not only still friends but roommates as well.

Kid Anarchy's injury-earned pride aside, this wasn't your usual crew of indie wrestlers. We weren't paying those wrestling schools or taking steroids in the hopes of making it to the majors. Your typical ISW wrestler either wanted to be Tor Johnson lumbering through an Ed Wood flick or El Santo drop kicking a vampire. We all longed to be part of a carnival sideshow from a bygone era or to create the kind of schlock that '50s low-budget moviemakers could put out with a kind of honesty we could only hope to approximate. We were all unavoidably tainted by our 1990s sense of self-awareness.

We could be funny. We could be utterly fucking nuts, but we could never create the kind of clueless camp that we really aspired to.

Audra hadn't arrived yet so Brett held court while we all waited for her. I took a seat on the floor and scrunched my large frame in between a pile of wrestling mags and comic books and a teetering stack of WWE and ECW VHS tapes.

"I don't want to get anybody's hopes up," Brett said while glancing down at his notepad, "but MTV called us the other day and they are very, very interested in making an ISW TV show."

Everybody let out a huge cheer and a kind of focused enthusiasm filled the room.

"And if they do make this show," Brett continued, "we are all getting paid." He lingered on the word "paid" for an extra beat as everyone cheered again.

"On top of that," he added, "there is a U.S. tour in the works for later this year and we are probably going to Europe after that."

It was then that it dawned on me. That ISW could be my ticket to the kind of rock and roll touring and fringe-level celebrityhood that I had always longed for. It had the potential to be bigger in and of itself than just helping me land some better gigs for my band.

MTV posed a bit of a quandary for me because everything that they touched turned to shit through all of their product placement and corporate kowtowing. I mean just look at what they did to Ozzy Osbourne! They took the fucking prince of darkness and put him into family counseling with goddamned Dr. Phil. Dr. Phil! *Dr. Phil!* My God! Make it stop! Please make it stop! I now hope I never see Ozzy or his talentless, annoying children ever again. Because of MTV, I can't even enjoy Black Sabbath anymore, which used to be my favorite band bar fucking none. It's driven me to listen to Cactus or Deep Purple just to get my heavy, pentatonic scale riffing fix. At least I can rest assured that the Purple's Ritchie Blackmore, hard rock's biggest asshole if ever there was one, will always be too bitter, recalcitrant and arrogant to ever subject himself to the Oprah treatment that Ozzy now regularly grovels for.

Still, the goal was to find a way to avoid working shitty, boring jobs in offices where everybody just kissed ass and hoped for a raise and a two-week vacation. With its promises of TV shows and touring the world, ISW seemed like it could give me everything I had ever wanted. As far as being a corporate, MTV-sucking sell out, I would have to burn that bridge when I fell off it.

Audra finally arrived and we gathered together and headed downstairs to the apartment building's weight room. There were maybe fifteen or twenty of us. We weren't midgets, pinheads or amputees but as we all barged into the place we still looked pretty odd and imposing to the pair of blonde secretary types that were trying to tighten up their buns on some stationary bikes. After we had stormed into the room, we started loudly throwing pulled punches at each other, and the secretaries cut short their workouts and took a powder. The gym had padded mats for us to tumble on, a universal weight set, those stationary bikes and not much else.

Missionary Man and Jefferson Monroe showed some of the large and lovely go-go girls how to do some basic karate rolls while Boris and Jose made me lie down on the mats while they leapt up and performed elbow drops on me. I was pretty nervous because they had a reputation for fucking people up, but not one of those blows managed to land with any force. Maybe they saved that kind of thing for the ring.

After I was done being a tackling dummy for the tag team of Chupa Suave and Doctor Loco, Tom and I went back to the familiar miming of our proposed match and Missionary Man showed us how to do a small-package roll-up and a few other mat moves. Like Tom Corgan, Missionary Man lacked formal pro wrestling training, but tried to make up for it with a combination of sheer enthusiasm and martial arts. It was a lot cheaper to take judo or karate lessons than it was to go to pro wrestling school.

Corgan showed me how to scoop him up for a proper body slam while Missionary Man weighed in with some pointers. We also reviewed the concept of being a prisoner of momentum once again. There were going to be a lot of missed clotheslines and running the ropes in our match. Tom told me that I was going to have to prepare to take some abuse because I wasn't ready for much else.

After about an hour of discordant chatter and rolling around the mats, we all started to leave. That was the end of our big training session. Our next big chance to work on our match was going to be on the day of the show during that short window of time between when the ring was finally set up and the club's doors were opened to the general public.

The two weeks before show time went by pretty quickly. Corgan and I scrawled an outline of our match on crumpled pieces of binder paper. We sure talked a lot about the thing, but we never ran through it again before the day of the show. We often mentioned going to one or the other's jiu-jitsu schools to do one more dry run of the bout, but never did. You'd think that the image of Kid Anarchy's arms propped up in casts would have made us go that extra mile, but there was only so much that you could do without an actual ring to practice in. Any further mat work would have only served as a scatterbrained repeat of the training session at the Missionary Man's apartment building.

I woke up too early on the day of the show. I had nothing to do but wait around my dirty apartment, gather my ring wear together and skim over that crumpled up outline of our upcoming bout. I was too nervous to do much else. I turned on the TV. *Demitrius and the Gladiators* was on the American Movie Classics channel. It was a 1950s biblical epic with Victor Mature as a Christian forced to fend for his life in the Roman coliseum. Ernest Borgnine plays the part of the sadistic slave master and William "Blacula" Marshall is also in it. There is a scene in the movie where Mature proclaims that he will not fight because he is now a Christian. The packed coliseum erupts with boos at Mature's spiritual pacifism.

"If you will not fight, Christian, then you will die!" Emperor Caligula proclaims giving the thumbs down sign.

You know, there could be a wrestling match there. . . .

I arrived at the Transmission around 1 P.M. to make use of that all too precious ring time. Corgan was already there and we quizzed each other over the points of our match like some grammar school kids preparing for a spelling bee while we waited for some space to open up in the ring. At any one time, two or three pairs of grapplers crowded into that squared circle to hurriedly work out their moves while the clock ticked away until those doors swung open and Audra made everyone hide backstage.

Corgan had added a spot. He wanted me to hurl him out of the ring and into the crowd for dramatic effect. He also wanted to body slam me to show off Three Mile Baby's plutonium enhanced strength. This wasn't going to be easy for him because I tipped the scales at nearly 300 pounds, but that only made him want to do it even more. Of course, I was to give him an assist with the move by leaping at just the right time so he could lift me up into a chest high position. He was going to do the same for me when it was my time to huck him out of the ring. Pro wrestling was all about cooperation. Most shows of strength are really only in the perception of your audience.

As I ran back and forth across the ring for the first time, I found it to be both springy and squishy. You didn't get hurt when you took a fall on its amorphous floor but its warped and buckling floorboards threatened to give way at a moment's notice. Brett had even taken the extra step of duct taping some X's over various spots in the ring that he didn't want us to land on for fear that we would fall through it. It was going to be pretty hard to work a match and be mindful of something like that.

The ring was a bit on the small side and I was told that it was an old television ring that Roy Shire had used at the KTVU studios. If that was the case it had to be at least twenty years old. That certainly explained a lot.

Showtime grew a little bit closer and it was time to vacate the ring. The band Manic Hispanic started off the evening with a brisk set, but I only grew more and more nervous as the fast paced, Mexican pop punk drew to a close. As with the previous show, my match was early in the first set. Tom and I went over our moves in a corner of the backroom while many of the other wrestlers around us did the same.

Manic Hispanic played their last power chord of the night, then started to carry their drums and amps into the backroom. There was about a five minute gap between the end of the band's set and the beginning of the wrestling. Some canned music through the house PA played but only for a few minutes before wrestling announcer Allan Bolte took to the stage, the wrestling portion of the evening about to begin.

Audra had somehow found Bolte in the backwaters of the Bay Area wrestling scene. The ring announcer for Roy Shire's promotion in its Cow Palace glory days, he still made a few extra dimes writing articles for all of those pulpy wrestling mags on the racks at 7-Eleven and smoke shops. Bolte's smooth but smoky voice added an incongruous touch of class to Incredibly Strange Wrestling and provided our show with an unlikely link to the Bay Area's wrestling heritage. Since ISW's over-21, club-going fan base related to pro wrestling as something that they used to watch on the boob tube when they were in middle school, Audra had Allan provide live commentary through the sound system while the matches went on. This made it all more like TV and less like a live sporting event, which was the way our audience wanted it.

There was something about Bolte using all of those stock wrestling blow-by-blow commentator lines — "I have never seen anything like this before"— that made ISW seem so much more real. So much more legitimate.

"ALL RIGHT, TRANSMISSION THEATRE IN SAN FRANCISCO," Allan said to near thunderous applause. My heart skipped a beat. "IT'S INCREDIBLE. IT'S STRANGE. AND IT'S WRESTLING!"

We were going to go on any second. All at once, I never wanted it to happen and also just wanted to get it over with. Finally, Allan announced the Three Mile Baby and then he announced me.

"I have seen this man wrestling all up and down the West Coast," he said, adding a background that I never had. "Here he is! COOOUUUUNTTTT DAAAAANTAYYYY!"

I ran into the ring as quickly as my flabby legs could carry me. As I made it through the ring ropes, fans stuck their hands in the ring for me to slap them five, which I did like any true baby face hero. Nothing blurs the line between fantasy and reality quite like pro wrestling. At that second, I was an athlete or a gladiator. Our characters were purposefully ridiculous, but Corgan and I acted like it was real and the whole audience followed suit. Everyone was in on it. Every audience member was an actor, extra or stand-in. The act of cheering, booing, fighting and losing subverted reality into a new paradigm.

Corgan slapped me hard across the face with an open palm to begin our match. It actually stung pretty good and (most important) it made a really loud noise, but it wasn't like it was going to kill me. We then went into our series of missed clotheslines and both found ourselves as crisscrossing captives of momentum over and over again. A nonplussed Boris with an ill-fitting, striped referee's shirt officiated our match.

Fans voiced their random bits of disapproval as we both ended up on the receiving end of head cranks and open handed slaps across the chest. I could see their upset or cheering faces in a blur and also noticed them grabbing handfuls of tortilla fragments from the ring floor and flinging them at us. Corgan attempted to whip me into the ropes one more time but I went crashing into Boris. Both of our round and weighty bodies went crashing to the duct-tape covered canvas with a dull thud. I don't know what kept us from going through that unstable ring floor right then and there but somehow those boards held.

I flung the Three Mile Baby out of the ring as we reached the conclusion of our match. He spun around the top rope and his knee slammed down hard on the ring apron. Fans cleared out of the way as he dropped down to the floor but then they started to close in on him while he made his way back to finish our match. He was limping pretty badly and I didn't think it was a put-on for the benefit of the fans. He still climbed to the top rope for a missed splash attempt and the end of our match got blurry after that.

Now I know I was supposed to beat him for the privilege of managing his stratospheric wrestling career, but for some reason I remember losing that match. It was my first match so that would only have been right, but for some reason I still ended up managing him anyway. So much for that storyline making any kind of sense — not that anyone was really paying attention.

As sad as this may sound, that may have been my best in-ring performance despite the near incalculable amount of missed clotheslines and the complete lack of training that led up to it. Corgan and I were pretty excited about it — like we had just won the Super Bowl and were going to Disneyland.

Still, our performance was not without its critics. An indie worker named Hanson on the rec.sport.pro-wrestling newsgroup wrote: "A big guy known as Count Dante takes on a guy wearing a La Parka outfit calling himself the Five Mile Baby [sic]. Again, weak non-wrestling. These guys definitely do not know how to work. The match ends when they work some kind of angle where Dante becomes Five Mile's manager and they leave the ring together."

Backstage, Corgan looked miserable as he propped up his injured knee. He decided to slam down a couple of beers followed

by a handful of aspirins before he made any important medical decisions. We ineptly iced down his leg but it was already turning three
shades of purple. He knew that he had to go to the Emergency
Room, but wanted to put it off for as long as possible before enduring the horrors of SF General Hospital on a Friday night.

In the ring, Chango Loco had accidentally set the Missionary
Man's receding hairline ablaze with a ball of fire. After suffering a
pyrotechnic indignity, Missionary Man tagged Chango in the ster-
num with a very hard Muay-Thai sidekick. For several minutes, you
could smell the stench of burning hair wafting into the backroom,
but that wasn't the only foul odor fulminating in there.

"Psycho" Johnny Pain, an indie worker with biceps that could
shatter walnuts, had decided to just pull down his tights and take a
dump right there in the backroom. He didn't want to go through the
audience and use the Transmission's public restrooms and no one
seemed inclined to stop the 250-pound bodybuilder from squatting
and pooping wherever he pleased. I always felt sorry for whoever
had to clean up that pile of oversized man-turds.

The rest of the show was the usual blurry mishmash of backroom antics and grind house punk rock washed in downed bottles
of free Corona and comp shots of bourbon. My work for the night
was far from over as Brett got the bright idea to make me referee the
last set of wrestling. I'd never reffed a match before but this was ısw.
That hardly seemed to matter.

I got overly ambitious with my ref chores and decided that
Count Dante should be a ball-busting enforcer of a ring officiate.
I had a character to consider. I couldn't go out there and be some
scared chump when I was the deadliest man alive.

I refereed a handicap match between Audra and three of the
dancers from Stinky's Peep Show. They were the large and lovely
go-go girls and they shook their stuff on Thursday nights in a rock
and roll burlesque that Audra booked at the Covered Wagon Saloon
on Folsom Street a few blocks down from the Paradise.

Most of the match consisted of Audra, their boss, throwing them around. The trio of go-go dancers always went off script (if there even was one) and pulled me down and dragged me onto the mat, but the payoff was a cheap feel and some boobs in my face. (Presiding over women's matches did have its prurient appeal.) One of the dancers had a crazed look in her eyes when she grabbed, groped and pulled me, and I kind of grew to fear the random nature of their violence as the match went on. When Audra stacked all of the hapless hoofers on top of one another, I counted the pin very quickly.

I reffed some more matches with Jose and Boris and masks and Lord knows what else. I got pretty full of myself and disqualified Shane Dynasty/Gran Fangorio for trying to bring a sledgehammer into the ring. I could tell that he wanted to belt me really bad but I was a little too big for him to shoot on. Luckily for me, he restrained himself from just cracking my head open with that sledgehammer.

It was pretty stupid of me but I never ended up having to ref a set again. At least I wasn't clueless enough to mess with Audra's match. That would have been a disaster. She was the big jefe and you didn't want to piss her off.

The show wrapped up with a set by the greaser blowhard outfit Deadbolt. They told bad jokes in between sludgy and slow Link Wray inspired instrumentals, but their main point of appeal was that they brought out a buzz saw and cut up a lot of junk.

Corgan finally hauled himself to the hospital, but that set off a convoluted chain of events that proved to be his undoing. Earlier that night, Tom had asked for and received payment of $50 for working his match. Asking for money was a previously unheard of practice among the untrained masses of ISW. We were supposed to be doing it to live out our adolescent fantasies — for the sheer love of it. Why did Audra have to pay any of us anyway with a seemingly limitless supply of wrestling wannabes knocking down her door and leaving messages on her answering machine? One group of us was just as capable of running through a crappy wrestling match as any other.

Still, Tom wanted to honestly say that he was a professional wrestler. For all I knew, he might have needed that fifty bucks, but it wasn't about that for him. He just wanted to be the honest to God paid professional in the world of sports entertainment to which he had always aspired. Being paid was an odd sort of honor for him. Audra agreed but also told him that he couldn't tell anyone about it for fear that such news of her paying somebody would upset her whole rock bottom pay scale.

While Corgan clutched his knee in the waiting room of SF General, he told some cop that he had hurt himself wrestling but was paid fifty whole bucks for the privilege. Don't ask me how, but Augie Ragone, who had a bunch of friends on the SFPD, found out about this and the news that Corgan had blabbed about getting paid not only got out to other incredibly strange wrestlers but also to Audra.

The next day, as Tom elevated his knee and took a steady regimen of painkillers and anti-inflamatories, Audra called and told him he was through. She had told him not to tell anyone about that fifty bucks and then she'd found out he had. She gave him the axe and there was nothing that anyone could do about it.

"I expect you to go on and keep doing this thing," he later told me over the phone. "You've got a future in wrestling."

Tom was a nobody — a strange loner. He wasn't part of the scene. He wasn't cool and he didn't have the right tattoos or listen to the right bands. I could have been noble and phoned Audra or Brett, fed them some hokey line like, "if Tom Corgan goes, then I go," but I was a nobody too. I thought that Corgan had gotten a raw deal. I wanted to do something for him, but I didn't have any pull whatsoever. I was going to have a hard enough time keeping myself hovering around the wrestling show that I was now addicted to. Getting Tom back into Audra's good graces would have to wait for later, if such a thing could ever be done at all.

# 5

# STINKY'S
# PEEP SHOW

IF I WAS GOING TO STAY in the wrestling show that was putting me in front of screaming club goers, getting me girlfriends and
possibly landing me on cable TV and a European tour, I was going
to have to find some friends. After Corgan got the axe, I was going
to have to find them fast. The place to find them was at Stinky's
Peep Show, which happened every Thursday night at the Covered
Wagon Saloon in South of Market.

Stinky's Peep Show was Audra's low-budget, rock and roll burlesque extravaganza, which was at its very best when it was so very
wrong. Audra booked three bands on every show. Between sets
she used a bullhorn to herd those club rats into a tiny backroom
where the walls were covered with red, crushed velvet wallpaper,
making the place resemble a Wild West brothel. Audra, always
clad in a constrictive corset for these events, served as the rough
and tumble, frontier madam, both loved and feared by the girls
who worked for her.

What ISW was to wrestling, Stinky's was to pornography. You had peep shows where John Pierre dressed in a construction paper pilgrim outfit while he mock raped the voluptuous, raven-haired Tigger LeTwang who played the part of a Sacajawea squaw in an Indian headdress even though her skin was as pale as printer paper. After the dildo raping was over Pierre then pretended to stuff Tigger's cavity with turkey legs and croutons all in a revolting Thanksgiving Day celebration. Around the Fourth of July, John Pierre did another holiday-themed shocker where he lubed up ballpark franks, shoved them up his rectum and then pooped them back out onto the grill of a Weber Smoky Joe. Audra and Pierre tried to sell the recently shat out dogs, but they found no takers.

There was also a show where John Pierre wore a housedress and spent ten minutes changing his male roommate's diapers. That show presented the audience with a bit too much full male frontal nudity. There was a tribute to Japanese giant monster movies with the bare-breasted female monsters Boobzilla and Muffra. When Audra got really desperate, she just had Jefferson Monroe drop his pants and twist his nuts into knots. He had an honest to God talent for twisting and turning his genitalia into an array of painful looking positions without breaking a sweat while every male in the audience winced and hid their eyes.

Most of these exhibitions didn't achieve that level of creativity, however. Many of the shows just featured some cute scenester gals like the Gomez sisters in vinyl bondage wear promising to show the pinks of their nipples but never actually baring their breasts.

Throughout each little lurid spectacle, Audra goaded the captive audience into hurling dollar bills onto the backroom's tiny stage. Of course the promise of unseen nipples was probably a better cash generator than Jefferson's twisted nuts or John Pierre in a housedress. After the show Audra snapped Polaroids for the sleazos in the audience who wanted something to display on their fridges. A particularly good peep show could rake in over 200 bucks for just a few minutes of stage time. In certain ways the peep shows did better business and were a lot more creative than the wrestling shows.

The Covered Wagon shared a building with a skid row hotel where the most out of it junkies and crackheads made their homes. No one who lived there bothered to complain about the noise coming from the club even when the Norwegian black metal band Mayhem played there. Nobody who lived in that hotel slept all that much.

The first thing that you noticed when you entered the dank and dirty cw to go to Stinky's were the "Large N' Lovely Go-Go Girls." They were the main attraction boasted about on the fliers taped to every telephone pole on Haight Street and then some. There was Tigger, Kink, Bria and Liz. They shook their stuff on a corner of the bar or top of the pool table while tattooed hipsters in trucker caps stood underneath them and ogled every one of their curves and rolls while begging to shove dollar bills in between their oversized but all-natural tits.

Stinky's was the place to be and everyone involved with isw hung out there. Jose and Boris swilled bottled beers by the coat check window. Chango Loco held court in the place and seemed like he knew just about everyone. The price for getting in for free and hanging your hat there was that you had to go into that back-room peep show. There was no getting out of it and if you tried you got royally bitched out by Audra until you caved in.

Sometimes guys got roped into being part of the peep show. Jose once had to don a G-string and perform a sumo skit with Tigger LeTwang. Craig Martins was railroaded into reprising the John Pierre diaper changing bit, which entailed crying like baby and letting a packed room full of perverts look at his newly baby powdered dingly dangly. Martins got the worst of it too. A German film crew captured the whole spectacle on tape for the entire European Union to see. As Martins entered the backroom wearing nothing but a pair of Depends and an oversized baby bonnet, a clueless Nordic cameraman shoved a steadicam right in his crotch and started shooting. The resulting documentary reportedly garnered very high ratings and was a popular repeat on Central European broadcast television.

It was because of this sort of thing that I just assumed that Craig Martins was as queer as Liberace's little lacey panties. He did break into isw by winning a dream date with El Homo Loco after all. That was the most m4m way to get in through the backdoor that I could think of.

After said dream date, he came back to isw as the strutting and swaggering masked s&m leather daddy known as the Cruiser. He was the bear to Homo Loco's pansy. All of their angles revolved around their off and on again love affair. Cruiser's first match was against Homo Loco, but they rekindled their romance by the end and formed a doubly gay tag team, only to break up once more during the aftermath of their next match. For the part of the Cruiser, Martins affected this macho snagglepuss lisp with a little bit of the New York Bowery thrown in for good measure. Little comic details like that put Craig above the rest of isw as far as characterization was concerned.

But I believed that Craig was gay before isw, the Cruiser and El Homo Loco entered the picture. San Francisco is a rotating fishbowl of a town where you run into the same people over and over again. I had met Craig at the Nightbreak on Haight Street while seeing a double bill of the weirdo rock bands M.I.R.V. and Idiot Flesh. I honestly believed that he was picking up on me because he was really into this Chinatown polyester tie with a playing card pattern that I was wearing. I was as high as a kite on mushrooms and he kept on clutching at my tie and staring at it, transfixed by its tacky design.

"Man, this is the raddest tie," he said while looking into my eyes with a disarming intensity that was probably the result of him being as stoned as I was. "Look, man, I work at the zoo. Anytime that you want to go to the zoo, just give me a call."

That had to be the oddest man on man pickup line that I had ever heard — even in San Francisco. A year or two later in ISW, it just made perfect sense that the gay guy from the zoo was winning a date with El Homo Loco and playing the part of the Cruiser. I was so confident in the man's raging homosexuality that I even went so far as to try to talk up Tigger LeTwang one night — completely unaware that Tigger was Craig's girlfriend and they were living together. When I found out that the gay guy from the zoo was Tigger's live-in boyfriend, I was a bit embarrassed, but luckily Tigger was completely oblivious to my feeble pickup attempts.

Tigger had fronted a trash rock band called the Hyperdrive Kittens and she was a fat chick fetish queen whose big, naked body had graced the cover and the double page fold-outs of such fine men's spank mags as *Big Butt* and *Plumpers*. She had legions of creepy fans and they all made their way to Stinky's sooner or later when they caught wind that she was shaking it there. She even lost a boring accounting job over an appearance she made on that HBO titillation-as-documentary show *Real Sex*.

But even with a centerfold like Tigger LeTwang as his girlfriend, Martin was just as big a nerd as I ever was. He had boyish blue eyes, but always looked about ten years older than he really was due to his long face and premature balding. He played guitar for this psychobilly band called the Disembowlers, but, like me, he was never quite part of that scene. He mostly played rockabilly just to gawk at all of the Bettie Page wannabe gals who came to the shows, showed off their cleavage and wore their grandma's hand-me-downs.

As good as he was at playing his gold glitter Telecaster, he was even better as a cartoonist. He did all of the artwork for the Stinky's Peep Show fliers in a style that was a combination of classic Disney, Jack Davis and Wally Wood with everything pushed to its most underground, grotesque outer limits. His most disgusting piece of flier art depicted a Looney Tunes style baby screaming at the top of his lungs while streams of piss and diarrhea streamed out of his overstuffed diaper. Martins also drew the infant with a disproportionately man-sized pair of hairy testicles that were bursting out the side of his Pampers. There was something unsettling about that image no matter how rendered it was. It might as well have been in Smell-O-Vision. I always wondered if that flier art didn't actually drive down Stinky's attendance the week that it was posted.

It was at those Thursday nights at Stinky's that Chango Loco, Craig Martins and I formed an unlikely but nearly inseparable trio. On the weekends that there wasn't an ISW show at the Transmission we piled into my '66 Oldsmobile and went to the Paradise, DNA, Covered Wagon or any other club that would let us in for free because we were with the wrestling show.

Loco knew every bouncer, bartender and doorman at every club that we went to, as he had seemed to work with all of them at one time or another. It didn't seem unusual that he had worked so many jobs in such a short time. I was temping a lot back then and avoiding permanent jobs like the plague because I always held out hope of going on tour with my band and making it big in entertainment somehow.

But Chango, Craig and I were still three guys and we gave each other plenty of shit. Chango once accused me of sleeping with Ruby, my costume maker. He had played drums in the White Trash Debutantes while Ruby was singing backups and writing songs for the band. "You hit that, didn't you?" Chango asked pointedly while I navigated my low and wide Oldsmobile through the maze of one-way San Francisco streets.

Ruby was like a crazy aunt to me. I could never even think of such a thing, but my fact-based denials only seemed to confirm Loco's suspicions. "I knew you fucking did it! Don't fucking lie to me! Admit it! You hit that!" he exclaimed while Craig Martins doubled over in my backseat with tears streaming down his face.

Even with Chango getting us into clubs for free, we often just ended up at Chango's or Craig's apartments where we watched

Mexican lucha libre B movies and old pro wrestling tapes. We gossiped about who was sleeping with who, compared notes on which rockabilly chicks we thought were hot and bitched about wrestlers that we didn't like. If we ended up at Craig's place, Tigger LeTwang added a lot of sarcastic levity to these all night bull sessions.

Having Chango Loco for a new best friend involved a descent into a world of ethnic mysticism. His apartment was a candlelit Santerian shrine surrounded by pop culture collectables, but even his shelves filled with *Star Wars* and Marvel Comics action figures held a religious significance for him. Carved idols of the black African, machete wielding Chango were sometimes posed with Chewbacca and other sci-fi heroes in a kind of religious diorama that was as meaningful to Loco as a Christmastime nativity scene is to a devout Christian.

On the staircase and in the hallways of his six-flat Victorian apartment building, Loco always left grisly piles of chicken feet and entrails accompanied by candles that he kept burning day and night to ward off evil spirits. He was in constant squabbles with his neighbors over those smelly and hazardous pagan displays.

In San Francisco, Santeria was both exotic and mundane since its ritual "Siete Potencias Africanas" candles were stocked at the Cala Foods right next to the "Hispanic Goods" section with its neatly arranged shelves of canned nopales cactus, Herdez salsas and dried chili pods. Most SF hipsters (myself included) couldn't resist the allure of those garish, glass candle holders with their overly saturated four-color designs, which depicted a scarred and pustule ridden San Lazaro healing the sick or a pre-decapitation John the Baptist. In the mind of Chango Loco, who knew what kind of charms we were unwittingly activating as we lit those candles just to give our overly cluttered apartments a little ambience.

Santeria originated in West Africa and was brought to Cuba and Latin America by the ugliness of the slave trade. African slaves who toiled in the Caribbean cane fields were forced to hide the worship of their original religion from their Christian masters by using images of the Catholic saints to represent their actual demigods. The orisha Chango, for example, was represented by the visage of Saint Jerome and worshippers of Ogun (the Lord of metals, minerals and tools) substituted the picture of John the Baptist for the deity that they really prayed to.

Many Mexicans throughout the Bay Area seemed to give the religion some lip service but with its freewheeling mixture of African magic and Catholic idolatry, it was often hard to tell where Catholicism ended and Santeria began. For some, Santeria was a full-time practice and for others, lighting those candles was the equivalent of carrying a lucky horseshoe or rabbit's foot. "We believe in God," Chango Loco once told me, "we just don't work with him directly."

Loco completely immersed himself in practicing magic, casting spells and levying curses. He often went into spastic convulsions claiming that he was "being mounted by spirits." After only a short time of hanging out with him, this kind of thing became just normal behavior and Martins and I both barely noticed when Loco went into his temporary spasms of otherworldly possession. He also tried to convince Martins, who still worked at the zoo at that time, to get his hands on some honest to Jesus chimpanzee shit. "You don't know the kind of power the droppings of such rare animals can have," Loco said as we both fought like hell not to laugh in his face.

You might be asking why we continued to hang out with Loco with so many idiosyncrasies bordering on out-and-out insanity. The simple fact of the matter was that we were all having too much fun. Loco may have looked intimidating but he was also jovial. He was a consummate prankster and he was as funny as all hell. He also seemed to be the most earnest person that I had ever met. Loco had a way of making you feel that you were his best friend in the entire universe. Mixed with street smarts he had a charisma that was inescapable.

I'm an atheist so I never worried about such flirtations with black magic, voodoo or hoodoo sending me on a one-way ticket to a tormenting hell. Even though I don't believe in Bigfoot or the Loch Ness Monster, I desperately wish that I could. Palling around with Chango Loco keyed in on that urge to accept so many Time Life Books' dubious *Mysteries of the Unexplained* as fact and live in a fantasy world of psychics, UFOs and spirit photography. Running even the most normal errands with Loco was like being trapped inside of an old episode of *In Search Of* except without any creepy Leonard Nimoy narration or the cheap synth soundtrack. There was an eight-year-old part of me that wanted that.

One time, when I met him at the botanica where he bought the herbs and potions for his rituals, he turned to me in all seriousness and said, "There are forces that are not meant to be tampered with!" It was a stock line from so many 1930s Bela Lugosi movies. At that moment, it was like I was the milksop protagonist of one of those films. The only question was if the movie was going to end with a horde of angry villagers armed with torches and pitchforks chasing Chango Loco into a pit of quicksand or if Chango was going to transform me into some kind of zombie-like ghoul and those villagers were going hunt me down with their packs of baying hounds.

It helped that Chango and I had an understanding of sorts. When he explained the power, fortune and romance that could be gained through so many rites involving copious amounts of chicken blood and Bacardi fire I simply told him, "Count Dante is a man of science." I had stock lines from old movies of my own, but saying that from time to time made him respect me. I will never know if it was due to my frankness or just because I wasn't such an easy mark.

But even with new friends as Chango Loco and Craig Martins in my corner, I was losing ground in ISW. Those meetings at the Missionary Man's place started to feel all too reminiscent of junior high school gym class where I was invariably picked last for the team. I went to those meetings and left with nothing. Everyone chose their partners and got their matches and I remained as a kind of hanger on with not much to do.

In one show I played the part of a manager in a very short match that ended with me unceremoniously having a flimsy acoustic guitar filled with baby powder slammed over my head by Brett/Borracho Gigante. I took the fall, passed out and rolled out of the ring. That was it.

Later on that same show, the Cruiser tangled with Chango Loco. After Loco made his grand fire breathing entrance through the audience, Craig returned the favor by holding a zippo lighter up to his denim covered ass and lit one of his own farts on fire. That burst of blue methane flame effectively stole Loco's usually considerable thunder.

In the show after that I wrestled a bouncer friend of Loco's in what quickly earned a reputation as the worst ISW match ever. The guy was adorned with all the latest modern primitive fashions and body modifications. He had large, wooden hoops placed in his earlobes that extended the cartilaginous tissue all the way down to his shoulders as well as the prerequisite stainless steel spike through his nose and the full sleeve of pagan tattoos. Chango Loco must have been a member of some kind of piercing of the month club with this guy or something.

I insisted that he wrestle as a bike messenger character called the Critical Master after this protest that was held the final Friday of every month called Critical Mass where hordes of people took to their bicycles and tied up financial district traffic for hours. The participants in Critical Mass were mostly just asking for more bike lanes but the SFPD, after being inundated with the complaints of suburban commuters, brutally broke up one rally with billy clubs and pepper spray. The TV news that night showed scenes of cops on their brand new Yamaha dirt bikes winding their way after defenseless bike messengers and throwing them to the pavement with more than justifiable force. That protest turned police-induced riot was a cause-celeb at the time and ISW's hipper audience was more than sure to get it. It was the first local/current events kind of angle that I had ever pitched.

The Critical Master got into the ring and didn't want to do anything at all. I had to judo throw and hip-toss him for real just to make anything resembling a fight happen during that match. If I hadn't done that, we would have ended up with a four-minute match that consisted of nothing but two fat guys standing around staring at each other. Such spectacles were not all that uncommon in ISW, but it wasn't like we needed any more of them. I finished him off with this jarring front headlock into a leg sweep that was taught to me by Royce Gracie himself. However, things got even worse for me when the Critical Master went backstage and spent the rest of the night clutching an ice pack to the back of his neck and complaining about how I had beaten him up.

As lame as this sounds, standing just shy of 6' 3" and weighing in at almost 300 pounds (in 1997), I was ISW's equivalent of Andre the Giant. Borracho Gigante was taller than me but he was all lanky and looked like he should be shooting hoops for some team in Slovenia instead of body slamming luchadores. Chango Loco and Gran Fangorio only hovered around the six-foot mark. In a not very tall promotion, I was ISW's ogre-in-residence. After having to toss Loco's pal to the mat a few times, I got a rep for hurting people — for being what wrestlers called "stiff" in the ring.

But even while I was somewhat sidelined as a wrestler, the wild and wooly and outright disorganized nature of the thing that was ISW presented me with many opportunities to have an impact on the show.

With the exception of Allan Bolte, the show's live commentary was sorely lacking. The Amazing Caltiki served as color commentator, but he mostly stunk up the joint when he got on the mic.

Everything was about him. He ceaselessly blabbed about himself and how he could kick the collective asses of the assembled might of the entire isw roster. Here we were trying to present these matches to paying customers and he did nothing but belittle the whole show. When matches ended, he just blathered further and delayed the beginning of the next bout by as much as a full five minutes making an already overly crowded show run twice as long as it should have. He was part of the original isw brain trust, but he never thought of the show as a whole.

They did sometimes have Cory McAbee split the announcing chores with Bolte. McAbee sang with this art rock band called the Billy Nayer Show and he put on these elaborate performances at the Castro Theatre where he screened his experimental short films followed by a set of new wave nursery rhymes with his band. As a wrestling announcer, he was a couple of steps up from Caltiki, but he knew nothing at all about wrestling in any way, shape or form. What he did bring to the table was a well-timed exclamation of the words "*Son of a bitch*" when something really crazy happened in the ring. Cory brought the house down with that one but that was all he had. I knew I could do better than the both of them.

I had all my spoken word experience. Alan Black from the Edinburgh Castle even wanted to send me to the U.K. where he was sure that I could hook up with Irvine Welsh and become some kind of performance art sensation. Half the appeal of seeing my band was the success seminar monologues that I laid out between songs. When I did spoken word open mics at the Casa Nova or the Nightbreak the bums on Valencia or Haight Street stopped pushing their shopping carts to cheer me on. I had ad libbed my way through more than my fair share of poetry slams and rock concerts. I had the voice. I may have sucked in the ring but I was damned good on the mic and I knew that I could make those wrestling shows better by standing on that stage and performing my own twisted brand of improvisational pro wrestling blow-by-blow commentary.

It didn't take a hard sell to get Audra to let me call a couple of matches with Bolte. "If you want to announce, go right ahead," she said as she stormed into the backroom while checking over some last minute details before the first band went on.

Bolte seemed a little confused when I first asked him about co-announcing, but when I explained that I was majoring in broadcasting at SF State he seemed more at ease with me. He actually needed the help. I was at those meetings and I knew who the characters were, whereas Bolte was just handed a computer printout with a list of the matches before every show. To make things harder, this printout was invariably littered with a confusing maze of illegibly handwritten revisions that were scrawled by the wrestlers themselves. With so many names crossed out and lines and arrows drawn all over the page, it was hard to tell who was wrestling who unless you were at those meetings.

As far as wrestlers' weights and places of origin were concerned, Bolte mostly just made that stuff up to have something to say out there. During one of my matches, Bolte announced me at 295 pounds but then during the match referred to me as weighing "at least 250 pounds!" By the end of that match, the Allan Bolte weight loss plan had me down to 235 pounds. Making shit up was a tradition of ISW commentary that I soon followed in.

Allan had his signature lines. A babyface wrestler was always announced as being "VERRRY POPULAR," with a little bit of a lilting emphasis on the "pop" in "popular." For a heel, Bolte's voice grew a bit more gravelly as he sternly said, "VERRRRRY CONTROVERSIAL" before announcing the wrestler's name. Bolte also made up little bits of banter before and after matches. He announced that he had seen Chango Loco wrestle "all over the circuit in Nashville and Shreveport" although neither Loco nor Bolte had worked shows out there. Bolte hated to travel much farther than Reno, Tahoe or Fresno for announcing gigs. Evidently El Gran Fangorio had recently defended his ISW title in Vegas, Reno and Phoenix as well.

It didn't matter to the beer swilling punkers and scenesters that made up our audience. It wasn't like they were reading the "Here & There" section of *The Wrestling Observer* for the latest updates on who was working in what indie leagues. What Allan Bolte was doing was creating an alternate reality where ISW champions toured the region and defended their titles just as the wrestling champs of old like Lou Thesz or "Strangler" Lewis did. With his pressed tuxedo and neatly coiffed and dyed hair, Bolte gave paper champions such as Gran Fangorio and clowns such as myself five minutes of respectability that we could have never manufactured for ourselves. With his old school radio announcer vocal mannerisms, he was something out of the past.

Backstage, Allan enthusiastically took swigs of his favorite tequila from the flask that he kept in his breast pocket while schmoozing the indie workers that he knew from handling the announcing chores for APW and other small-time Nor Cal outfits. He never snubbed the amateur ISW talent though and he talked up this article that he was writing about our shows for *Pro Wrestling Illustrated*. The story did eventually come out but seemed to dwell on the appearances by Shane Dynasty and "Psycho" Johnny Pain more than it mentioned the crowd-pleasing crotch-thrusting antics of El Homo Loco.

Bolte was also a fountain of real behind-the-scenes wrestling gossip from working so many WWE and WCW house shows in the Bay Area and the Central Valley. One of these anecdotes concerned this time that WWE champ "The Heartbreak Kid" Shawn Michaels threw a real, first-class diva hissy fit. Michaels was a longhaired pretty boy who wore an unintentionally homoerotic chain mail vest and a pair of skintight, red spandex pants adorned with the kinds of little broken heart designs that nine-year-old girls would draw on the backs of their school binders. He had a reputation for being a backroom manipulator with no equal and no shame.

"Oh, it was just awful," Allan said in his less booming but still resonant conversational voice as a small gathering of ISW wrestlers changed in and out of their costumes. "Shawn was throwing a real tantrum. He was slamming lockers, kicking stools. So I went up to him and said, 'Shawn, do you remember the days when you slept in your car and drove 500 miles to wrestle a match for thirty dollars because of your love for the sport?'"

Bolte took a breathy pause and concluded: "And then Shawn looked at me said, 'Thank you, Allan. You really just put it all in perspective.'"

Now anyone familiar with the arrogance and petulance of Shawn Michaels and how he had so often jetted out of a pro wrestling territory without dropping his title belt in the ring, found this tale hilariously hard to believe. But Allan didn't have any reason to lie to us, and he tended to be the least full of shit of anyone who had spent so much time in the creepy carnie world of pro wrestling.

As I made my way to the stage to call a couple of matches for the first time, Audra stopped me right before I made it to the creaky wooden steps.

"Somebody's throwing fucking pita bread!" she screamed trying to make herself heard over the crowd noise. "What kind of sick, granola fuck is throwing fucking pita bread?! You've gotta get up there on the mic and tell them to only throw corn tortillas! Only the corn ones! They fucking fly! Pita bread doesn't fly!"

I looked around and the pita bread seemed to be flying pretty good to me but it had a lot more weight to it than the uncooked corn wafers did and probably hurt a lot more when you were tagged in the face with it.

I got up on the stage, took a look at Bolte as if for final permission, grabbed the extra Shure-57 microphone and did my duty.

"Ladies and gentlemen," I said in my best, booming racetrack announcer's voice, "Please do not throw pita bread, lavashes or any other Middle Eastern food products at the wrestlers! Please only hurl corn tortillas. Yes, you call it corn, but my people call it maize.

Corn tortillas really fly, while flat bread just falls, well, flat!"

Of course telling that unruly mob of paying club goers that they couldn't do something only made them want to pelt me with whatever they could lay their drunken little hands on. Tortillas, crumpled up plastic cups and handfuls of ice cubes were flung at me from all directions, but that's what we were all there for — the wrestlers, the announcers, the referees — to have stuff flung at us. A longhaired little dweeb in the front row kept on gathering handfuls of previously thrown tortilla fragments and then continuously flicked them at me like it was some kind of game.

"Hey, hippie!" I shouted as I singled him out. "Phil Lesh and Friends is playing at the Warfield next week. Why don't you hitchhike over there and catch a miracle!"

The friends that he had come to the show with laughed right in his face. "Hey hippie," they said, taunting him. It also got some scattered laughs from other people in the audience who picked up on the Grateful Dead "I Need A Miracle" reference.

I took care of that little runt and I was quick on my feet with the other hecklers. I had always been a big fan of Don Rickles, also Rudy Ray Moore from the *Dolemite* movies so when I had to I could resort to putdown comedy and one-liners at other peoples' expense. Doing live commentary for isw, I had to a lot.

But even with my forays into stand-up as ring announcer, I knew more about wrestling than Cory McAbee did and I kept the show moving a whole lot better than the ramblings of the Amazing Caltiki. This was good because, although I could be funny and possessed the right voice, I stepped all over Allan's lines and cut him off right and left my first couple of times up there. I got excited when an idea for something clever or fucked up to say popped into my head or when a wrestler pulled off a top rope move. I just blurted it out as soon as I thought of it. Allan and I never discussed what kind of cues he was going to give me and it was all off the cuff and from the hip — like all of early isw.

But Bolte was very patient with me and directed me as best he could with facial gestures and body language. After that first show, he showed me the ropes and mentored me in the ways of wrestling announcing. He gave me a much-needed break after the expulsion of Tom Corgan.

By the second and third time that I was up there, we started giving each other lanes to speak in. I ended rants with a simple "back to you, Allan" line and Allan often handed over control of the conversation by asking me for my "professional opinion." I handled the color commentary and Bolte did the blow-by-blow and most of the ring introductions. After a while, however, we became akin to an old school 1940s comedy duo like Abbott and Costello with Bolte as the straight man and me as the funny guy.

ISW almost never had any angles or storylines back then. Many matches were still being put together in the backroom after the show had already started. I took it upon myself to make feuds up off the top of my head the same way that Bolte did with the wrestlers' heights and weights. Why was Chango Loco fighting Doctor Loco? Well, because "Doctor Loco is a man of science and reason and he wants to turn back the tide of superstition represented by Chango Loco and his brainwashed followers!" That seemed to be as good an explanation as any.

I referred to the rotund Chupa Suave as "ISW's greatest lover." El Gourmexico (Jefferson Monroe's chef character who originally spoke only in unintelligible faux French) was bringing internationally acclaimed cuisine to the unsophisticated palettes of the ISW masses. The continuous matches between El Homo Loco and the Cruiser "illustrated the dysfunctional nature of relationships in today's society."

"Is true romance dead, Allan?" I asked. "Please tell me that it isn't so, because if these crazy kids El Homo Loco and El Cruiser can't make it work, then who can? They should be in some kind of couples' counseling instead of in that wrestling ring!"

"I suppose, Count Dante," Bolte replied rolling his eyes. "I suppose."

"I suppose" became a common Allan Bolte retort to my crazed tangents. If we were on a sitcom, that line probably would have made the live-studio audience break out in rabid applause after the first season. There may have even been Bolte lunchboxes and T-shirts with that line on it in bubbly, fluorescent, block letters.

Doctor Loco once took off his shirt and exposed his flabby physique to the entire crowd. "Doctor Loco isn't ashamed of his body the way the rest of this overly clothed isw roster is, Allan!" I said frantically as if something more exciting than a thirty-year-old Mexican removing an article of clothing had just happened. "Look at that manly chest, Allan! Look at it! Women at ringside, please, control your animal passions!"

There was a spell during this match where Jose/Doctor Loco and his opponent just stood there and stared at each other not really knowing what to do next as was common in isw. But after I had talked up his courageous act of disrobing, Doctor Loco jumped out of the ring and started making out with this drunk chick at ringside and she actually drunkenly kissed him back with tongue, clawed at him and wouldn't let go of his sweat soaked body to let him get back in the ring and finish his match.

Unlike a regular wrestling show, most of our audience had a shred of a college education and at least half of our audience were women. I got away with using ten-dollar words, was able to make people laugh by using surrealism and absurdity. isw allowed me to be a Dadaist sportscaster — something that many experts would have previously dismissed as utterly impossible.

After having some success on the mic at the wrestling shows, Audra gave me the bullhorn duty at Stinky's. After those neo-glam, surf instrumental and gutter punk bands stopped playing I had to pace through the well-weathered dive bar with that RadioShack loudspeaker to coax those micro-brew guzzling poseurs and party girls into that backroom. Audra was always better at browbeating those types into shelling out a dollar for the peep show than I was, but I could get them to throw paper bills at the go-go girls once they had already submitted to being a captive audience.

You didn't let the dancer flash her boobs all at once. You had to draw it out. "How many of you people want to see this lovely lady's boobies?!" I called, building up their anticipation of glimpsing a twenty-three year-old's mammary glands. "Well, let's see some more dollar bills on this stage!" There were always a few dollar bills that made their way onto the stage that wouldn't have been parted with without my being there.

By manning the bullhorn at Stinky's, I probably freed Audra to count cash and keep the dancers and bands in line. With my mic skills, I discovered my niche in the whole lunatic, all-night, club-hopping world of San Francisco's South of Market district. Working the wrestling shows and even those small, backroom nudie shows seemed so much more real, so much more substantial, than my mind-numbing temp jobs shelving books and loose-leaf filing at downtown law libraries — or my square broadcasting classes at San Francisco State. Being totally immersed in that music and showbiz scene is why I left the calm quiet of the suburbs and instead endured the broken car windows and aggressive panhandlers of the city. I wouldn't have had it any other way.

# 6

# CELEBRITY GANG BANG

IT WAS JUNE OR JULY 1997 and it was uncharacteristically clear and hot by the standards of fog-enshrouded San Francisco where it's often as chilly in the summer as in the dead of winter. I was at Stinky's Peep Show and the Covered Wagon was only about half full. This was either because some lesser-known local bands were playing or that the warm weather had given rockers options like hanging out in the open-air courtyard at this bike messenger bar called the Zeitgeist. San Francisco didn't offer you all that many nights where you could hang outside past midnight without being bundled up like you were about to go off on an arctic expedition. You had to appreciate those rare nights when you got them, but I was still there at the cw.

On the bar, Bria was unenthusiastically sashaying to whatever uptempo 1990s Fat Wreck Chords release Audra's boyfriend Spike was spinning on the turntable. On the pool table, Liz was putting on a dazzling display of kicks as if she were in front of a packed house. It was hard not to admire and contemplate those kicks of hers and dream about them as her foot went way above her forehead. Liz and Tigger were the prettiest of the Stinky's dancers and they always gave it their all when they were up on the pool table or the countertop. Liz never coasted on her pouty, baby doll good looks and Tigger wasn't one to let her double-D's do all of her work for her.

I was chatting with this brown-haired coat check girl named Laurel whom I had an unrequited crush on. Laurel looked as good in a miniskirt as any gal in all of San Francisco but what made her even more attractive was that she had a Master's degree in military history. I could argue about George Kennan's *The Long Telegram* with her and discuss its implications in shaping the Truman Doctrine. Sadly, I wasn't her type and she always ended up going for skater-punk tools and effeminate fashion nerds who could never appreciate her for her ability to delve into Barbara Tuchman's *Stilwell and the American Experience in China* the way that I could.

In the world of dating, skinny guys with glasses were always my arch nemesis. As a smart guy trapped in a big man's body, I always found myself losing out the bookworm women of my true desire to skinny guys with glasses who may have "looked smart" but weren't necessarily. This human condition only grew worse for me after the "geek chic" phenomenon of the late 1990s kicked in. Callow, sexist scammers could affect nerdiness and still be the same jerks that they were when they wore pegged acid washed jeans.

When the women that I really wanted ended up on the arm of one of these dreaded skinny guys with glasses, I was always told that at least she went for some bespectacled beanpole instead of some muscle man. That was supposed to give me some kind of solace. It was supposed to make me feel better that some oiled up, steroided out Hulk Hogan wannabes weren't taking all of my women. After a while I realized that bodybuilders with perfectly sculpted biceps and iron clad lats weren't my true enemy. They had never kicked sand in my face and walked off with my girl like in the Charles Atlas comic book ads. My true foils were those skinny guys with glasses. They were the ones who were taking the girls of my dreams and making me miserable. Just once, I wished that some art girl that I had my eye on ran off with Randy "Macho Man" Savage. Just once. At least that would have been funny.

That night at Stinky's, Chango Loco strutted up to me with a really intense sense of purpose about him. Laurel was allowed to sell shots at her coat check window. I offered Chango a swig of Cuervo Gold but he didn't take it. He was straight-edged. He didn't drink. He didn't do drugs. He even had a chance to "party" with Rick Nielsen of Cheap Trick (read: do rails of coke on the tour bus), but Chango even turned that down despite his acute star fucker tendencies. It always kind of astonished me that a guy could be as constantly amped as Chango was without ever being wasted. If anyone needed to just calm down and smoke a joint once in a while, it was him.

I slugged down the shot of tequila and ordered a bottled beer to wash it down with. I always liked ordering bottled beers from Laurel because she had to bend over to get them. It was a good idea to select the Red Stripe, because they were on the bottom shelf of the fridge. I never would have bought that brand of brew anywhere else for any other reason.

Chango took me off to the side out of earshot of the coat check window. "You know Brett doesn't like you," he said bluntly. "He doesn't like the whole Count Dante thing. He likes the band okay, but he hates you as a wrestler. He doesn't want you in the ring."

There was plenty left to be desired concerning my ring work, granted, but I was no worse than seventy percent of the ISW roster. Why did Brett single me out?

"Because you're not lucha," Chango answered giving me what he thought was some heartfelt advice. "You don't wear a mask. You've got to be more lucha."

Chango Loco then stood straight up and tried to loom over me to better make his point and added, "Think lucha! You've got to think lucha libre. Mexican wrestling. It's *Mexican*."

The idea that Incredibly Strange Wrestling was some kind of traditional Mexican lucha libre promotion and that any of its regulars were legit luchadores was plainly ridiculous. Putting a mask on pasty white boys like Brett Kibele and Jefferson Monroe wasn't going to make them into technicos no matter how many times they dove off the top rope. Chango Loco and Doctor Loco may have been Latinos but they had a long way to go before being lucha. Lacing up a mask wasn't going to transform someone like me — an uncoordinated, overweight gringo with a Scottish surname — into Mil Mascaras anytime soon.

We were all just amateurs. Our wrestling was composed of odd combinations of karate classes we took as kids, judo and jiu-jitsu classes we took as adults, and high school Greco-Roman mat wrestling with a few ring moves that we either learned by slowing down videotapes of old WrestleManias or by getting pointers from some indie worker during a rare moment of helpfulness. Of course a lot of us didn't even go that far with our pro wrestling studies. The first time that Cruiser Craig went up to the top rope he fell off and hit the mat with a painful thud. Nobody bothered to tell him how to take a fall and he never took the time to ask. He had to learn from bruising experience.

Lucha libre has its own rules and guidelines and none of us had a clue about any of them. If we were a real lucha promotion, we would never do interviews or make wrestling speeches. We would have completely shied away from having any angles or storylines whatsoever. Our tag matches, as chaotic as they were, still had people tagging in their partners. Lucha tag matches are a free-for-all ballet with colorful characters acrobatically springing into the ring at will. Brett never followed that formula and neither did the rest of us. The indie workers like Shane just put on masks and affected vaguely

Spanglish names, but they still wrestled in a strictly American style with more rope work thrown in to placate the promotion. The only people who worked lucha on any of those shows were the actual, goddamned luchadores that Audra brought up from Mexico.

At best, we were a parody of lucha libre (with wrestler names like Chupa Suave, La Chingona and El Homo Loco), but at the very worst we were just no-talent, poseur luchadores.

But the 1990s were the golden era of poseurati. The SF scene had become so dominated by aspirations of retro chic that any attempts at true creativity or envelope pushing were frowned upon and fretted over. Fears of being labeled "uncool" ran at an all time high in the city's club scene and this forced many a hipster to work only with universally agreed upon "cool" aesthetics lifted from earlier decades and originated by other people. Like so-called "ironic" punk rock cover tunes, it was safe to do things this way because everything had already been tried and tested.

ISW couldn't actually be lucha libre any more than Quentin Tarantino's *Kill Bill* movies could be 1970s exploitation flicks (unless Tarantino actually traveled back in time to 1976 and managed to cut a drive-in distribution deal with Samuel Z. Arkoff). ISW could only strive to be an inspired homage but it was better off as an amalgamation.

Sure, the ISW fans wanted the masked pageantry and high-flying ring work of lucha. There is no doubt that the masks were a major selling point and anything off the top rope always got an enthusiastic response. But they also wanted Andy Kaufman craziness, Southern wrestling sleaze and 1980s WWE bluster with a good helping of social satire and surrealism thrown in. They wanted a cross between Ed Wood *and* Monty Python inanity (both accidental and contrived) all wrapped in politically incorrect ironies. And as far as lucha, our fans wanted ISW to be more like those weird El Santo monster movies than his actual matches.

Brett/Borracho Gigante wasn't so worried about whether I was or wasn't wearing a mask as much as he was concerned about the total takeover of his little rockabilly social scene by a collection of feisty nerds and nutcases. The ISW backroom was no longer a place for the swapping of pomade styling hints and tips on where to buy flaming dice decals for the side panels of your Dodge Dart.

Brett had seen ISW meetings presided over by the Missionary Man and Kid Anarchy. He probably wanted to get rid of them too, but they had the best work rate of any of ISW's non-pros and they had both created an entire short set's worth of characters including the Twinkie (who spoke in a Hindi accent and looked like a golden Hostess sponge cake) and Calibos, whose sole mission was to lose every match he ever fought no matter who was wearing the mask. Calibos was the emergency jobber character that anyone could play as long as they agreed to hold up the tradition of failing miserably. Also Missionary Man and Kid Anarchy could pull off that accursed Frankensteiner. That made them invulnerable to even the most well connected attempts at ouster.

The sad part about this was that Brett had read just as many comic books and collected just as many action figures as I ever had. He was a geek through and through. The second that he perceived that he was "cool," he became as cliquish as any of the trendies and jocks that tormented us in high school.

Brett wanting me gone only made me more determined to stick around. Going into ISW, I never thought that I would wrestle more than two or three matches. My mission was to get my name and my face out there in front of the hundreds of rockers, greasers and party gals that crammed themselves into the Transmission for every ISW show. Once I did that, I reasoned that my target audience would know who I was and that they would naturally want to check out Count Dante's kung fu rock and roll success seminar. (Why wouldn't they?) After wrestling a few times as Count Dante and without some mask covering my beautiful face, I would be connected. I could then get the better gigs at the better clubs like the

Bottom of the Hill or the Paradise. At the very least more people would show up to see me play at the Nightbreak, which wasn't such a bad thing either.

When you're plugging away with your band, you have to get those better shows at the better clubs opening for the bands that people actually give a shit about. If you can't pull that off, you just end up playing free shows on Sundays at punk rock dives in front of a thinning audience of dirtheads who would much rather be listening to somebody else. You can find yourself relegated to a punk rock purgatory of demo tapes coming out right before the band breaks up and fading, photocopied stickers of groups no one remembers permanently affixed to that always empty paper towel dispenser in a really foul dive bar bathroom on Haight Street.

But ISW was starting to be more than just a promotional tool for my band. ISW was in fact my one-way ticket to San Francisco celebrity. Being a celeb in San Francisco occupies a universe all its own — just like every other aspect of the place that Bay Area residents refer to as "The City." Once you make it in Baghdad by the Bay, you are almost destined to never make it anyplace else. When right wing radio shitbags like Rush Limbaugh proclaim that San Francisco "isn't part of America," you know they're right. They really are. Thousands of gays, weirdos and activist types move their asses to San Francisco every year because it isn't part of America. Can SF become part of the European Union? It would if it could.

San Francisco has its own scene with its own celebrities and artists. To San Franciscans, their city's mayor is just as important as the president of the United States if not more so. Oddly, our mayors are some of the few famous San Franciscans that somehow become known outside of San Francisco. Whether it is corrupt Willie Brown with his impeccable fedora collection or Gavin Newsom and his stand on gay marriage, SF mayors are some of the only big city executives that the national media pays attention to at all. Only the mayors of San Francisco and New York City get press coverage outside of their general metro areas. Nobody knows who the fuck the mayors of L.A. or Cleveland are and Marion Barry had to be caught on tape smoking crack for anyone to take notice of him.

San Francisco is its own place. It's different from the rest of the country and even different from the rest of California. Fuck Fresno, the Central Valley, Disneyland, Orange County, the pope and the president. We're going to let middle-aged bull-dykes with buzz cuts marry each other. If you don't like it, we'll see you all in hell. The city doesn't give two steaming shits about what is going on in the rest of the country and, conversely, the rest of the nation doesn't bother to ever ask San Francisco what it thinks either.

Sure, there are always busloads of tourists pouring out of their chartered buses to walk around in shorts through Fisherman's Wharf in fifty degree fog. Hollywood occasionally stops by to shoot some establishing shots for a forgettable thriller with Michael Douglas or, even worse, a Robin Williams comedy. Karl Malden used to push Rice-A-Roni and AmEx travelers' checks off the backs of moving cable cars around the same time that Dirty Harry was busy torturing perps on the green at Kezar Stadium where the 49ers used to play (until the residents of Haight Ashbury realized that the football fans pissed all over their neighborhood even more than the hippies did). There was also that mediocre 1990s cop show *Nash Bridges* where Don Johnson palled around with Cheech Marin (sans the monster doobies). The times that I saw ol' Don around town waiting for the cameras to roll, he wore so much stage makeup that he looked like a wax museum version of himself. That damned *Nash Bridges* show always seemed to tie up my favorite cheap Chinese diner for hours as they shot a street scene in front of the place, thus denying me a truly massive amount of greasy chow fun for only $2.50.

isw was my key to entering the San Francisco zeitgeist that was occupied by the likes of Jello Biafra, light table wielding grunge poster artist Frank Kozik, gay stand-up comic turned city supervisor Tom Ammiano (who almost became the first openly gay mayor of a major U.S. city) and a whole host of bitter feminist performance artists who provocatively shoved yams up their asses in the name of art. This made ISW worth fighting for. The only question was how?

If Chango Loco's warnings of my imminent ouster were right, they weren't borne out by the results of the planning meeting for the August 16, 1997, ISW show (which appropriately fell on the anniversary of Elvis Presley's toilet bound death). ISW was too chaotic for Brett or anyone else to have issued any directives to deny me matches. Maybe Brett only cared when he was drunk or on alternate Tuesdays.

Dragging that short-circuited bullhorn around Stinky's Peep Show every Thursday was really a godsend. It put me in Audra's good graces. If she had allowed her old friend Brett to purge me from the wrestling roster, then she would most likely lose her peep show barker as well. She didn't want to go back to doing that detail herself and there wasn't anyone else rattling around with quite my level of oratory expertise. I was sticking around by being useful. At first that was just an accident of wanting to be accepted and wanting to ham it up in front of an audience — any audience. Later on, when I saw what was working for me, it started to be by design.

For that August show, I defaulted into realizing the lifelong dream of every heterosexual male: I was going to wrestle two women. They were friends of Audra's that she wanted to give a match to. That's how a lot of people ended up in that ring — they were just friends of Audra's. Nobody was stepping up to take on two girls. For some reason, Jose was bent on wrestling Boris again for the umpteenth time and Missionary Man and Kid Anarchy were of course fighting amongst themselves as usual. I was just standing around at the right place at the right time. I lucked out and got the match.

One of the gals was Audra's hairdresser and she wore a mask and Jose or somebody gave her the name of Culo de Muerte. Roughly translated it meant "Ass of the Dead." It was a name that didn't really speak well of her hindquarters. She was a pretty faced gal with meat on her in all the right places and there was nothing inherently deathly or deadly about her ass at first examination. In fact, I sometimes admired it from afar when she showed up to Stinky's. Her partner was a blonde with nice, perky breasts who took the name of La Coqueta.

Not only did I get to wrestle two women, but Audra also booked my band on the show. The first thing that I had wanted from isw was to get more exposure for my band and playing the show was going to do a lot more for me than just prancing around the ring in a custom-made karate suit. It was like I got to take home what was behind door number one *and* door number two. And talk about sending mixed messages: one day I'm about to get my ass tossed out the door and the next day I'm getting everything that I could possibly want. Strange. Well, Brett did supposedly really like my song "Redwood City Rock City." He often blurted out its repetitive refrain despite himself.

Maybe they gave me the show just to shut me up. Maybe they thought that if I got what I wanted, I would leave. I didn't know and I really couldn't care. I was going to play some rock and roll and then I was going to get into the ring and wrestle some girls. Every juvenile fantasy that I had ever dared to dream while carefully penciling an ac/dc logo on my uncomfortable eighth-grade desk was about to come true.

There was no way this match could actually be what anyone would call "good." I still didn't know article one of working a match and my lovely opponents had never set foot in a ring before. The match could be memorable however. It involved working the crowd. It meant making them care and pissing them off. I wanted people to like my band. I wanted the band to really take off and play the Paradise and Transmission more often after this, but when I stepped in the ring, I had to be a bad guy. Nobody is going to cheer for you when you're smacking around girls.

I possessed the raw vocal talent to whip up the frenzied passions of so many inebriated tortilla tossers, but I was still a work in progress. This called for a real pro. I needed a manager to be my mouthpiece for this bout. I needed Dennis Erectus.

Dennis Erectus was a friend of a friend. He was a Bay Area broadcasting legend. In 1977, he quickly established himself as the most subversive, sleazy disc jockey on the raunchiest rock radio station in the Bay Area: KOME 98.5 FM. All of KOME's DJs referred to their station as "cum radio" and their on-air motto was the disgusting, "Don't touch that dial, there's cum on it!" With regular bad taste skits like "Celebrity Gang Bang," where a small studio audience made grunting and groaning noises while Erectus played sound bites by such conservative stalwarts as Maggie Thatcher and Nancy Reagan, Erectus' show was what you didn't want your parents to catch you listening to on your transistor radio headphone set.

Erectus perfected the shock jock shtick a good decade before Howard Stern crowned himself "The King of All Media." The Bay Area has never been a media market to sneeze at, but the East Coast rules radio. Simply by virtue of making it in D.C. and then New York, Stern got all the national press and became a mega-star who played himself in a big budget biopic, while Erectus was condemned to spin Foreigner and Foghat sides in San Jose.

By the mid-1990s, KOME had switched from its hard rock roots to the more confused modern rock format. When the station picked up Stern's syndicated show, Erectus was forced to move to his former competition at KSJO 92.3 FM. His show's salad days were definitely in the early 1980s when things like Reagan Youth and the first lady's "Just Say No" campaign served as potent conduits for Erectus' ire, but in 1997 he still had his diehard cult following.

Erectus and I were both monster movie nuts. That's how we got to know each other. Sooner or later, you get to know just about all of the monster movie nuts in any given area because you're always looking to trade tapes. Through a friend of a friend of a friend you find out that somebody has some rare-assed Bela Lugosi, thought-to-be-lost, zero-budget, almost unwatchable, piece-of-shit programmer produced by Monogram Pictures in 1938 and you just have to see if your letterboxed, taped off laser disc VHS copy of *The Giant Behemoth* was enough to strike a deal. I was such a nerd that I had a laser disc player and a Sony Betamax because there were certain movies that you could only get on those nearly defunct mediums. (Remember, the DVD explosion was still a year or two away at the time.) The uncut, letterboxed copy of *Vampire Circus* with all of its original Euro softcore interludes (and the added bonus of Japanese subtitles) was on Beta after all. Having a way to record both lasers and Betas always gave me lots of tapes to bargain with.

Just about the only prominent Nor Cal monster geek that I never had any business with was Kirk Hammett of Metallica. Hammett was on a whole different level of monster geek. He had the scratch to buy a 1970s Godzilla suit from *Famous Monsters* editor Forry Ackerman's fire sale. One thing that Bay Area monster nerds shared was that we all bitched about Kirk Hammett. "That little fucker never returned *The Corpse Grinders* to the Cinema Shoppe," was a common complaint.

Besides his devotion to Boris Karloff, the Three Stooges, decaying drive-ins and atomic scare sci-fi flicks, Erectus was also a pro wrestling fanatic. He was a constant subscriber to Meltzer's *Wrestling Observer* and he had even been to Meltzer's house once.

"Meltzer kept trying to show me all of this really arty Japanese wrestling," Erectus later recounted. "I was getting bored of all of the high-flying and said, 'This is great but can you show me that tape that you said you had of a couple of hillbillies fighting in a hot dog stand?'"

Erectus had emceed wrestling cards and had also managed a local Nazi wrestler as well as the 1980s NWA tag team champs the Rock and Roll Express, who looked like what you'd get if Brad Gillis and Jack Blades of Night Ranger were tag team partners. Erectus loved the lowbrow spectacle and the race-baiting theatrical aspects of pro wrestling more than he cared for any kind of acrobatic artistry in the ring. To him, ISW's tastelessness and bad production values were actually its virtues. When I got a hold of Erectus, he was pretty psyched to manage me against two women and he even agreed to put some of the wrestlers on the radio.

KSJO's dinosaur rock format wasn't exactly the kind of image that Audra wanted for ISW, but if she was going to continue to run a show every month at the Transmission, she had to attract that bridge and tunnel crowd. You could only ride the backs of urban retro scenesters for so long. I was pretty confident that landing ISW a spot on a high wattage station with reach to the entire circumference of the Bay Area scored me some major points and beat back the calls for my expulsion. Audra seemed happy with the development, but she wasn't going to fall all over herself while singing my praises either.

On the Friday night before the Saturday show, Chango Loco, the Cruiser and I all piled into my 1967 Plymouth Valiant. I was driving a boxy art-girl car by that time because my Olds Starfire lived up to its name and actually burst into flames a few months earlier while I was coming back from L.A. It was a mini-tragedy that had me riding back to Gilroy on a Greyhound bus filled with Mexican migrant farm workers.

We were going to meet up with Brett and the Ku Klux Klown at the radio station and throughout his shift Erectus was going to run interview segments with us touting the following night's matches. When we got to the station, it looked like any other sterile South Bay office building. It may have been a rock radio station, but from the look of it they could have been just coding software in the place.

We were buzzed in and shown into a room where Erectus, with his stringy, longhaired classic rock DJ look, was hurriedly taking compact discs in and out of trays. A lot of radio's glamour was lost when they switched from vinyl to CDs. Listener calls were piped in through a pair of Infinity studio monitors and Erectus answered them through his oversized DJ mic.

"If you had any balls at all, you'd play some fucking Pantera," one caller said, throwing down a heavy metal gauntlet to the AOR veteran.

"I don't have balls; I have a cunt," was Erectus' off-the-cuff reply as he pressed the disconnect button on his console. Chango Loco seemed really impressed with Erectus' comeback.

"Dude, I just got out of county," another caller pathetically pleaded, "and I really need to hear 'November Rain' by Guns N' Roses."

Erectus said that he would see what he could do and then turned to us holding a detailed spreadsheet. "These marks just keep calling in asking me to play songs but we haven't played listener requests in years," Erectus told us, letting us in on one of broadcasting's dirty little secrets.

"Rock jocks used to be able to program some of their own material," he continued, "but now we get these computer spread-sheets from the program director where our whole show is timed down to the last second of airtime. Sometimes our playlists come straight from the goddamned corporate HQ in Texas. You end up with some suit in the South programming a rock station in San Francisco, man. It really sucks."

Having popular DJs hip their audiences to emerging artists was a system that had served rock and roll well ever since it all began in 1956. Everyone from Elvis to the Ramones had some local jock spinning them somewhere and giving them a regional following that served as a springboard to greater stardom. Erectus himself was the first major market DJ to play Metallica at a time when all other rock radio stations shunned speed metal in favor of safer Van Hagar ballads. In the age of Clear Channel consolidation, radio music programming is now the sole province of high priced marketing consultants and computerized research models. What plays in Peoria is now foisted on New York and San Francisco. Record sales and ratings have been slipping ever since. One can only wonder where Metallica would be today without Erectus' airplay.

At KOME in the 1970s, Erectus was able to feature two people humping live in his studio while he called play-by-play. By 1997, KSJO only afforded a few short segments at the top and halfway mark of every hour where he could still engage in a smidgen of the audio theater that he was locally famous for. During one break, Erectus touted me as his newest protégé and I ran off with an Ali-inspired rant about my ring prowess — in rhyme.

Later, Chango Loco and the Cruiser painted a picture of mutual animosity that was capped by an in-studio scuffle, which consisted of Dennis Erectus slamming down a garbage pail filled with Diet Coke cans to simulate a brawl. It was an old "golden years of radio" chestnut that Erectus had used every time he had wrestlers on his show.

During another station break, Brett blathered on about ISW being "authentic Mexican lucha libre" to an unimpressed Erectus who just wanted to hear about the show's more bizarre attributes. This quietly confirmed all of my misgivings about the direction of the show. People wanted to hear about the freak show. They didn't really give a damn about the Mexican traditions to which we weren't really adhering anyway.

Then it happened. Erectus finally gave the microphone over to the Klown. The Klown's rap about polishing his swastikas wasn't nearly as well thought out as any of the other wrestlers' speeches that night. The Cruiser's earlier line about having a brown thumb should have stirred some level of passions from the listening audience — especially since they seemed motivated enough to call in just to hear a tired GN'R keyboard ballad. San Jose is fifty miles away from San Francisco, but it's still part of the Bay Area. One would expect homophobic responses from people who think that Poison's

"Every Rose Has its Thorn" is an example of stellar songwriting, but they never came. However, thirty seconds of the Ku Klux Klown over the public airwaves inspired a deluge of furious phone calls. The mere concept of the Klown far outweighed anyone else's delivery.

"Hey, dude, is that Klown there?" one pissed off caller asked. "I'm gonna come down there and kick his fuckin' ass! How about that?!"

"Me and a bunch of my buddies are gonna come down to that wrestling show tomorrow night and beat the living shit out of that clown," threatened another outraged caller.

All of the calls started to sound the same after a while but they kept on coming. "I have black friends man. You're fucked up…"

"That fucked-up clown better not show his ass in San Jose ever again…"

"Kick his fucking ass…"

"Beat that clown's fucked-up ass…"

It was a cacophony of threats of impending ass-kicking but when we got out in the parking lot, it was just as empty as it was when we had arrived. There were no pickup trucks filled with long-haired stoners looking to kick the Klown's ass. Hopefully, they would still be pissed off enough to show up at the Transmission and part with some of their beer money for the show. Enraging your potential fan base was a marketing strategy that had put asses in seats at pro wrestling shows ever since a couple of fat, hairy guys in tights first figured out how to fake a fight. The Ku Klux Klown, as ridiculous a symbol of racism as he intentionally was, was following in a time-honored tradition. Not a Mexican tradition, but an American one.

The next night the bell was ringing repeatedly and La Coqueta and Cula de Muerte were already in the ring, running around and slapping peoples' hands. They were entirely too well clothed for the event. La Coqueta at least lived up to her name and showed some cleavage. But with those masks on, the two gals resembled curvaceous Rock'em Sock'em Robots more than squared-circle seductresses.

I ran into the ring wearing a rayon snakeskin gi. Dennis Erectus followed me at a more measured pace. I was brimming with nervous energy as Allan Bolte handed Erectus the microphone. Erectus was decked out in dark shades and a cheap, black sports coat. It was his best bad guy wrestling manager attire. He launched into a tried and true sexist spiel that had never failed to fan the flames of what wrestlers refer to as "crowd heat." In other words, it made a hall packed full of wrestling fans care. It made them hate Dennis and, by association, it made them hate me too. It was mostly the same wrestling speech that worked like a charm for Andy Kaufman when he grappled women during his after-hours comedy club shows and no doubt also served the likes of Freddie Blassie, Ray "The Crippler" Stevens and Gorgeous George very well.

"I have a message for all you San Francisco socialists," Dennis emoted with just the right amount of disdain for the audience that now surrounded him. The crowd realized he was talking about them and they instantly began a mad chorus of booing, hissing and groaning.

"Men are superior to women," he continued emphatically. That was enough to really bring on the bile. The crowd hated Erectus for that remark but that didn't stop him: "Women have genes in their chromosomes for washing! Women have genes for shopping, but *women do not have genes for professional wrestling!*"

At previous isw shows, the tortilla throwing was always inter-mittent at best. Dennis changed that. Hails of broken up tortillas started pelting him from all directions. Flecks of cornmeal wedged their way behind his sunglasses. Hunks of soft taco shells clung to his hair. Erectus' radio audience may have absolutely hated the Ku Klux Klown the night before but the crowd that actually showed up to the Transmission fumed at Erectus.

Dennis may have been building up to something with his

speech, but I have no idea what it was. La Coqueta and Cula, not really knowing what to do, ran over to him and started yanking at his long locks. I tried to separate them. It was a bit of ad libbing on their part. The Missionary Man, with a full understanding of our voluminous shortcomings, had painstakingly worked out our match. If we all stuck to the script, with its bulldog DDTs and numerous crotch shots, we should have been okay — at least by ISW standards.

I was going to win the match. It may have been a bitch move for me to insist on winning, but my band had just played. I can't go around losing after I just got off the stage. Also, with two or three matches under my belt, I was a grizzled ring veteran compared to them. We had worked out that the women were going to make a comeback after the double leg lock submission and brain both Dennis and me with steel chairs. It was a way for me to assuage my big ego and get my victory and for them to go out with the crowd cheering them on. It was pro wrestling's way of letting everybody win. The drawback was that nobody really lost either. It was the kind of late 1990s booking that totally destroyed Ted Turner's WCW and made Vince McMahon's WWE almost impossible to care about. Done sparingly however, it was a good way to go about things.

La Coqueta was a spaz though. Either she didn't pay attention to the script that we had worked on or she was pissed off that she had to lose her very first match. She kept on ad libbing. Cula didn't, but Coqueta did. The biggest problem with ad libbing when you don't know a goddamned thing is that the results don't look like a real fight or even a staged one. It just looks like a couple of six-year-olds clumsily playing at kung fu with each other after they've just seen a Jackie Chan flick. It was that bad.

La Coqueta was pulling at my hair, generally freaking out and feebly trying to slap me around. I didn't dare pull a real judo move on her the way I did with the Critical Master. The Critical Master was bigger than me and he was a dude. These two chicks were friends of Audra's. I would have never worked in ISW again if I had hauled off

A barefoot Dante the Baptist delivers a fire and brimstone sermon before one of the Christians to the Lions matches.

*The End of Times Match*
(December 11, 1999 at
the Fillmore).

LEFT: In the role of the Whore
of Babylon, the Poontangler
kisses the rear of Roman
potentate Flamius Caesar.
ABOVE: Dante gives Flamius
a backbreaker.

The Poontangler mauls Dante the Baptist as Bob the Ref looks on (note the cigarette in Bob's hand).

El Pollo Diablo, the Devil Chicken.

BELOW: Señor Bueno slams a chair over the back of El Pollo Diablo during their oft-repeated arm wrestling match in 2001.

El Pollo Diablo waits to lock up.

RIGHT: The Cruiser courts El Homo Loco in the Mission High School men's room.

BELOW: The Cruiser takes marital vows during ISW's gay wedding.

RIGHT: Safe words fall on deaf ears as Wally cuffs the Cruiser.

BELOW: El Gran Frangorio puts Bad Boy Corey in an airplane spin at Homomania on October 6, 2001, at the Fillmore.

Intergender action as Irene Butterfly cranks El Homo Loco's arm at the
Transmission Theatre in early 1998. (Photo: Brandi Valenza)

The Ladies' Man enters the ring at Homomania in October 2001.

Libido Gigante suggestively strokes his baseball bat.

El Gran Fangorio goes for the pin on Bad Boy Corey of 69 Degrees while Dancin' Joey attempts to run in for the save.

After catching the Cruiser on the top rope, Macho Sasquatcho sends him crashing back onto the canvas with a Ric Flair–like arm drag.

The ring being assembled at the Fillmore.

Left to right, masked wrestlers only: Chicano Flame, the Cruiser, El Gran Fangorio and Chango Loco in the Fillmore balcony. Note that Chango Loco is wearing a "Fuck You Willie Brown" t-shirt.

Mextacy rallies against Dead Man Walking.

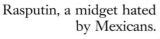

Rasputin, a midget hated by Mexicans.

Covered in whipped cream and chocolate syrup, Desperation Squad frontman, Mr. P. a.k.a. Pandaman, sets the stage for Homomania at the Fillmore.

The Mexican Viking kicks out from a pin by ISW softcore icon Niko After Dark.

ABOVE: Man from M.O.N.K. poses with pig guts at Shoreline Amphitheatre (Mountain View, CA) on June 16, 2000.

BELOW: Bumpin' and grindin' with the Sheik of Physique and the Poontangler.

(The Sheik worked for NOFX label Fat Wreck Chords and became one of ISW's more surreal stars.)

Construction worker tag team Damage Inc. climbs through the ropes at the Transmission Theatre in 1998. (Photo: Brandi Valenza)

LEFT: Doctor Loco's Alien Autopsy.

The Dwarves' He Who Cannot Be Named, masked but by no means covered, headlining ISW at the Fillmore.

The Bands (OPPOSITE PAGE CLOCKWISE FROM TOP): The Toilet Böys push glam rock androgyny to its obvious extremes. Desperation Squad frontman Mr. P. twists his own nipples. Lee Ving of Fear.

The Clermont Lounge in Atlanta claimed to be "The Bible Belt's Oldest Strip Club." It also boasted some of the Bible Belt's oldest strippers. (Photo: Craig Martins)

ABOVE (left to right): Vampiro, Count Dante, Tim Armstrong of Rancid and an unidentified roadie at the Toronto Skydome during the 2001 Warped Tour (Photo: the author's collection).

LEFT: After begging to get into the ISW ring, Fred Durst of Limp Bizkit is ignored by Latina hotties at Shoreline Amphitheatre (Mountain View, CA) on June 16, 2000.

TOP: With the Bay Bridge onramp in the background, El Gran Fangorio stomps around the ring at the San Francisco Warped Tour show on June 30, 2001.

BOTTOM: Count Dante works the crowd at the Warped Tour show in Pittsburgh, PA (Photo: the author's collection).

The Lion locks up with El Pollo Diablo during the "When Animals Attack" match.

One of ISW's sickest creations: Uncle N.A.M.B.L.A.

and used that really nasty neck crank take down on them. Instead, I had to just lamely prod them into the right position as if they were wayward lambs so I could attempt the next move in our little sequence.

In the end, everything fell into place. We hit the double DDT. I ducked their double clotheslines. They delivered double forearm blows to my crotch and once I was down on the mat, they sat on my face while I writhed around in utter agony. I should have won a Tony Award for that little bit of stagecraft. I slammed both of their heads into my stomach, which knocked them out cold because you know it is just too devastating to have your noggin rammed into a fat man's gelatinous mid section. After that, I slapped on that double leg lock submission. The ref, who was just as clueless as the wrestlers, counted it as a pinfall.

After the closing clang of the bell the women rallied and slammed Dennis and me with the steel folding chairs. Before the bout, La Coqueta actually wanted to drag this oversized oak chair into the ring and conk us with it. Shane had shown her the trick to properly smacking us across the back with steel folding chairs so it made a loud noise that would impress the audience without hurting anybody. Coqueta didn't seem to have the time for the finer points of the craft. She just wanted to brain us with a heavy piece of aged hardwood that she could barely carry. That girl must have had a lot of pent-up hostility. Luckily, common sense prevailed (which was really an uphill battle in the ISW backroom), and the two wrestling women stuck with time-tested aluminum.

Erectus sold the chair shots like a pro. He stayed in the ring as if he were unconscious for several minutes. He looked like he was dead. When he finally got up, he staggered around as if he were seriously injured. As dumb as the whole spectacle was, some people openly wondered if he was really hurt or not.

That was the night that I had everything I could have possibly wanted. My band had already played before I set foot in that ring to publicly grope two buxom, masked women. There were pervs who paid good money for that sort of thing you know.

Count Dante and the Black Dragon Fighting Society had gone on right after the club's doors opened. We were tucked away on one of the Paradise's smaller stages to warm up the crowd as they filtered in for the wrestling show next door at the Transmission. It wasn't like playing that little opening slot got my band signed to some of the bigger indie labels like Sub Pop or Lookout! Records, but it was at the Paradise/Transmission. It was on an ISW show — the Holy Grail of gigs to every unknown rock band with that right combo of retro and punk influences in the San Francisco Bay Area.

As I said before, I had had to beg and bother booking agents just to get a Wednesday night show at this Mission District dive called The Chameleon. That club was a dump. It was little more than a decrepit wooden hallway with bathrooms that were often overrun with fecal sludge and beer taps that overflowed with scurrying cockroaches when you dared to unscrew them. But it was a place that people actually went to despite how rancid it was. Still, the Paradise was definitely a step (or six) up from that.

With this show, I had stuck my foot in the door that I had been struggling to pry open for over a year. It was an incremental turning point for me where I graduated from having my demo packages tossed in the trash by unfazed booking agents to actually getting something resembling the gigs that I wanted. My ambitions were big, but my needs were small. For this show, my band rose to the occasion. My drummer Ed and I had worked out a bunch of vocal and hand signals to begin each song so we were tight as hell. The early club goers had sung along to "Redwood City Rock City" and danced around to "I Don't Care if You're Married." In between songs, I'd hyped my match with more Ali/*Dolemite*-inspired rants.

"They say that hell hath no fury like a woman scorned," I'd howled, "But that was before Count Dante was born!"

My next poetic boast had been a little more on the raunchy side but tempered with a classical Greek sensibility: "I mounted Athena and Aphrodite on the same day and had them both moaning and groaning the name of Count Dan-te."

It was the best way that I knew how (besides riding on Dennis' coattails) to make a room full of rockers care about seeing a 300-pound guy duke it out with two chicks. We'd held the attention of everyone who was there until this goth surf band called the Ghastly Ones starting playing on the big stage next door. After that, just about everyone bolted from the small lounge stage, except Dave, the crazy overalls wearing doorman at the Paradise who seemed to like us a lot. So did the sound guy. That had to count for something.

After playing my set and wrestling Cula de Muerte and La Coqueta, I made my way into the backroom. The surreal scene of masked luchadores cavorting with beer swilling wannabes in thrown together wrestling costumes was starting to be commonplace for me. It was just my Saturday night. Dennis was in a corner shaking the tortilla crumbs out of his coat and combing them out of his hair. We were both soaked with sweat.

"You can take any drug you want to, man," Dennis said with a Cheshire Cat grin, "but nothing can beat that high. I've taken everything under the sun, especially working in radio back in the '70s, but making a room full of people hate you like that, making them all want to kill you, is the best high that I've ever felt."

# 7
# THE FORCE FIELD

THERE'S A FORCE FIELD. It emanates somewhere out of Redwood City or Menlo Park and it keeps people living in the Bay Area suburbs for far too long. There are probably similar force fields maintained and operated out of places like Queens, Long Island, Orange County and/or San Berdoo. I am not personally acquainted with their apathy-inducing pull, but my personal experiences with their San Francisco Peninsula counterpart assures me of their existence.

I was once a captive of the force field. I was in my early and even mid-twenties but I was still living in the same room at my mom's house where I once used mixtures of *Star Wars* action figures and Micronauts to determine whether or not Baron Karza could kick Boba Fett's ass or if the plastic Ice Planet Hoth Stormtrooper was any match at all for the die-cast metal Galactic Warrior.

I was a grown man and I collected gadgets and gizmos, bought bass amps and stockpiled laserdiscs and comic books. I was a captive of apathy and chickenshit fear. I was going on five (or was it six?) years at a two-year college. Sooner or later, you actually take those statistics and math classes you were avoiding and transfer to State. You finally have decisions to make. You don't really want to just manage the Kinko's copies or sling coffee at the local bookstore/espresso house. You want to be somebody and a dirtbag in the city seems so much more spectacular than a loser in the burbs.

I didn't have an Obi-Wan Kenobi to deactivate my own personal tractor beam, but eventually, the city exerted a far greater gravitational pull on me than suburban security, sterility and convenience.

Paul Van Dyne, on the other hand, was a proud prisoner of that suburban force field. He still lived at his parents' house in the upper, upper, upper middle-class suburb of Palo Alto, commonly referred to as "Shallow Alto." He was a round-faced cherub who resembled a younger, longhaired surfer version of John Goodman. Van Dyne had hair down to his forty-inch waist, but he chopped it off after a confused five-year-old in a Redwood City bank parking lot exclaimed, "Look mom, it's a man-girl!"

After the haircut, Van Dyne's resemblance to Goodman only grew more profound and Mexican guys on the beach started calling him Fred Flintstone or King Ralph. Recently dumped secretary types, who had no shame over their love of the then-waning sitcom *Roseanne*, always wanted to go home with him. This must have been its own private kind of hell.

Like me, he played bass guitar, but he never seemed to be in any bands. The extent of his musical drive centered exclusively on the accumulation of new axes with ever increasing amounts of strings and wider and wider necks. He liked those too expensive, gazillion stringed basses that looked like your grandma's overly lacquered coffee table. Basses like that were only suitable for backing Yanni at the Acropolis during those really desperate PBS pledge drives. You couldn't be seen in a rock club with them.

With the amount of money that he shelled out on those things, he could have paid first and last month's rent on a really nice apartment in the Marina, but he didn't seem to care. He just acquired more CDs, more basses and more extravagant widescreen TVs that only he possessed because it wasn't like anyone wanted to hang out with his crazy family just to catch some boxing on satellite TV. He also had a penchant for raising these really yappy puffball show dogs that constantly nipped at your ankles while you waited for him to get his ass out the door.

But Van Dyne had potential. He had a really fucked up sense of humor and some crack comic timing to match it. He could say the most depraved, wrong, godawful thing, at the exact right time to make you laugh uncontrollably no matter how guilty you felt about it.

I used to have all these ratty, old paperback books in my car, dimestore novels that I'd bought at rummage sales. Small collections of them somehow gravitated to the vast expanses of my car's backseat. One afternoon, I was pulling up to my apartment with Paul in the passenger seat. As I negotiated a parking space for my LBJ-era land yacht, we both noticed this blonde professional looking woman in her mid-thirties sitting down on the sidewalk and bawling her eyes out. She looked as if someone just died or her husband had just left her. Something terrible must have just happened.

As I put the car in park and killed the engine, Paul pulled this aging paperback out of the rear seat of my car and said, "Hey maybe we should go give this to her to cheer her up."

The book had a crudely painted cover with big, bold, black type over a yellow background. It was titled *Wounded, Dying but Still Killing Japs!* The cover art depicted a desperate GI in tattered fatigues clutching a gleaming bayonet while waiting behind a coconut tree as a Japanese patrol stood unknowingly in the distance.

Van Dyne just sat there, staring at me with this impish grin that revealed the small gap between his two front teeth. I couldn't help but laugh. It was so inappropriate. It was so wrong, but I was too busy cackling and chortling to care that this poor woman, who had just lost someone or something very dear to her, was sitting in plain view of a car filled with fatsos laughing uncontrollably during her moment of true sadness. It was the juxtaposition of the crying woman and that dog-eared piece of hoary racism. I couldn't help it. Paul Van Dyne caught me at just the right time. He could do that to you.

Paul's depravity went a little bit further than well-timed quips and comments here and there. He loved barfing and he loved porn. He liked drinking until he heaved, especially in public places or all over his suburban neighbor's nicely manicured lawns. As far as pornography went, he often spoke of the "healing power of smut" — usually when he was nursing a really nasty hangover from hurling in his neighbor's yard only hours before.

He had the odd habit of making you buy his X-rated reading material for him. He didn't make you pay for it. He always had plenty of cash because he clocked at least $50,000 a year and still lived at home with his parents. It was as if he couldn't take the stern looks of the mustachioed shopkeepers at the local liquor stores with their porn racks burgeoning with three packs of *Barely Legal*, *Swank* and *Cheri*. Either he was shielding himself from a small piece of embarrassment by having you walk up to the counter and put down some cash for the latest copy of *Oriental Twat*, or he was having a silent laugh at your expense. It must have had something to do with his Calvinist upbringing that my Catholic-raised mind couldn't begin to fathom.

isw needed people like Paul Van Dyne. With the "rockabilly dudes with masks" motif quickly growing stale, it needed them desperately. Could he wrestle? Who the hell knew and who in the hell cared? Could anybody in isw wrestle? Did that matter? No. It didn't. He'd done some high school wrestling. That was it. But Van Dyne was funny and he had a big disposable income rattling around to buy costumes with. He might have to forgo buying some rack-mounted, digital whatchamahoozit that no one but him would ever hear, but he would have the glory of staging ludicrous conflicts in that rat trap of a ring in front of hundreds of tattooed ladies and urban slicksters.

With him in the fold, I could actually pull off those historical spectacle matches that I had always wanted to do. He could buy the lion suit. He could buy the Caesar drag complete with laurel leaves. We could do that "Christians to the lions" match that I had conceived during the hours of dead time before my first bout. He could buy a lot of other crazy-assed costumes that we hadn't even thought of yet at the oversized House of Humor in Redwood City. We could do with props and costumes what we could never pull off with athletic ability. Sure, I felt a little guilty for always tugging at his shoulder and urging him to put down his plastic for so much stitched together acrylic fur and molded latex, but at least it kept him from buying another one of those decadent bass guitars.

In October 1997, isw attempted its first national tour since the nearly disastrous string of Lollapalooza dates back in 1995. This time around, there wouldn't be any Johnny Legends or Courtney Loves to deal with. Audra simply crammed twelve sweaty wrestlers into a Ford passenger van and took her Transmission Theatre club show to similar venues in the Northwest, Southwest and Midwest. The tour went as far east as Chicago, then cut through the Pacific Northwest on the way back to the Bay Area. The wrestling van was going to be closely followed by a Ryder moving truck carrying that ramshackle ring and the ring crew, which oddly included Brett's gray-bearded dad.

Since the August show the ring was only in worse shape as Brett had thrown a kind of wrestler appreciation party at his house in the somewhat suburban Excelsior District. For the party, he had set up the ring on the uneven dirt and gravel surface of his backyard and then left it set up that way for over two weeks. The continuous tension from the ring ropes actually bowed the aluminum ring posts until they all started to curve in towards the center of the mat. As a result, the ring's surface became even less symmetrical than it already had been, and it was never what you would call smooth to begin with.

Coming along for the ride (but in their own presumably less crowded vans) were the bands. You couldn't have ISW without the bands. "This isn't a wrestling show [like] in Mexico City," Audra told the Chicago mag *Punk Planet* in an interview conducted during the tour. "The music is as important to ISW as the wrestling. It's not your usual night at a club with three bands either. Garage, punk rock, surf — it's just this big crazy night of music and wrestling." The dialectic of booze, bands and brawling was the whole point of the show.

Headlining the tour was going to be the ironic punk rock cover band Me First and the Gimme Gimmes. Me First had Fat Mike (not to be confused with Fast Mike) of NOFX on bass and Audra's hipster heartthrob boyfriend Spike on vocals. They took perennial AM radio hits by Neil Diamond and Barry Manilow and sped them up with thrashy guitars and punked out 1-2 beats. It had been somewhat of a punk rock tradition to play inappropriate cover tunes ever since Sid Vicious croaked out "My Way," but it somehow lost all of its intentional irony when all you did was play inappropriate cover tunes.

When the Dead Kennedys did "Viva Las Vegas," it was ironic because they contrasted it with nice little numbers like "I Kill Children" and "Holiday in Cambodia." When Black Flag did "Louie Louie," it usually included a monologue by Henry Rollins where he told every suburban punk kid in the concert hall to go out and knife some cops. It was a tune that had been cranked out at every high school dance for over twenty years and Rollins used it to incite near riots (back when Henry was something more than just a talking head on VH1). Me First and the Gimme Gimmes just gave you the punk rock covers without any of the hardcore sentiment. This approach shockingly foreshadowed the playlists of so many episodes of *American Idol* in the process. If there was any irony there, it wasn't solely intentional by anyone involved.

Still, unlike so many other singers of the 1990s, Spike could hit the notes. He could croon and with a set that consisted of the works of some of the greatest pop songwriters of all time like Diamond, Leiber and Stoller and Burt Bacharach, it was really hard not to like the band no matter how bubblegum they were. As embarrassing as it sounds now, I used to get the chills when they played the opening to "I Write the Songs."

Bringing up the middle of the show (in between the first and second set of wrestling) was the Detroit experimental band Calvin Krime. With their heavily distorted keyboards they didn't seem like the right fit for ISW but their bandleader, Sean "Na Na" Tillman, had deep connections in the Midwest scene. Despite being only seventeen at the time of the tour, he had a hand in booking most of the dates. Today Tillman fronts Har Mar Superstar (another band whose name is a slight twist on words) and he takes the stage either shirtless or wearing day-glo 1980s workout clothes.

Kicking off each show were SF soapbox racing enthusiasts the Demonics. Their singer Russ usually had the band come out in drag, devil horns and other goofy costumes, but their happy, unabashedly Beach Boys–influenced sound never really fit with their hell-spawned name. Still, Russ was an evil genius in a surfer dude kind of way and he was never above producing a "Revolution No. 9"–esque track that amounted to sixteen solid minutes of nothing but noise. The SF retrobilly crowd should have shunned that kind of experimentation out of hand, but because "Russ was cool" in their estimation, they never clawed him out of the pecking order for his heretical forays into psychedelia.

The wrestlers that were being packed into two tons of Detroit steel for that tour were Cruiser Craig, Chango Loco, Jefferson

Monroe, the Missionary Man, a French-Canadian friend of his named John Pierre LeButt (probably not his real name), Audra's hairdresser Cula de Muerte, Brett/Borracho Gigante, the Inbred Abomination, Audra herself and a couple of indie workers from San Bernardino who nobody knew.

One of the indie workers claimed to have been Doink the Clown #2 in the WWE. He boasted that he wrestled the massively obese former WWC champ Yokozuna although the ISW regulars later found out this was a total lie. The two supposedly trained wrestlers only lasted one show before they faked concussions, got lap dances at a Denver strip joint, then quickly disappeared never to be heard from again. They just bolted as soon as the coast was clear.

Then there was Bob the Ref. That tour was his ISW debut. Bob was a bulgy-eyed bald man who looked like he was in his early forties even though he was still in his late twenties. He worked the door and security at Stinky's Peep Show and got roped into refereeing by Audra. He was her friend, and probably in between jobs at the time.

His ref shtick was the same as every other ISW ref's. Bob strolled around the ring with a beer in one hand and cigarette in the other and paid absolutely no attention to the match whatsoever. Jose did this when he reffed and so did his brother Juan, but Bob did it better than anybody else. It was something about the perpetual bags under his eyes, his bad posture and the fact that he really didn't give a shit. He was for real and the fans knew it.

Bob always voted democrat and even subscribed to *The Nation*, but he had the most foul-mouthed racist sense of humor this side of the Mississippi.

"What do you get when niggers fuck buffalos?" he once asked during a break between peep shows.

"Samoans," was the simple yet revolting punchline.

There were jokes about raping three-year-olds and of course, there were jokes about nuns, priests, rabbis, Jews, Arabs and gays.

He had a never-ending supply. Like Paul Van Dyne he could catch you with them at just the right time so that you couldn't help but bust out laughing no matter how horrified you were at yourself for having done so.

There were almost no amenities on the tour. The nightclubs where they wrestled didn't come with showers. The crowded passenger van was their only home except for the nights that Audra was able to convince one of her friends in some other town to allow her oversized cast to crash on their floor space.

The wrestlers were paid a meager $20 per diem and the only thing resembling catering were late night swings through the Jack in the Box or McDonald's drive thrus. All of the Big Mac meals and plastic encased 7-Eleven sandwiches were paid for out of those per diems.

Just about all of the wrestlers had to pull double duty using an assortment of masks and outfits to change their characters from the first set of wrestling to the second. Jefferson Monroe grappled with Audra in the first set as El Gourmexico and then wrestled Cula de Muerte in the second set as the combustible Buddhist Man from M.O.N.K. Craig fought it out with Chango Loco for the second set and donned some absurd pancake makeup and gaudy imitation designer wear to become the Ghost of Versace whenever an extra grappler was needed.

The Ghost of Versace was probably Craig's most inspired creation although it didn't have as much stretch as the Cruiser as far as plotting wrestling matches was concerned. It was hard not to laugh at the mere sight of Craig acting like a bad cartoon specter while wearing faux Versace purchased from homeless guys on Market Street. Washing off all of that white face paint between sets so he could put on the leather and denim for his match as the Cruiser was pretty daunting. Doing it without access to a working sink (as he often had to do) was almost impossible.

I wasn't invited on the tour. Nobody asked me to go and since I kept hearing how Brett wanted to axe me, I didn't feel right going hat in hand begging for a space in that overstuffed van. But I had a plan to subvert ISW from the inside. Part of that plan was bringing in Paul Van Dyne. The tour gave me my shot.

Everybody was bringing people into ISW back then. Audra brought in her hairdresser. Audra brought in a lot of people, but it was her show. She could bring in her Cuisinart bread machine and put a cubic zirconium studded championship belt on it and nobody could say anything. Brett brought in people and so did Chango Loco.

Chango once brought in this dumpy bleached blond delivery truck driver, put a hat with dingle balls on him and called him Rauncho Villa. Their ensuing match was comprised entirely of shoulder blocks. It was one shoulder block after another. In fact the shoulder block was the only move in the entire match besides that old ISW chestnut of standing around the ring, looking at each other and not knowing what to do next. Why did Chango bring this guy in? It didn't make sense. If Chango did drugs (and this guy had the killer chronic) then it would have made some kind of sense, but Chango didn't do drugs.

When Brett, Chango and everyone else brought in their pals it was like they were teenaged kids working at Dairy Queen and giving away free fries and shakes to all their friends. Instead of so much deep fried fare, Brett and Co. had wrestling matches and they were giving those away whenever they could to win some kind of popularity contest. They weren't thinking of who could wrestle, who was funny or who could afford a whole menagerie of furry animal costumes. It often seemed like they were just bringing in the last guy they talked to before the show began.

I was going to be successful because I was going to do things differently. I was actually going to have criteria for bringing my cronies into the show. I was going to only bring in people who could actually make the show better in some kind of thematic way — people who could work towards making the show "incredibly strange." At your average San Francisco ISW show, I was in no position to bring in anybody. I brought in Dennis but he had a major market radio show. Paul Van Dyne was just some nerd who lived in Palo Alto. If those retro heads ever got a load of his seven-string Zon bass guitar collection, they would've never let him into the show even if he paid double admission.

Van Dyne and I both had friends in Portland that we could stay with so I asked Audra if me and a friend could work a match at the Portland show if we flew up there on our own dime. Either I had promised Audra that my buddy was going to wear some kind of animal costume into the ring that night or maybe it was something that Paul came up with all by himself. I wanted to do the Christians to the Lions match, but I knew we hadn't quite gotten to that stage yet. Either way, Audra agreed to let us work a match in Portland if we got ourselves up there.

She really had no choice. Portland was one of the last shows on the tour. The likelihood of wrestlers breaking their legs and arms during that road trip was very high. It was almost to be expected. Kid Anarchy broke both his arms at an art show for Christ's sake! Who knew what kind of mayhem would ensue when a crowd of Robitussin addled pre-teen punks in Green Bay, Wisconsin, got a load of the Cruiser. For all Audra knew, one or more of her wrestlers was probably going to leave several crucial bone fragments somewhere between Denver and Milwaukee. Best-case scenario had no major injuries but her entire cast was going to have numerous nagging ones no matter what. Sleeping in that van alone was going to give everyone extreme lower back pain even if they weren't wrestling two matches a day. The tour hemorrhaged those two indie workers after the first gig. Right there: two wrestlers gone, out the door, never coming back and not being replaced any time soon. By the time ISW got to Portland, she was going to need us.

"I just got back from the House of Humor and we have two choices . . ." Paul Van Dyne murmured over the phone. To use

*Seinfeld* terms, he was a quiet talker. You almost always had to ask him to repeat everything he said.

"I can get a chicken suit or a Wookiee costume," he said as many times as it took me to hear what he was trying to say.

The chicken suit was a bit more expensive ($120) as Chewie clocked in at only ninety bucks. For some reason, being able to beat Chewbacca in Portland appealed to me more than pinning a six-foot tall chicken. It wasn't as if the State of Oregon Boxing and Wrestling Commission was going to be keeping the results of these bouts on file, but I liked the idea of having a victory over Chewbacca on my official ISW win-loss record as if there really was such a thing.

In actuality, the State of Oregon Boxing and Wrestling Commission was the last governmental regulatory body that we wanted to have anything to do with our little one ring circus. I didn't know it at the time and Audra sure wasn't aware of this, but the Boxing and Wrestling Commission enforced such a draconian drug testing policy that it inadvertently resulted in a statewide ban on the pseudo sport. The two major promotions of the time (WCW and the WWE) assumed that the vast majority of their rosters could never hope to pass such a test so they steered clear of Oregon despite any money to be made off its mostly white, rural populace.

This unofficial ban on pro wrestling in Oregon lasted until the passage of Bill 3581 by the Oregon House of Representatives in 2003. This bill was sponsored by a representative with the decidedly un-statesmanlike name of Tootie Smith and was actually referred to as "The Professional Wrestling Economic Stimulus Plan." The bill abolished most of the regulatory authority that the Boxing and Wrestling Commission had over what was then dubbed "entertainment wrestling." In an official state press release, Rep. Tootie touted her bill as "one of many steps that will be needed to help revive this state's economy."

In 1997, the Oregonian economy was still reeling from its lack of professional wrestling and there was really no end in sight.

Luckily, ISW skated under the radar. It probably helped that ISW was booked as part of Portland's annual North by Northwest music festival. ISW did get some ink in their newsweeklies up there but the state's wrestling commission probably thought Incredibly Strange Wrestling was just another name for a kooky, crazy rock band if they even paid that much attention.

Nobody had to pee in a cup and this was a very good thing. If the lunatic fringe of luchadores that made up ISW's roster were made to take a piss test in order to be licensed to wrestle, then the straight-edged Jefferson Monroe and Chango Loco would have been the only ones wrestling in Portland and Eugene on that tour.

NXNW was an annual showcase of unsigned indie rock bands with every pizza parlor, pool hall and dive bar in Portland was converted in a makeshift music venue. Hundreds of bands paid their submission fees and played the festival in the hopes of being seen by recording industry talent scouts (referred to in the biz as A&R reps) and getting signed to a record label. With everything I now know about the insular nature of Hollywood, it is really hard to picture some L.A. recording execs leaving their Burbank offices for two days to catch some college radio bands in Portland. Still, somebody at some point in time must have been signed after being noticed at NXNW, because otherwise, why would bands actually pay for the chance to play some crappy sportsbar in Oregon? Maybe Sub Pop Records in Seattle (the label that was the epicenter of the whole Northwest grunge explosion in the early 1990s) actually bothered to send a couple of interns down for the thing. Maybe NXNW was all part of the Oregon State government's "Indie Rock Economic Stimulus Plan" of 1995. You know crazier things have happened up there.

Meanwhile, Van Dyne bought the Wookiee suit and we bought the plane tickets. The day before our big match we lamely tumbled on some of our friend's couch cushions in an inept attempt at preparation for the next night's bout. We also drank whiskey and shot pool. Van Dyne did not, however, consume enough whiskey to barf although he did talk a lot about vomiting as the perfect workout regimen for his new athletic venture.

Before we went to the venue and met up with the other wrestlers, we had no idea what to expect. In 1997, cellphones still weren't commonplace. Most people who needed some form of mobile communications still carried pagers, so it wasn't like I could call Audra or any of the wrestlers and find out how the tour was going. The huge proliferation of cellphone use was still a year away. The only communication that I had with any of the wrestlers after the start of the tour and prior to arriving in Portland was a postcard from Chango and the Cruiser that was sent from the Denver Waffle House and cleverly addressed to "Cunt Dante." The postcard didn't really tell me that much except that they were both in awe of the Waffle House's oily hash browns and the laminated four-color menus.

During the two weeks leading up to the Portland show, Incredibly Strange Wrestling almost fell apart. It was as if the 1997 tour was hell-bent on finishing the job started by Lollapalooza two years earlier. There were the predictable things. The things that were expected from any low-budget tour ambitious enough to feature a wrestling ring, a group of very green grapplers and three rock and roll bands.

At some of the shows, such as Chicago or Minneapolis, the wrestlers felt like they were on the verge of hitting the big time, only to reminded just how small-time they were at the next night's gig. The ring couldn't fit into the club in Lawrence, Kansas. In La Crosse, Wisconsin, the wrestlers had to hump the ring up three flights of stairs. The show in Detroit was canceled because the promoter stopped booking shows and decided to wipe out his previous calendar while he was at it.

In Green Bay, Demonic Russ drove an oversized Econoline over his drummer's foot. Stillman's tour diary from *Punk Planet* has an account of the incident: "Everyone wanted to leave when the ultimate drama occurred. Courtney Demonic, who had done nothing but bitch and moan about every aspect of the tour was ready to get some action from some Green Bay girl, and he was excited. As he honked and yahooed from in the van Tim Moss (Inbred Abomination), of ISW, pulled him out of the driver's seat to mock wrestle. Some horseplay ensued, and an unknowing Russell Demonic jumped behind the wheel and attempted to pull the van forward. Crunch! Everyone looked on in disbelief as the rear tire of the van sat atop Courtney's right food for at least ten seconds. It was definitely broken."

The drama over Courtney's smashed foot didn't end there. Chango Loco actually took credit for the accident, citing a Santerian curse he'd put on Demonic Russ the day before in La Crosse. Several of the wrestlers witnessed Chango as he lit candles, waved his machete and sprayed sacramental rum all over the room while he invoked the forces of black magic. The next day, when they heard the crunch of Courtney's foot under the steel belted radials of Russ's E-250, they were all convinced of Chango's blossoming mastery over the occult.

Apparently, Chango spent a lot of time on that tour trying to convince his fellow wrestlers of his mystical powers. The crazy conditions, the isolation and the massive sleep deprivation made them all very susceptible to the spirit realm. As the caravan passed by the Little Bighorn Battlefield National Monument in Montana, he claimed that he was being "mounted by the spirits" of the dead Indian braves who fought under Sitting Bull. Why he wasn't mounted by the spirit of Colonel George Armstrong Custer is anyone's guess. If anyone who died at the Little Big Horn had an ego big enough to A) not realize that he was dead and B) possess the bodies of Chicano wrestlers from the world beyond, it was Custer.

Also, why Courtney had to go to the hospital and wear a cast on his foot for God knows how long is another psychic inconsistency. Despite being the one cursed, Russ was, at most, inconvenienced by

Chango's occult utterances. The next night, the Inbred Abomination filled in on drums for the Demonics and the band had a replacement drummer at the show after that. In Portland, Russ didn't clutch his head or wring his hands. He did talk my ear off about his inexpensive Rat stomp-box distortion pedal. "This is the only thing you need, man," he told me while hanging out of the van that he'd driven over his drummer's foot only days before.

"All I need is this stomp-box and my Fender amp," he continued. He did not sound like a cursed man.

As if the foot squashing, ancient curses and general misery weren't enough, Brett and Audra got into a fist fight in the hallway of a Kansas hotel. The squabble started over who got which room and quickly erupted into what was later described as a "full-on brawl" by author Sarah Jacobson in her 1999 Gettingit.com article. The rumors that have surrounded that tour ever since hold that Brett actually hauled off and kicked Audra. Brett may have been my behind-the-scenes arch nemesis from those days, but he always seemed like a level-headed enough guy. Something actually drove both of them to wage a very real intergender shoot fight over what were probably identical suites at the Cozy 8. Some kind of road rage or mass hysteria made Brett kick a woman.

Audra's own comments in Gettingit.com confirm the physical nature of the confrontation. "The only reason we didn't get kicked out of the hotel was because we gave this whole bullshit story that we were practicing our matches," she said, recalling the infamous spat.

The fallout from the fight had everyone taking sides. With her usual managerial flair, Audra had screamed at everybody a lot on that tour, so many musicians and wrestlers found it easy to side with Brett even though he was the one who descended into misogyny. Spike even broke up with Audra and the two were still separated when the show pulled into Portland. Incredibly Strange Wrestling had taken the brown acid, drank the purple Kool-Aid and was suffering from one hell of a mescal hangover mixed with meth that had been cut with strychnine. Everyone was half-crazed. Everyone hated each other and hadn't been to sleep in days. That was what Paul and I were getting ourselves into when we called a cab for a ride to the venue on the day of the show. We didn't have a clue.

# 8

# LEG BITING RIOT!

THE WRESTLERS WERE LATE. The clueless kids who worked the venue seemed to know more about the goth show downstairs than they did about Incredibly Strange Wrestling. The truck with the ring showed up before the wrestlers did. Inbred Abomination and Brett's dad stood by the truck as if in a holding pattern. They looked too tired to talk. There was a problem with the venue. The room had low ceiling beams. Anyone attempting a Jimmy "Superfly" Snuka dive off the top rope risked smacking his head into a solid piece of oak and collapsing into the middle of the ring as an unconscious, bloody hulk. Unconscious, bloody hulks were usually desirable in pro wrestling, but they were seriously uncool when they were the result of nothing more than building codes.

The venue itself wasn't very impressive. It was a drab, gray rec center on the east side of town. It was the kind of building where the local Kiwanis or Ladies' Auxiliary held their weekly meetings and annual pancake breakfasts, but from the look of things, the old folks and do-gooders had long since abandoned the place. It felt like we were trying to put on a rock and roll wrestling show at an aging branch of the Department of Motor Vehicles.

The wrestlers arrived looking beat-up and bruised from the most severe form of on-the-job training imaginable. Before the tour, Cruiser and Chango may have had three matches apiece. Their only training came from tumbling on the mats in the weight room at the Missionary Man's apartment complex. On the tour, they were hitting each other as hard as they could, night after night, just to get a reaction from often-indifferent audiences.

The wrestlers didn't know how to fall and they didn't know how to land. They didn't know how to distribute their weight properly when they hit the mat so each body slam and back fall jarred and jammed their spines with a savagery born of amateurism. They were play-acting with pain as a major stage prop. Long drives, nightly beatings and bad food pushed their minds and bodies beyond the limits of human endurance.

Chango Loco attempted to walk with his usual macho swagger but looked more like he was nursing a minor toothache. Cruiser Craig had the thousand-yard stare. "I haven't been to sleep in days," he said while looking straight through me. He babbled almost incoherently about the wonders of tiger balm. He held up a little plastic jar with Chinese writing on the label and beheld it in awe as if it were some kind of magic talisman.

"This is the only thing that has gotten me through this tour," he said as he rolled up his sleeve and started to apply the smelly ointment. Patches of his skin were a sickly shade of purple from all the knife-edged chops and flying elbows he'd received. His skin was made even more ghastly by his liberal use of "tan in a can" as he believed that the butch, queer Cruiser character probably spent a lot of time in a tanning salon. To live his character, he smeared his body with this vile, orange-brownish concoction that was produced and distributed by Ernest Borgnine's wife Tovah and purchased at the Walgreens beauty counter. Every inch of his body took on an unnatural tint. You felt as if you needed to adjust the color levels on your television set just to look at him in person.

Paul Van Dyne shot me that devilish grin of his, clearly taking delight in Craig's misery. Van Dyne got off on that sort of thing. Hell, we all did at one time or another, but Van Dyne just wore it on his sleeve a little bit more than most. Van Dyne may have only planned to have a few yucks flopping around in that fur suit of his, but if he stuck with ISW, then bruises, bloody noses and broken bones were his exciting future: our twisted little showbiz fantasy world.

The hours until the show crawled by. Everyone was either too tired to talk or they all hated each other too much to strike up a conversation. The ring was set up at an odd angle to account for those low ceiling beams. There was only one corner where you could do a dive off the top rope. Even then, it was suggested that the shorter Jefferson Monroe be the only person to attempt any aerial maneuvers, which was fine with him.

Van Dyne's Wookiee suit still didn't have a name. In lesser professional wrestling hands, he would have just gone out there as Chewie or the Wookiee Monster. There would have been no life for that suit beyond just running with the *Star Wars* angle. Van Dyne wanted a more terrestrial origin for his character. He wanted to be a sasquatch.

"Dude, we can just say that we found him rooting around in the trash outside," he said with as much enthusiasm as he ever had about anything. "It is Portland after all."

He was right. With a Wookiee, all we had was Lucasfilm, sci-fi nerd bullshit. There might be some humor there but not a whole bunch. After a point, it would all just get too stupid, and when something got too stupid for ISW, it really was too stupid. Being a Bigfoot opened up all kinds of possibilities. We could parody those low-budget speculation movies that they actually used to show in theaters in the 1970s like *The Mysterious Monsters*, which was narrated by a seriously out of work Peter Graves, or the immortal *Legend of Boggy Creek*. Van Dyne's Chewbacca suit was seriously better than the shadowy, out-of-focus glimpses that you caught of the swamp sasquatch from *Boggy Creek*, but that flick still managed to scare me when I stayed up to watch it on *Creature Features* when I was six years old.

Often times, the cheaper monsters, aided by bad camera work and lo-fi audio were much more fear inducing than any big-budget computerized creation could ever hope to be. The feel of Sunn Classics exploitation-speculation flicks like *In Search of Historic Jesus*, where you could clearly see the boards underneath Christ's feet as he walked on water, were a big isw inspiration for Paul and me.

Bigfoot was really the way to go with this thing but Audra insisted that he somehow be Mexican. "It's isw. It has to be lucha. It has to be Mexican," she said, reiterating the advice that Chango Loco had given me at Stinky's weeks earlier.

"How do you say Bigfoot in Spanish?" I asked.

There was a moment of uncomfortable silence until Chango chimed in and said, "Zapato Grande."

"Shit," I answered back, "That means 'big shoe.' Even I know that!" isw was about as Mexican as one of those Jack in the Box tacos with that conspicuous slice of American cheese sticking out of it.

"How about Macho Sasquatcho?" Audra said and it stuck. It was better than anything any of us could have come up with using either proper Spanish (had anyone in isw actually known how to speak Spanish) or the King's English. It fit the show and had a ring to it. Macho Sasquatcho was born.

The doors opened. At show time, the hall was about half full, mostly with those snot-nosed skater punks who were there to worship Fat Mike, only there was no Fat Mike. Like the later day Brian Wilson or Berry Gordy that he was, Mike sat the tour out and stayed in San Francisco to develop new material. He sent a Gimme Gimmes comprised of hired hands out on the road with Spike. It was a smart move, but it made for a lot of pissed off Fat Mike fans. The punk kids at the wrestling show were the really nasty, redneck Portland variety. They probably huffed glue or snorted d-CON before the show. They were high on something and whatever it was you didn't want any of it.

The debut of Macho Sasquatcho was mostly uneventful. I got on the microphone, ranted and capped it off with a chant of "Dante wants it all so the Sasquatch has to fall." A few people joined in. That was something. When the Sasquatch entered the ring, those that cared made up their minds and were solidly on his side. He was in a fur suit and he was announced as being found rooting through the trash in Portland. There were probably a few people there who had done some dumpster diving so the Sasquatch was the inhuman Everyman against that fat, loudmouthed asshole from California. Still, despite Paul Van Dyne's best efforts, the fans kept screaming "Cheeeewwwwwiiiiie" at him. Macho Sasquatcho was always going to have one foot in Wookiee-dom. It was unavoidable.

Van Dyne didn't know which way was up and I didn't know much more so the match was a fairly one-sided affair. There were some judo throws and clotheslines. The Sasquatch got a rally, but I used that monkey flip that Royce Gracie had taught me at a seminar at the Academy of Fighting Arts. It's that move where you fall on your back, take your opponent with you and flip him over with your feet. The audience never expected me to pull off something that athletic so they cheered a little bit when I did it. It kind of became my one big move. It was the one move that I could pull off that looked halfway decent.

I put Macho Sasquatcho out with a sleeper hold and then rubbed his tummy for that little bit of comic levity. It was an ignominious demise for the Sasquatch in his first match. Bob the Ref raised my hand in victory. A few people booed. A few others chanted for Chewbacca.

The wrestling set went on. The Missionary Man fought the really strange-looking, gangly John Pierre LeButt. After their match, LeButt hobbled backstage and had a complete nervous breakdown. He sat in a folding chair and sobbed wildly while still wearing his Montreal themed tights with the royal cross on his kneepads. Nobody talked to him. Nobody tried to comfort him. He was almost too disturbing to look at.

Van Dyne and I took a powder during Calvin Krime's set. There was no booze at the venue so we went across the street to this bar called My Father's Place. It was kind of a cool bar really. It had an old school democrat theme. There were lots of framed pictures of FDR and Truman up on the walls. As we got our drinks and sat down in a large wooden booth, Van Dyne overheard some hippie kids from the show carrying on about our match. "There was a fat, crazy guy fighting a Bigfoot," one of them exclaimed like it was the wildest spectacle he had ever seen. Van Dyne was impressed by that. He was hooked.

Van Dyne and I returned to the venue after a couple of shots. I was emceeing the second set. The first match was the Cruiser vs. Chango Loco. I announced Bob the Ref. He greeted the crowd by giving them the bird. This didn't set too well with them and pissed off those fucknuts a little more than it should have.

Then the Cruiser stomped into the ring with that exaggerated strut of his. He held out his hand for the microphone and I handed it over to him. He surveyed the audience with complete disdain and disgust. "Hello Portland Oregon," he said in his incongruously macho Snagglepuss affectation. "I am gonna fuck each and every one of you up the ass!"

The crowd went utterly crazy-assed ape-shit nuts. In a burst of incredibly repressed homosexuality, one kid jumped into the ring and latched onto Bob's leg. I made a few pleas on the microphone in an attempt to calm things down. It didn't do any good. I got into the ring expecting a brawl. Cruiser was hitting the kid across the back of his head with all his might. Bob was hitting the kid. I jumped onto the kid's back. I wanted Bob or Cruiser to lift his head up so I could slap a chokehold on him. They didn't hear me. They were too busy hitting the kid across the forehead. The kid chomped into Bob's thigh and started to draw blood. I raised myself up and came down on the kid's back with all my weight but it didn't do anything. Some other wrestlers joined in and pulled the kid away. Bob kept trying to kick the kid. Bob understandably wanted to kill the little shit.

This pissed off the crowd even more and some more skater kids jumped up on the ring apron and got in the Cruiser's face. "You're beating up a little guy!" they yelled. "You're twice his size!!!" Shit, two wresters and a ref couldn't take that kid out. It didn't matter how small he was. That kid was caught up in some kind of PCP induced homoerotic berserker rage. He was indestructible.

We waited for security to do something. They did nothing. We were on our own. Chango Loco got tired of waiting to hear the Bad Brains song that he used for entrance music. He saw the aggro kids on the ring apron. He took a swig of rum and breathed fire at them. The fucking punks were totally devoid of all natural animal reactions. They weren't even afraid of fire. Chango then broke a broomstick over one of their heads. Shards of wood splintered and flew all over the ring. The kid just stood there. He didn't even flinch. It only enraged him until veins were popping out of his neck and forehead. Even Chango Loco seemed at a loss for what to do next.

Missionary Man got in the ring. Van Dyne pulled one of the kids off the ring apron. The kid grabbed the ring post and held onto it for dear life. Van Dyne grabbed his belt and tried to pull him away. The kid's pants gave before he did and Paul ripped his Wal-Mart jeans right off him until the kid's ass was hanging out.

The security people got brave. They started throwing people out in a half-assed way. They tossed Van Dyne out with a bunch of the skater kids. Van Dyne somehow got away from them and snuck into the venue through a back door after being worried that he was going to get jumped by a gang of pissed off Fat Mike fans.

Audra called the wrestling set and rushed the Gimme Gimmes onto the stage like the Old West piano player who launches into *Camptown Races* right after a barroom brawl. Things didn't get any better from there. The Gimmes Gimmes were consistently pissed off during the days that had followed the hotel room brawl between Brett and Audra. They'd been drinking all day and could barely stand up. Barry Ward, a hired gun guitarist who had played with Gwar and Rich Kids on LSD and now fronts the trucker punk band Crosstops, kept hitting the bassist in the arm instead of playing the songs. Spike was so shitfaced that he fell off the stage several times. Like the wrestling set, Me First and the Gimme Gimmes' set was cut short.

All hell had broken loose and kept breaking loose. Chango Loco and Brett got the bright idea that they wanted revenge. They found one of the kids quietly being escorted out of the hall by security. Brett ran up and broke the kid's nose right in front of all of the ticket takers and NXNW volunteers. The cops showed up. The college kids working the venue told them what Brett had done. Of course, everyone sided with the townies. The cracker skate punks seriously sucked but they were the locals. One of them had blood streaming down his face and a bunch of witnesses saying that one of the wrestlers from the hated Golden State did it. The cops wanted to throw Brett's ass in the clink. Brett ran into the backroom wanting us to hide him. He quickly changed his clothes and shaved off his John Waters pencil mustache to alter his appearance. There was some talk of putting some of the Ghost of Versace's white facepaint on him and sending him to the goth dance party downstairs, but Audra somehow bullshitted Brett's way out of a night in the Multnomah County hoosegow.

This made her more pissed off than she was already. Brett and

Audra had come to blows only days before and now she was keeping his ass out of jail. She stormed into the backroom and let all us all have it, except for Brett who had conveniently disappeared.

"What fucking genius gets the fucking bright idea to go off and break some kid's nose?! We had already thrown him out for Christ's sake! You people are just fucking stupid. You are fucking idiots! The kids were already gone! Now the fucking cops want to run us all in! Fuck! God damn it!" She went on in that vein for a while. Then she calmed down a little and kept saying, "Thank God I know how to lie to cops. Thank fucking God I can lie to cops."

Chango stormed off and got on a payphone to his padrino. He came back to the venue convinced that he needed to get on the next Greyhound bus back to San Francisco. "This is it," Chango said, "I'm done with isw," and he stormed off again.

Brett caught Van Dyne and me on our way out. He begged us to drive down to Eugene, Oregon, for the show the next night. John Pierre LeButt wasn't coming back and Chango Loco was gone. Things weren't looking good for isw. Somehow, Brett must have appealed to our masochistic natures. We agreed to rent a car at the airport and drive down to Eugene. You'd think that Paul wouldn't want anything to do with isw after the leg biting riot and getting hollered at by Audra, but Paul only had a private little laugh at Audra's freak-out. It was funny to him. His sadistic sense of humor was his best defense. He probably hoped that it would happen again the next night.

Eugene, Oregon, is known for two things: the University of Oregon and its irrepressible love affair with meth amphetamine. Saying that Eugene is the meth capital of Oregon is like saying it is the meth capital of the world. More people are treated for addiction to the drug there than in any other state. This is truly alarming when you consider that Oregon barely has three and a half million people — not even half the population of the San Francisco Bay Area.

Cooking up meth with household chemicals and over-the-counter cold medicines accounts for much of Eugene's industry and many of the university's students put it up their collegiate noses to extend their all-night cram sessions ad infinitum. With the utter debacle that was Portland, it was hard not to picture the Cruiser or Count Dante being torn to shreds by a horde of cranked out psych-Lit majors.

But the show in Eugene didn't further our descent into tweaker punk hell. Where the dumpy rec center in Portland was foreboding almost from the get-go, John Henry's Bar in Eugene was warm and welcoming. The club was owned and operated by a half-crazed mountain of a man named Bruce Hartnell. Hartnell played crunchy, overdriven guitar for a twelve-piece Latin-tinged instrumental ensemble called Los Mex Pistols Del Norte. His band was very good at blending galloping toreador music with surf rock sensibilities and one can only wonder if they wouldn't have been bigger on the cult circuit if they had been from Los Angeles or Austin instead of Eugene. Out of all the venue owners and club bookers that hosted isw during that tour, Hartnell was the only one that got it. His band could have easily provided half the theme music for any isw tv show.

In contrast to Portland, Eugene seemed to want isw there so badly that the restaurant next to John Henry's even altered their menu to serve Gimme Gimme Green Quesadillas, Cheese and Garlic Calvin Krime Fries and Incredibly Strange Rice Pudding. It was nice to be wanted and everything awful from the night before seemed to be gone as we gathered to set up the ring. Chango Loco was back. He didn't make the Greyhound and someone convinced him to finish out the tour. Audra and Spike (who'd broken up after the Brett incident) were back together and if there were any lingering animosities between Audra and Brett, neither showed it.

Once we got into town, Van Dyne wanted to rent a hotel room. I was flat, busted broke so I was fine with wrestling our match and driving back to Portland to sleep on somebody's couch. Van Dyne was a creature of comfort however and he sprung for the room. Paul had shelled out enough cash on this little jaunt already so I felt kind of bad about it. That's how it usually went. Van Dyne footed the bill. He worked that steady, higher mid-income job and lived at home with the parents. I lived in my cruddy apartment, worked a rotating roster of low paying temp jobs, burned through my student loans while making things like ISW and my band top priority. Hanging out with Van Dyne had a way of making you feel like you were taking advantage of him. Then again, Van Dyne never got behind the wheel of a car for some reason. If I didn't drive him all over the place, he would have never left home.

Craig and Chango went to the hotel room with us. Chango Loco was fastidiously clean by nature and it must have driven him nuts to be so dirty on that tour. He immediately hit the shower and used up most of our towels. Craig parked himself in front of the TV and looked like "man discovering fire" as Van Dyne later put it. Craig just sat there and stared at MTV and clutched a rolled up copy of *Family Circle*.

"Where did you get that?" I asked. Craig didn't strike me as the kind of guy who regularly read *Family Circle* or *Ladies' Home Journal* for that matter.

"Oh, I bought it, man," he replied.

Now I was even more confused. "Why did you buy that?" I asked.

"Oh, it has Oprah on the cover, man," he answered. "It's Oprah."

I just left it at that until it was time to walk back to the venue.

The Demonics kicked off the show that night wearing tight, pink one-piece swimsuits. Even though they were wearing women's swimwear, they didn't look like transvestites. They just looked like guys who got too stoned while shopping at a dirt-cheap thrift store. It was still pretty funny though and that's what made the Demonics so much more enjoyable than any of the other bands from that SF retro scene.

Van Dyne and I went through the same match again from the night before with me winning. I wanted to have him win but we really didn't know enough to go changing anything. We didn't have another finisher for the Bigfoot. We just stuck with what we knew.

Chango Loco called the first set and he wasn't that bad at it. La Coqueta showed up to the Eugene show and spent nearly ten minutes groping and clawing at some lady friend of hers in a cat suit. You couldn't really call it a wrestling match even by lax ISW standards.

I called the second set and botched some kind of drunken battle-royal match that they had planned where wrestlers took a shot after they got tossed out of the ring. Nobody told me about it and I didn't even have a sheet of paper to work from. "What's the matter, Dante?" Missionary Man kidded me after the show, "Don't you remember the battle-royal from last night?" Of course the second set never got that far in Portland.

After the show, Brett asked us to work the Olympia, Washington, show, but we had a flight to catch. We could have eaten our tickets and ridden back on the van, but after hearing so many horror stories about it we decided to make our flight. It was only Olympia after all. Seattle may have been a bit more tempting but not much more. Van Dyne had a job to get back to. I also thought I had a job waiting for me on Monday, but I'd made the mistake of telling the head librarian at one of the Kaiser hospital libraries in Oakland that I was going up to Portland for the weekend to wrestle a guy in a Wookiee suit. On Monday morning she called my agency and told them that they had no further need of my services.

Friday, October 24 was the last show of that tour. The van with the wrestlers had rolled back into town a few days earlier but this was the capper at the Paradise. It was ISW's big return to its home base.

I was pretty assured that Van Dyne and I would get to wrestle on this show. Brett had asked us to go to Eugene and we did out of our own pockets. That should have counted for something. That should have canceled out any kind of brewing backroom bullshit between Brett and me.

The morning of the show I got a message from Brett. He told me that there wasn't space for us on the card and that there was nothing he could do about it. He had gone and crammed the show with rockabilly types and other scenesters like he had always done. None of these people were pros and none of them had bought a Wookiee suit or hauled their asses to Eugene. I felt betrayed — like I had been had all along.

I felt like a bitch but I called Audra. What else could I do? She sounded like she'd had enough hassles already but told me that Van Dyne and I should show up anyway. When we got to the Transmission, we were still bumped. It was one last little fuck you to me from Brett and this was after he'd begged me to drive down to Eugene to save his little show and I did.

As I walked around the Transmission with nothing to do, there was a TV crew there. They were from some local TV show aimed at teenagers. Brett and the rest of the rockabillies were too cool for school when it came to television. They only cared about their insular clique of Bettie Page look-alikes and guys who dressed like they were from the 1950s but drove around in muscle cars from the '60s. Audra needed a wrestler to talk to the cameras and she gave me the go-ahead to be on TV. The one thing that I excelled at was addressing the public. That was how I was going to outlast Brett and the other neo-greasers. I was going to show up and do the work. I was going to work the media. They could have all of the people from the Greaseball, the blessing of the cars or the last Reverend Horton Heat show. I was going to be the one that the general public associated with Incredibly Strange Wrestling.

On the TV show, I voiced over some blow-by-blow commentary

while Kid Anarchy demonstrated wrestling moves on a teenaged Asian reporter. Then one of the show's newscasters asked me what it took to be a pro wrestler.

"It takes a willingness to live the life, to be there in the sawdust, to be there in the ring, to have tortillas thrown at you," I said with a rapid-fire delivery. "You got to push all that aside and say, 'I'm gonna live in the grit and the dirt and the dust and I'm gonna love it, and I'm gonna be famous!'"

# 9

# THE POONTANGLER
# AND THE DEVIL CHICKEN

IT WAS THE LAST ISW SHOW of the year: New Year's Eve 1997. Brett was gone and so were some of the other people who had been with the show since the Johnny Legend days. Audra had stripped them of their power and cast them out of the show that they had helped to create. It was inevitable, and had been coming on even before Brett kicked Audra on the tour or before the over-crowding of the October show caused so many problems. It had been the way things were shaking out ever since Audra got rid of Legend. Incredibly Strange Wrestling was Audra's and all Audra's. It always had been and always would be.

While the expulsion of Brett and company from the ranks didn't leave much of a power vacuum, it did leave a creative one. The age of the rockabilly dudes with masks was rapidly drawing to a close. The nerds were poised to take over. Uncool weirdos like Paul Van Dyne, Craig Martins and myself had the creative capital that the show needed more than ever.

But Audra wasn't about to hand out promotions. She had been burned or at least kicked by her second-in-commands before so she wasn't going to recreate that post anytime soon. Audra had a certain fascination with fascism and she often joked, "I'm not a Nazi; I'm a Fascist" as an open retort to her most vicious detractors. So when Audra finally wrested complete control of ISW, she ran it like a totalitarian regime. Audra's supreme leadership was unquestionable, but the ranking of everyone else in the show was left purposely vague to maintain a constant struggle for power amongst her underlings. ISW never had a booker or creative director or co-producer. Giving anyone official titles other than wrestler, wrestling manager or announcer would have implied a level of authority that Audra wasn't going to share with anyone.

For me and the other nerds to prove our creative worth, we still had to pass through the crucible of the wrestling meeting. While the meetings were definitely a good idea in principle, in practice they devolved into shouting matches among blowhards. The king of all the blowhards was Dave Steele, better known as U.S. Steele.

Steele had started as a company man who struggled to fit the show's lucha libre aesthetic as much as he possibly could (considering that he was a white guy in his mid-thirties from Concord). With a patch of thinning dishwater blond hair on top of his head that ran in long strings down past his shoulders, he worked concert security for Bill Graham Presents (later SFX Entertainment, later Clear Channel). At first he wore a mask as Audra had demanded and wrestled under the name of Risa de Muerte or "Smile of Death." A few years later we had him just wear the star-spangled parachute pants and Old Glory bandannas that he always seemed to have with him and he became the super patriot U.S. Steele. Gaudy displays of nationalistic pride were just another element of '80s kitsch when Clinton was still president. The fans chanted "U.S.A." during Steele's matches mostly as a joke.

Steele brought his little brother Josh and all of Josh's suburban teen friends into isw. This provided Dave with a steady stream of opponents who always lost to him. Those wrestlers from the 1980s who never, ever won matches (like Salvatore Bellomo in the wwe or the Mulkeys in early wcw) were called jobbers in the wrestling business. They were the squared circle equivalent of cannon fodder. They existed solely to be fed to the Junkyard Dog or the Macho Man. Losing a match is thus called "jobbing" or "jobbing out." If a promoter booked you to fail miserably, you were "jobbed." U.S. Steele found a way to make jobbing a family affair.

Most of Steele's ideas for matches consisted of Risa de Muerte entering the ring and proceeding to beat the living shit out of Josh. When Risa was done beating up Josh, Risa then pulverized all of Josh's puny pals. It was a brutally one-sided sibling rivalry played out before paying customers. Unfortunately the dynamic of the sadistic older brother mercilessly pounding on the weaker younger brother (until, presumably, the worm turned and the bullying brother received his comeuppance) would have made a far more interesting storyline than any match that they actually did before a crowded Transmission Theatre.

Back then Steele tended to dominate those wrestling meetings through the sheer force of his personality and it would have been really easy to hate him if it weren't for a few things. Dave Steele personally took in all of the teens that he regularly beat up in the wrestling ring. They were fuck-ups and runaways from abusive or uncaring family situations. Dave and his wife gave them a place to stay when no one else would. Dave also loved his wife and to him she was the most beautiful woman in the world. Behind Steele's boastful public persona lay an honest sweetheart of a guy and once you discovered that, it was almost impossible to dislike him no matter how much he got in your way.

Steele was also one of the best wrestlers in isw. This made him even more frustrating because, while he had the moves in the ring, he didn't always work well with other people. In Steele, we had this decent worker (which was a rarity in the lower, non-pro tiers of ISW) but it was hard to do anything interesting with him. As we moved the wrestling show in an absurdist comedy direction and away from its faux-lucha model, Steele's tough guy style of putting together a wrestling match gave us all ulcers.

My suspicions of those wrestling meetings went beyond Steele's influence on them. I had come out of them a few times holding the short end of the stick. I figured out that the best way to continue my plans of subverting ISW while improving my match's quality (at least thematically) was to go into those meetings with my match and opponent already worked out. Planning your match with twenty-plus pro wrestlers crammed into Audra's or Chango's claustrophobic flat was a bad idea. You ended up just drawing lots, which meant you and your opponent were saddled with each other. Putting on a show that way it was impossible to develop characters or a storyline. Although it may sound absurd to be concerned with character development and plot elements in a show where the audience was encouraged to throw food at the performers, we had to move beyond the "two guys in masks who hate each other" plots.

For the New Year's Eve show, my match was already planned. Count Dante was going to once again face Macho Sasquatcho, with the Sasquatch winning this time. It was the match that we should have done in October, but Brett had nixed it. Audra was as good as her word. Our bout was even on the Chuck Sperry four-color poster this time around, but we still had to go to the wrestling meeting anyway.

This time the meeting was held at the Transmission itself. The club was closed the day before New Year's Eve, so we were actually able to set up the ring and work on our matches the day before the show. This was luxurious.

Most of that show was going to be the usual ISW fare of the time: U.S. Steele vs. Jefferson Monroe and Boris and Jose vs. Boris and Jose (or some combination thereof). Audra also wanted to have a late Christmas match with the character of Santo Claus, which was Jose wearing a Santo mask and a red, fuzzy Santa Claus costume. Santo Claus needed an appropriately holiday-themed opponent and everyone in the room started yelling out ideas so awful that I have completely blocked them from memory.

After this went on for a while, Audra clearly wasn't satisfied, so I said, "How about Super Kwanzaa?" The African-American alternative to the overly commercialized Christmas had only been in the public consciousness for a short time and it had been getting some news coverage that year. Audra almost died laughing. That was it. Super Kwanzaa was happening.

When Super Kwanzaa was realized during the opening match on the following night, the character was played by a spear-wielding white woman in blackface and a dashiki. For that extra touch of tastelessness, Audra got the idea to have Kwanzaa toss chaffs of buckwheat to the audience. A menorah wielding yenta named Matzo Mama was added to the bout at the last minute so that Hanukkah would be properly represented. At one point Matzo Mama brained Santo Claus with an oversized plastic menorah and Claus took the time to catch a much-needed breather on the filthy mat. This led to several long minutes of Kwanzaa and Matzo standing there and throwing Manischewitz baked goods and buckwheat at each other. The match eventually trundled to a confusing conclusion several minutes later.

I always had more than my fair share of white liberal guilt over coming up with the Super Kwanzaa concept, but people who were at that show still come up to me and tell me that it was the funniest thing they had ever seen. Some of them look like goobery white boys. Others look like grad students. But that match did a lot to cement my reputation as a backroom creative force, and it came at the right time. Audra praised the concept to various punk rock publications for years afterwards.

Following the Christmas vs. Kwanzaa vs. Hanukkah three-way

was my rematch with Macho Sasquatcho. For this bout, I was once again managed by Dennis Erectus. He got on the mic and boasted about how we were both from San Jose. "It pains two sophisticated gentlemen such as Count Dante and myself," Erectus said with his trademark sneer, "to have to come to this filthy, dirty, decadent city!" San Franciscans are programmed to hate everything about their suburban neighbor to the south so the fans hurled a blizzard of tortilla fragments mixed with matzo and buckwheat down upon Dennis until he could barely be seen amidst the hurtling culinary debris.

Erectus and I kept the crowd's ire at a fever pitch by double-teaming Macho Sasquatcho. We did all of the cornball heel moves that we could think of. Dennis choked him in the corner with a rope while Allan Bolte exclaimed, "Somebody stop it!" This kept the crowd involved in the match and also kept them from noticing how godawful it really was. It was programming for short attention spans. We needed to feed our audience a lot of crazy shit in no more than five minutes. That was the Dante formula I'd come up with. Everyone else in ISW seemed to want to wrestle fifteen-minute classics even though they were incapable of wrestling three-minute classics. There was some strange instinct to eat up as much time as possible once you were in that ring. I just wanted to get my match over with and leave the crowd thinking that they had actually seen something.

The bout was supposed to close with Erectus getting into the ring and attempting to hit the Bigfoot with the dreaded steel chair but missing and hitting me instead. Somehow, our little environmental psychodrama actually spurred some acid-addled hippie kid to get in the ring to save the hairy woodland creature from those evil men from San Jose. The auburn haired Phish fan jumped into the ring and pulled the Sasquatch out of Erectus' way as the rock deejay was about to lower the chair. Erectus still hit me with the chair anyway, which was the plan in the first place. I didn't know what was going on when Jose and Dave Steele hit the ring. Jose pulled the hippie down by his long hair and sent him face first into the mat hard. Dave and Jose then proceeded to stomp a mudhole in some hippie ass in the corner of the ring until security dragged the tree-hugger's limp, broken body away.

I stayed down on the mat for several seconds while Van Dyne collected himself and pinned me for the three count.

Looking down on the spectacle from the balcony of the Transmission was Tom Corgan. He had paid his admission to get into the show just to see me wrestle. He wanted back in and he wanted back in bad. I was rising through the ranks and he knew as much, but I still didn't have the clout to bring him back although most of the people who had thrown him out were now gone. Bringing him back was going to take some time but it was something that I had to do. I owed it to him.

Tom and I discussed the match, the show and the hippie beating. He was especially excited about the hippie beating. I was happy to see him but I had to abandon him for the free flowing beer and champagne in the backroom. It was New Year's Eve: 1997 was giving way to 1998. Mike Watt was headlining the show but by the time he went on, I was too far gone to enjoy his ceaseless bass guitar noodling. I felt like I was at a *Bass Player* magazine clinic. Watt may as well have been Victor Wooten that night. It was New Year's for God's sakes! I was drunk as a skunk. I wanted to hear Motorhead goddamn it! Most of the rest of the crowd did too and the room seemed to empty about three songs into Watt's set, leaving behind only a corps of his diehard fans right in front of the stage. As I looked around I realized that I had to stagger home all by myself. Everyone I knew was gone.

By 1998, Incredibly Strange Wrestling was the hottest underground rock spectacle in San Francisco. Despite the terrible wrestling, the infighting and the often nonexistent prep work, it had somehow grown by word of mouth and bits of media to the point where we were doing a show every month. Shows that didn't sell out the

Transmission were rare. But the whole country and maybe the whole world seemed to be wrestling obsessed in the late 1990s. There was as ongoing ratings war between Vince McMahon's WWE and Ted Turner's WCW that was consistently skyrocketing their respective Monday evening programs into the two top cable ratings spots week after week. Although *Monday Night Raw* (WWE) and *Monday Nitro* (WCW) ran opposite each other, the competition between the two promotions had millions of people tuning into both shows every week.

There is a misconception that because professional wrestling is a lowbrow form of entertainment most commonly enjoyed by slobbering sister-fucking hillbillies, it draws its biggest audiences during economic downturns. The truth is just the opposite. Pro wrestling's biggest boom periods have always coincided with times of economic prosperity. The first national wrestling boom of the 20th century was during the Eisenhower '50s. The second wave of wrestling popularity was right in the midst of Reagan's economic recovery in the mid-1980s and 1997's wrestling craze occurred as Bill Clinton turned the U.S. economy around and presided over budget surpluses and a soaring stock market.

These periods of pro wrestling popularity also shared one other crucial element: a massive leap forward in communications and entertainment technology. The 1950s saw the rise of television and with it Gorgeous George became one of the "Golden Age of Television's" most recognizable celebrities along with Lucille Ball. In the 1980s, cable super stations like USA and TBS brought Hulk Hogan, Roddy Piper and Ric Flair into millions of living rooms and gave Vince McMahon a way to make his WWE a truly national phenomenon — undreamed of during the previous decade when UHF syndication deals were the means by which regional wrestling promotions got on the air.

In the late 1990s, there was a great expansion of cable and satellite television along with pay-per-view technology and, of course, the Internet. The greater access to pay-per-view in peoples' homes is what really floated the boat for wrestling in the late 1990s. Throughout most of pro wrestling's history, live attendance and tickets sold accounted for most of a promotion's revenue. In 1997, pay-per-view buy rates were the measure of a promotion's success.

Because of cable TV in the 1980s, I was able to watch *Georgia Championship Wrestling* out here in the San Francisco Bay Area. There was always a lot of mystique to the Southern product because those crudely designed, pulpy wrestling mags that you could buy at 7-Eleven endlessly hyped Dixie's "American Dream" Dusty Rhodes and "Nature Boy" Ric Flair. The publisher of most of these mags, Bill Apter, had an axe to grind against Vince McMahon at the time so he published article after article proclaiming that WWE champion Hulk Hogan couldn't last five minutes in the ring with NWA champ Flair.

In my adolescent mind, Hulk Hogan, with his self-proclaimed "24-inch pythons," was the most perfect male specimen of all time. Ric Flair, on the other hand, as pictured in these magazines, looked like a much smaller, Camaro driving cracker with feathered platinum hair and brown eyebrows. Hair bleached so blond it was almost white accompanied by dark facial hair actually seemed to be de rigueur in Southern wrestling circles during the go-go '80s. Many other grapplers decided to pass up dabbing a little peroxide on their eyebrows in order to sport this hideous look. The idea that "Nature Boy" Ric Flair could somehow survive and even eke out a victory while Hulkamania was running wild seemed patently ridiculous.

But the grainy, black and white pictures of Southern wrestling piqued my interest. There were photographs of an obese white man with a platinum blond perm and brown eyebrows named Dusty Rhodes who always seemed to be bleeding profusely from several lacerations in his forehead. There were also pictures of an even more morbidly obese black man named Abdullah the Butcher, also bleeding like a sieve while digging a dinner fork into his hapless opponents' foreheads. There were rednecks wrestling in steel cages. There were cowboys and Indian chiefs tied together with leather straps and chains and beating each other with boots.

In Vince McMahon's bid to go national, he had rendered his promotion into a piece of family friendly entertainment. There were many moments of greatness like when Roddy Piper beat Jimmy "Superfly" Snuka with a coconut, but nobody seemed to bleed very much in the WWE. The WWE had the star power. They had Andre the Giant and Hulk Hogan. Their wrestlers definitely had the look of superhuman athletes of the future, but those images of Vince McMahon's Southern fried competition displayed a marvelous barbarism that was at once more realistic yet surreal at the same time.

I got really excited the first time that I saw *Georgia Championship Wrestling* (later *World Championship Wrestling*) on Ted Turner's TBS. The show definitely lacked Vince McMahon's production values. The matches were filmed in a stark soundstage with a smattering of fans seated in a few rows of aluminum bleachers. The set's walls were painted black and an incongruous collection of flags of the world hung from the rafters.

While Southern wrestling lacked the slick look of the WWE, it did have high drama. The WWE's shows were nothing more than a series of squash matches where jobbers showed up to be pummeled in minutes by the show's superstars. *Georgia Championship Wrestling* featured the working class hero Dusty Rhodes' endless efforts to wrest championship gold from the elitist Ric Flair's waist. Week after week, Rhodes would almost have the title in his grasp only to be put down by the Nature Boy's cheating cabal, the Four Horsemen.

To a fat, socially ostracized teenager such as myself, Dusty Rhodes quickly became a role model and inspiration. The announcers constantly and glowingly spoke of Rhodes' amazing athletic prowess. Rhodes was fat as a house and he clearly spent more time scarfing down chili dogs than he did pumping iron, yet he was an athlete. My adulation of Rhodes was furthered when a sculpted Adonis-like Lex Luger had to resort to illegal tactics such as leaning on the ropes just to have a chance of beating Rhodes. The announcers assured me in their high-pitched Southern twang that if Luger had only played by the rules Dusty would have won for sure. In a supreme display of wish fulfillment, I opted to believe these respected pro wrestling tele-journalists.

Turner's wrestling also gave me a weekly clinic in sheer shit talking. In the WWE, Hogan definitely had a distinctive interview style with his frequent invocation of the word "brother" and Piper had the gift of gab, but Ric Flair, that man that the Hulkster supposedly couldn't last five minutes with, elevated trash talking to a high art form. He had enough catchphrases to supply any other wrestling promotion for an entire year. He punctuated everything with that trademark "Woo" of his and boasted about riding in limos and private jets. But the best saying in his repertoire seemed to transcend merely defeating Magnum TA or Dusty Rhodes and spoke to some higher meaning or personal philosophy. "In order to *be* the man," Flair exclaimed before pausing for a few beats for dramatic effect, "you have to *beat* the *man!*"

As the 1980s trudged on to its conclusion, I started to outgrow my interest in pro wrestling. Inevitably I started to play bass and discovered that girls really didn't want to talk about fat bloody guys wearing tights, but what really pushed me on to other interests was the Ultimate Warrior. Ultie was a character so incredibly stupid that his emergence in the WWE effectively killed my interest in pro wrestling altogether. The Warrior was a real scorched earth policy. With his inane interviews and his silly shaking of the ring ropes, he sealed a Pyrrhic victory between Vince McMahon and his competition — at least as far as my viewing habits were concerned.

When I started wrestling in ISW, I hadn't watched pro wrestling in years, but Chango Loco, the Cruiser and I soon found ourselves gripped by the same kind of pro wrestling fever that infected millions of adolescent males of all ages at that time. It's funny how you can believe you are bucking the mainstream but end up following trends despite yourself. Sometimes there is just something in the air. At least we had the excuse that we were watching *Raw* and *Nitro* for business purposes.

Chango was convinced that we needed to watch as much pro wrestling as possible in order to improve our ring work and he was right about that. A lot of the silly and easy moves like having my head rammed into the turnbuckle or my face dragged along the ring ropes that no one else in ISW ever bothered doing were rediscovered while watching pro wrestling.

Chango, Craig and I could get through four hours of wrestling programming every Monday night because the Turner's TNT network was still broadcast on Eastern Standard Time on San Francisco cable, while the USA network was delayed for the West Coast. This allowed us to catch both *Nitro* and *Raw* back-to-back. When WCW added another two hours of wrestling called *Thursday Night Thunder*, we forced ourselves to watch that too. When *Nitro* added an extra hour on Mondays, we struggled to watch all seven weekly hours of wrestling offered by both promotions plus monthly pay-per-view extravaganzas without our brains turning into grayish sludge and seeping out our ears.

While it may seem strange that ISW's popularity paralleled that of pro wrestling's big leagues, it really wasn't at all. There is only the demand for an alternative version of something while there is high demand for its mainstream component. Rock music was never more popular than it was in the arena rock era of the 1970s. That was why, during that post–*Frampton Comes Alive* period (where even bands like Styx could go multi-platinum album after album), you had the Ramones and the Dictators stripping down rock and roll past the point of its primitive roots and offering a three-chord, two-minute alternative to the overly orchestrated major label output of Fleetwood Mac.

As the hardcore punk era developed in the early 1980s, the same conditions remained. Rock was still popular. The Go-Go's, a group that was barely above one-hit wonder status, sold out the 13,000-seat Cow Palace no sweat. People wanted rock. They wanted a lot of rock so there were also people who wanted Black Flag and the Butthole Surfers.

In the 1990s, pro wrestling was a massive, pay-to-play machine where so many would-be grapplers shelled out thousands of dollars to those wrestling schools to even have a shot at the stardom that they craved. Even Paul Heyman's revolutionary Extreme Championship Wrestling, which was a distant third in pro wrestling's big three and run like a cottage industry out of Heyman's own kitchen, worked well within these confines. Of course this was a necessity for ECW due to its emphasis on match quality and risk taking. Sure, ECW had guys like the Sandman who did nothing more than slam down beers and hit people with sticks, but the organization also had some of the best matches of the period with high flyers and technical masters like Chris Benoit, Chris Jericho, Tajiri and Super Crazy.

Where the Ramones defiantly reminded the world that you didn't have to go to Juilliard to play rock and roll, Incredibly Strange Wrestling was the do-it-yourself answer to pro wrestling's corporate structure. Our matches may have been incoherent wrecks for the most part, but like early punk rock, we still had the ability to entertain and enrage with almost none of the budget or training that the entertainment establishment deemed indispensable. Still, if nobody wanted wrestling, than no one would have wanted us. So just as Rollins was reportedly spinning Dio's mainstream metal epic "Holy Diver" during the recording sessions for Black Flag's *Loose Nut*, the brain trust of ISW wasn't above catching *Monday Night Raw*.

Paul Van Dyne could no longer resist the siren's call of the chicken suit that he had originally considered buying for our trip to Portland.

It was still available. It haunted him in his dreams. The icon of caricatured poultry was beckoning to him so he up and bought it. Like his Chewbacca suit, it needed a name. Of course El Pollo Loco was the obvious choice. Although being named after a third-tier fast food franchise had some appeal, ISW was awash with "Locos" at the time. There was already Doctor Loco, Chango Loco and, of course, El Homo Loco. What ISW didn't need was another Loco.

"How about 'El Pollo Diablo'?" Van Dyne asked during one of our long bullshit sessions that preceded every coming show. "It seems like ISW could use a Diablo?"

Van Dyne was right on the money with this one. ISW didn't have a Diablo or a Satanico or Diabólico for that matter. How ISW could have avoided creating a character with Diablo in the name is really a mystery when you consider that every post-modern gearhead had Coop drawn cartoon decals of chubby, big-breasted devil girls stuck to their Mopars. Velvet paintings of Satan and strings of little devil head Christmas lights seemed to decorate almost every hipster bar in the Bay Area. Interest in family-friendly devil kitsch was at an all-time high, but ISW still had no Diablos. I guess that's what happens when almost no one in the supposedly Mexican wrestling promotion can speak Spanish. Lucifer had never been cast out, but merely left out due to an unfortunate oversight. But no longer, the Devil was about to get his due.

To give the newly purchased Devil Chicken more of a satanic edge, Van Dyne even went through the trouble of convincing these old ladies at this suburban costume store to sew large yellow horns to the side of the helmet-like headpiece. One can only wonder what went through those women's minds when they got that request, but they ended up doing a really good job on it.

El Pollo Diablo, the Devil Chicken, the cock from the barnyard of hell, looked like it was otherwise destined to be a zany high school mascot leading a homecoming parade in downtown Cupertino until Van Dyne intervened. The suit was made up of yellow and brown synthetic fur and the oversized head had two goggly cartoon eyes and a red, overstuffed pillow shaped into cockscomb. El Gallo Diablo, or the "Devil Rooster" would have been a more appropriate name for it, since the thing actually was the male of the species. But let's face it: the word chicken and the name Devil Chicken are just funnier than Devil Rooster.

While Van Dyne was piecing together his chicken suit, I had to work on my match for the next show so I would have everything together before one of those meetings. Craig's girlfriend Tigger had a great name for a wrestling character. She wanted to play the part of the ultimate trailer trash, gutter slut, a brawling bitch called the Poontangler. Now you can't say Poontangler for the first time without laughing at it and no one could possibly play that part better than she could. Tigger was a big woman with really big jugs. She also had presence and presence is the one thing that you just can't work on. You can work on comic timing, but you either have presence or you don't.

Now if we had waited until the wrestling meeting, the Poontangler would have just been booked with Cula de Muerte in a very non-descript match with two large women rolling around on each other. I had the idea to have a palimony or custody suit match between Count Dante and the Poontangler where the Poontangler would claim that Dante was the father of her son and Dante would steadfastly deny this. Both parties would then fight it out in the ring, Jerry Springer style. I actually wanted the match to look like the hair pulling, white trash brawl that Springer's security guards always denied you by pulling the toothless, screaming biker bitch off her spindly, mustached, no-good husband just as the really hard shots were starting to fly.

With this match, we could spoof Springer, which was a true ratings juggernaut at the time and was often blamed for speeding up the decline of American civilization. We could also develop much needed back stories for both Count Dante and the Poontangler, which we never could have done with whatever matches were thrown together for us at those accursed meetings.

I had to act quickly to get to Craig and Tigger before somebody else got the bright idea to set up matches before the meeting. I called their house and Craig answered the phone.

"Hey, do you and Tigger know who you're wrestling in the next show?" I asked.

"No, we don't," Craig replied, "We were going to just wait for the meeting."

"Don't wait for the fucking meeting," I shot back, "you'll always get fucked at the meeting! You'll end up wrestling Dave Steele for two hours!"

"Listen," I continued making my big pitch. "You want to go into those things with your match already laid out. If it's a good idea, Audra will go along with it because that's one less match she has to worry about. You get a better match out of the deal and she gets her job made easy for her. It's a win, win."

I told him how funny I thought the Poontangler idea was and how Tigger had all the potential to be as big a hit with the ISW crowd as El Homo Loco. The problem was that Tigger had already teamed up with Jose under the name of Azúcarota (roughly: Sugar Girl). She wore a Santo mask and basically helped Jose beat up on Craig for fifteen minutes.

"Well, she already wrestled as Azúcarota," Craig said.

"What, are you talking continuity here?" I asked. "Look, nobody remembers Azúcarota. Nobody cares. Poontangler is funny. That's Tigger's big money character. Forget about the Santo mask. Go with the Poontangler."

"Well, we were thinking of maybe Azúcarota: The Poontangler," Craig interjected, floating the idea.

I took a bit of a pause and said, "Naaaaaawwww — too many words. Don't confuse the audience. Poontangler's funny. The Poontangler is what they are going to remember."

"Doesn't it have to be lucha?" Tigger asked in the background. They were all still cowed by Audra's lucha libre mandates although there was really nothing lucha about Super Kwanzaa and Matzo Mama and Audra loved those two characters.

"Forget about lucha," I said in my best reassuring tone. I was trying to close the deal here. "Nobody's going to think that Tigger's Mexican. Besides, we shouldn't limit ourselves creatively this way. The Poontangler should be a masked American heel in the old school tradition. She represents something far more than we could manage to portray with the Spanglish thing."

It took some convincing but Tigger came around and agreed to work the match. She liked the whole idea behind it. Audra liked it too and gave it the green light. Now to Audra's credit: she may have talked up the lucha libre thing to every journalist who would listen, but if you gave her a good, funny idea, she was all ears. As much as the rest of us she wanted things to be funny or subversive or somehow confrontational.

Our only concession to Mexicanicity in that match was that the disputed child in our little one act drama was going to be named El Niño and the kid was going to be played by some relative of Jose's. The kid ended up having such golden brown skin that it was pretty obvious that he didn't come from my pasty white Irish stock, but that only made it all funnier — the joke being that of course the child is not Count Dante's, but yes, Dante has slept with the Poontangler on several occasions although he ineffectually attempts to deny it.

It was the night of the show. We didn't have TV. We didn't have those pulpy magazines to keep the fans informed. We didn't have programs either. We didn't even have a website. I had to get over the whole twisted love affair between Count Dante and the Poontangler, as well as the stipulations of this very special custody suit match with about two minutes of blustery testament before the bell rang and the Poontangler started hitting me.

Allan Bolte introduced me. I was 6' 4" and 280 pounds this time. He had me about an inch taller and fifteen pounds lighter than I actually was. Thanks, Allan.

"Tonight is a very serious matter," I said as I grabbed the microphone. People started booing the second I opened my mouth. Tortilla fragments sailed by my head.

"For I am fighting in a custody suit match," I continued. "This woman, the Poontangler, says that I, Count Dante, am the father of her child, El Niño! I am going to say right now that the Count would not soil his sacred genitalia with her foul fetus! But since Count Dante's heart is as big as this here arena, if I win this match, I will take custody of this child and he will be a ward of the Estate of Dante and I will provide for him. If she wins, she will get a child support check that she will spend on booze and drugs and…"

The Poontangler stormed the ring. She wore black with pink trim and a crazy pink wig. There was a kind of meanness conveyed in her mask that was almost scary. She grabbed two handfuls of hair and started pulling it as hard as she could. She was jerking my head around violently. I wanted this match to have a kind of realism to it but this was too much. She could have just held my head and I would have gladly moved wherever she directed me. It was the heat of the moment. She was carried away with it.

She slapped me hard with an open palm strike across the face. I fell to the mat like an old sack of potatoes and then she jumped on me with every ounce of her 240 pounds. She hit me hard with elbows and boots. The match was predetermined but the blows were real. Tigger was a strong woman with some weight on her. She was as tough as a gal could get without being an out-and-out bull-dyke.

I started to feel blood well up in my nose. I started to freak. For a second I thought that if blood started gushing out of my nose that the ref would stop the match like it was a jiu-jitsu tournament or something. After a few seconds I came to my senses. We were going to the finish no matter what. Then I wanted the blood to start pouring out of my nose. I wanted blood to get all over the ring but it never came.

We did the corny moves that I was starting to remember from my youth. She raked my head across the top rope. She pulled my hair some more. She rammed my head into the top turnbuckle, clutching a handful of hair the whole time. The audience counted off every time my head crashed into the turnbuckle padding.

It was a battle of the sexes. Men were cheering for me. Women cheered for the Poontangler until she started biting me on the forehead. "Is it a bite or a kiss?" Allan Bolte asked on the microphone. The audience turned on the Poontangler. They weren't new school "heel as bad-assed baby-face" wrestling fans. They were people who watched wrestling when they were kids in the 1970s and '80s and they reacted to things the way that fans reacted back then. The biting was a good reason to boo. The fans liked booing and they paid their money to do it.

I got up and started stomping my feet like Dusty Rhodes. I was about to mount my big comeback. I was going to land the bionic elbow. I was going to pull off that monkey flip of mine and maybe a couple of other moves that I had seen Captain Kirk do 100 times. The Poontangler was a woman. She was my friend but I was going to lay a couple of knuckles across her forehead as payback for all of that hair pulling. But then El Niño ran into the ring with the steel chair. The kid got excited and jumped his cue. He hit me with the chair. I went down. Tigger fell down for no reason so that El Niño could pull her onto my unconscious body. El Niño won the match for his mom, but he didn't have to. She'd kicked my ass from pillar to post.

The debut of El Pollo Diablo followed my bruising defeat at the hands of the Poontangler. The Devil Chicken was fighting Jefferson Monroe's luchadore chef character El Gourmexico. It was pretty

Sonny and Cher humor-wise, but it made sense. It got a laugh. Van Dyne also figured out that with that oversized beak of his, his head was well protected so that Gourmexico could land hard punches and kicks to it at will without doing harm to Van Dyne's actual nose and jaw. Gourmexico was also to rake the chicken's big, goofy eyes to get a laugh from the fans, who were quick on the uptake.

When that oversized mascot of a devil chicken entered the ring, the fans cheered like they never had before in isw. It was the kind of thing that they had always wanted to see from a show called Incredibly Strange Wrestling. That was the moment the show had changed. The nerds had taken over.

# 10

# ASHIDA KIM, THE NINJA

IT WAS ALMOST SUMMER in San Francisco and the weather oddly reflected that. I was meeting a friend at a sidewalk café across the street from my rundown apartment building. My little South of Market shoebox room may have been only one small step above squalor, but the tucked away circle of buildings across the street from it was becoming just the opposite.

When I first moved into the neighborhood there was nothing there but abandoned warehouses, forgotten outlet stores, and vacant lots. Homeless guys pushed shopping carts that were so weighed down with aluminum cans, plastic bags and scrap metal that one more patch of uneven sidewalk was going to send the whole thing tumbling all over Third Street. Now the area was being touted as "High Tech Gulch" and Internet startups were springing up in the district's vacant buildings as fast as domain names could be registered.

At the center of "High Tech Gulch" or "Multimedia Gulch" was a tucked away circle of buildings called South Park. It wasn't named after a cartoon on Comedy Central, but was actually one of San Francisco's oldest planned developments. The small one-block enclosure was built around an oval-shaped park in 1856. During its earliest days, the park was closed off by a wrought iron fence and at its eastern end there was a large wooden windmill facing what would some day be the Bay Bridge. By the time I moved there, the windmill and the gate had been gone for over a century but the park was still there and the raised concrete ring around it recalled its earliest days. The neighborhood was originally envisioned as a place for San Francisco's elite, and as the 20th century drew to a close, South Park was returning to its roots.

Adam, the friend I was meeting for coffee, had nothing to do with pro wrestling. I had known him since we were both in grammar school, but he was a bass player. I hang out with a lot of bass players. Ironically, Adam was also a founding member of the bass guitar–less trio the Fucking Champs back when they were still just called the Champs. He played an old Silvertone guitar in that band.

The Fucking Champs played under the name of the Champs for a few years before some talent agency that represented the remnants of the band that played the 1958 hit "Tequila" (also called the Champs) served their little Santa Cruz stoner asses with a cease and desist. Like the type of oldies act that served as their accidental namesake, the Fucking Champs tour around these days with only one original member. However, they still pack nightclubs full of indie rockers with Mr. Spock hairdos who want to hear harmonized heavy metal guitar solos but need their six-string wanking delivered with the proper amount of post-modern irony.

Adam worked down the street at an audio-visual company where a lot of other SF musicians earned their livings. A lot of people that I knew from my band's flophouse of a practice space held down jobs there. I met Adam in South Park during his lunch break.

"You know, I never had one chick wanting to go home with me after I played music," I said while waiting for my cup of coffee to cool a bit. Somehow it became okay to refer to women as chicks again in the late 1990s.

"Never — not one," I continued. "It never happened. But the wrestling show! Man, sometimes they're throwing themselves at me after I get out of that ring."

"No way," Adam said drawing out the "O" in "no" to accentuate his disbelief. "Really? You've got to be kidding."

Adam didn't believe me. He thought it was absurd that a guy could get laid by grappling Paul Van Dyne in a Sasquatch suit and fighting women, and he was right. It was absurd.

Then, as if on cue, a cute waitress who worked at the coffee place gathered up her courage and walked up to our table.

"I don't know how to ask this," she said nervously, "but are you a wrestler?"

"Yes, I am," I replied taking a little too much pride in the moment. "I am Count Dante — the deadliest man alive." I put on a little show for her, assuming that's what she wanted.

"Oh, I thought it was you," she said putting her hand on my shoulder. "I saw you wrestle Macho Sasquatcho. You're great with the commentary too. You're really funny."

I thanked her profusely but didn't get her phone number, thinking that I would probably run into her again as I lived across the street. I looked over at Adam and he had nearly fallen out of his seat.

This was starting to happen more and more. People recognized me from the wrestling show. Bike messengers on Market Street yelled, "Hey Count Dante!" at me as they rode past. Bartenders flowed me free drinks. I almost never had to pay to get into a show — especially at the Paradise or Transmission. There was always some bouncer or door guy who would let me in. Some teen girls at a Redwood City thrift store kept staring at me one day. It was only later on that I figured that they had probably seen me on that local teen show aimed at teens that I had been on. KRON Channel Four seemed to replay the segment with me in it at least once a month.

On another occasion, I was shelving books at one of my day jobs at the library in St. Mary's Hospital. The AV guy, who usually kept to himself in his back office, walked up to me while I was reorganizing the current journals shelf.

"Did I see you wrestle two women at the Transmission Theatre?" he asked slowly. It wasn't the kind of question that you just asked anybody. Of course it was me. Who else could it have been?

Other co-workers from other dead end temp jobs also recognized me while I was performing daily duties that were even more mundane when you compared them to slugging it out with the Poontangler or dealing with a speed freak riot in Portland.

My band started doing better too. Audra booked us at Stinky's and we played the Transmission. We played the Bottom of the Hill. All my attention-getting with my crazy gimmick at the wrestling could land us the better clubs, but we still played the dives. We played the Purple Onion in North Beach a lot. In the 1950s it was considered a classy joint and everyone from the Kingston Trio to Barbara Streisand performed there. The Smothers Brothers recorded a live record there and a dusty copy of it hung behind the bar.

By the 1990s, the Onion was owned by a clinically insane burnout by the name of Tom Guido. The bar had been reduced to serving cans of cheap beer that looked like they had been bought in bulk at Food Co. Guido had these gnarly acid flashbacks and he used to pull the plug on bands mid-set. He then got on the microphone and delivered incomprehensible monologues that went on for almost an hour. He was obsessed with bringing back the '60s and the place became a base of operations for wacky retro bands like Phantom Surfers, the High Fives and the Count Backwards (who wore zany pirate hats and looked like they should be hassling the Banana Splits on *Danger Island*).

Count Dante and the Black Dragon Fighting Society was too '70s obsessed for the Purple Onion. We played grinding distorted rock instead of twangy rock but the older guy who handed us cans of beer from behind the bar (it would be a stretch to call him a bartender) liked us because we could actually play our instruments. Most of the bands that played the Purple Onion couldn't. He convinced Guido to keep having us back. Later, Guido liked us too. I got in a bit of trouble over an incident where Guido started kicking people at a house party after I had given my kung fu rock and roll success seminar at the Onion the night before. I was a bad influence on Tom Guido.

I got mentioned in the papers. The band got written up in the newsweeklies. I had my first taste of local celebrity and I wanted more. The problem was that there really wasn't anything more to it. That's all the bands I patterned myself after got of out the whole scene. They got some ink in the newsweeklies. They put out their own self-released records or they were signed to some local label with a bit of a name but they still had to pony up a lot of the cash for the recordings anyway. Their members still installed fiber optic cable, worked crappy temp jobs or slung coffee and home fries at Mission District bohemian breakfast joints. There were no mansions. No penthouse apartments. No endless recording sessions on some mega corporation's dime with Rick Rubin manning a computerized mixing board. The musicians that were my peers maybe crammed themselves into a twenty-year-old van and played other Purple Onions across the country. Maybe they charted on one of the college radio stations and some weird indie rockers and college kids gave a shit about them. But that was really about it.

I had these notions of not selling out to MTV or corporate America, but there was really no way to gain more fame, and make something resembling a living off being a kook and a weirdo, without going Hollywood at some point. Luckily, producers weren't banging down my door so I didn't have much of a problem with being a fame whore while maintaining my lofty principles. Principles are easy to maintain when no one is putting money on the table.

The band also opened for Los Super Elegantes a couple of times at a packed Chameleon. Sure it was still the Chameleon. It was still rancid as all hell and served stale, roach infested beer, but if you are going to play somewhere, you want it to be packed. Los Super Elegantes was the perfect band for ISW that never played ISW. They were a punked out band outfit with a flaming queer Argentine guy on vocals and a Latina babe sharing the stage with him. They drew equal parts Mission Mexicans and new Bohemian types.

My friend Powers played bass for the Elegantes. He got us the gigs. I tried to introduce Powers to Chango Loco one time. Chango and Powers were both kind of shady and crazy characters in the same sort of way. I thought that they would hit it off, but Powers would have no part of it.

"Is that the Santeria guy?" Powers asked with one part disgust and one part worry in his voice.

"Listen, I grew up in Miami," he explained. "I have had enough of Santeria guys. They're nothing but con men and scam artists. They're crooks. They're just looking for ways to bilk people. It's like a religion based on blackmail. They convince you that there's some curse on you, or that your wife or girlfriend will only love you if you give them cash so that they can keep casting their spells. It's like spiritual protection. Take my word for it. Stay away from that guy."

Powers had that wrong side of the tracks air to him. I probably should have listened to him.

The World Wide Web and the information age, which had been touted by Al Gore and trumpeted by *Wired* magazine throughout the 1990s, had finally arrived during the decade's waning years. The Internet and the Clinton-era prosperity that came with it slammed San Francisco's club scene like an 8.5 quake on the Richter scale. It was called the end of history, and for people in the local music scene, it felt like it.

People used to relocate to San Francisco for the purpose of being eccentric in a way that whatever red state hellhole they hailed from wouldn't allow. They came to come out of the closet. They came to bang on amplified pieces of scrap metal in art noise bands. They came to protest something — anything. They came to shake their bare asses in suspended cages at the Folsom Street Fair. They came to drive as many pieces of metal into their faces and genitalia as they could stand and still be able to get a job serving the public while looking like an H. R. Giger etching. The dot-com boom changed all of that. In 1998, people came to San Francisco to get rich.

The streets were once again paved with gold. With this new El Dorado came not prospectors, but young urban profession-als with a desire for pricey Napa merlot. This overflow of people earning six figures spilled out from the swank Pacific Heights and Marina neighborhoods (which had always been populated by the city's stock brokers and business lawyers) into SF's South of Market nightclub district.

The neighborhood's warehouses, meat packing plants and machine shops were torn down and live-work lofts were indiscrimi-nately built in their place. The city's new elite of graphic designers and web developers shelled out hundreds of thousands or even millions to move into these concrete and steel townhouses with their track lighting and gourmet kitchens. Ironically, the sidewalks in front of these lofts were often littered with needles and broken crack pipes just like they were before the boom. The one-way streets still stank of panhandler piss.

A passel of lofts sprung up around the Paradise Lounge and Transmission Theatre. Another high priced live-work develop-ment was slated to start construction right behind the Bottom of the Hill. The Holy Cow, the Covered Wagon, the DNA and a whole host of other rock clubs and dance clubs started to feel the heat. The loft dwellers didn't like the noise coming from the clubs even though they had gone out of their way to move next door to them. They called the cops and complained to the planning commission.

They lobbied the mayor. They bitched to the board of supervisors. They had money, stock options and they were all part owner of the new media companies that they worked for, but they were the least of anyone's worries.

Only a few months earlier, the city's motley collection of club owners could afford to buy off any complaining neighbors or nosy city officials in order to keep the booze flowing and the music playing. But soon the club owners found they couldn't compete with the big time developers that had set their sights on SOMA. Construction was becoming a billion dollar business in San Francisco, and a few booze peddlers didn't have the scratch to stop it. Graft in San Francisco was now the sole province of the developers who sought to spur the loft-building bonanza by any means necessary. Mayor Willie Brown, in his pinstriped suits and $500 fedoras, presided over it all like the modern-day Boss Tweed that he was.

With the boom, rents more than doubled in the Mission and the Haight. Some musicians moved to Oakland and the East Bay in the hopes of finding affordable apartments and places to practice. Others fled to Portland or Los Angeles because they could no longer afford to live in the Bay Area on the wages they were making at grocery collectives and coffee houses. Practice studios were torn down to make way for even more loft projects. The rent at the music studios that remained started to skyrocket in the same way that the rent on flats did. Unless you had a good rent control deal or were somehow grandfathered in somewhere, you couldn't afford to plug in an electric guitar or set up a drum kit anywhere within city limits.

Every wrestling show that we did at the Transmission and every Thursday at Stinky's started to feel like it could be the last. The demolition orders could come at a moment's notice. ISW responded to this crisis with an awful skit with a few moments of inspiration. A wannabe wrestler who ran an artsy Mission District metal label out of his overly hip Japanese monster store played the part of a sneering yuppie. He carried his laptop into the ring and wore an unbuttoned thin lapelled sports coat with a *Wired* magazine T-shirt plainly visible underneath.

He called for the show to be shut down and said that "according to the internal clock on [his] personal computer" it was too late for "all of this noise that you people call 'entertainment.'" The crowd started to boo and told him to go fuck himself.

"I'm a normal person," he continued lingering on the word "normal." "I'm having fun like normal people do. I'm watching *Friends* with a girl that I met at 24 Hour Nautilus and drinking some Amstel Lights."

After a few more minutes of ad-libbed vitriol, a masked Jefferson Monroe entered the ring and delivered a profanity filled rebuttal followed by a stiff punch to the yuppie character's face. Monroe legitimately shattered his nose and really sent the poor guy to the hospital with blood streaming out of his swollen mouth and nostrils. Monroe was beginning to have difficulties separating the competitive nature of the various martial arts that he studied and the cooperative aspects of professional wrestling. Monroe never pulled his punches and he had a strong straight right for such a little guy. The complaining yuppie skit wasn't the last time that Monroe sent that record label owner to the emergency room but the guy kept coming back for more. He kept wrestling Monroe and kept on having to get stitches and casts because of it. Maybe they were pals from the S&M clubs that Monroe often frequented and sometimes worked at. That would have explained a lot.

The Count Dante website had only been up for a short time before we started getting some really strange e-mails. Of course, that sort of thing is to be expected when you claim to be the "deadliest man alive" and take your name from a comic book kung fu master. The web was still a new and unfolding universe in 1998. Its ability to put you in touch with people that you would otherwise never want to talk to was just being discovered. Its capacity for enabling unending harassment was largely unknown.

Everything that I knew about the original Count came from those full-page Marvel Comics ads. Count Dante was the undefeated grandmaster of the fighting arts. He sold a book called the *World's Deadliest Fighting Secrets*. You got a really cool looking Black Dragon Fighting Society membership card when you bought the book. Dante defeated "the world's top masters of JUDO, BOXING, WRESTLING, KARATE, AIKIDO, etc. in Death Matches." Did Dante actually kill these top masters? The ad copy didn't elaborate.

The ad was a triumph of crude cut-and-paste design. Its image of a racially ambiguous, sneering, Afro-sporting Count fermented in my mind and served as my inspiration twenty years after it ran in every copy of *Ghost Rider* and *Giant-Size Man-Thing*. But for all I knew Count Dante could have been alive and well and coming to rip out my throat with some kind of Ancient Himalayan death blow for hijacking his name. I was only a pretender, but he was the "authentic" deadliest man alive. One thing was certain though: he may have claimed to have defeated the world's top masters of boxing in death matches, but I think I would have remembered if somebody named Count Dante had killed Muhammad Ali.

The first odd e-mail came from somebody calling himself Yoshi. "Master Dante," it opened, "Master Ashida Kim is under attack and needs your assistance!"

I thought that it was just a joke and filed it away in a received messages file without sending a reply.

A little while later, Yoshi wrote me again and better explained himself:

Greetings from the _REAL_ Black Dragon Fighting Society!

We are pleased to see you keeping the name of Count Dante alive. Would you like to meet with us and become an officially sanctioned member of the BDFS? Ashida Kim is the current Grandmaster, and he says he would be happy to appear with you on stage (he judges a number of wrestling events himself). Looking forward to your reply.

Yoshi — Black Dragon Tong of Retribution

Yoshi included a hypertext link to Ashida Kim's website at the end of the e-mail. Kim's web page was one to envy for its combination of utter lunacy and P. T. Barnum self-promotion. Ashida was only pictured in full black ninja regalia with most of his face covered. Like the original Count, he was racially ambiguous. He could have been Asian but may have been just a strange looking white guy underneath all of those hoods and cloaks.

He was the author of several sensationalistic martial arts manuals with lurid covers that recalled the spirit, if not quite the verve, of Count Dante's comic book ads. Most of the books had the word ninja in the title. There was *Ninja Death Touch*, *Ninja Mind Control* and *Ninja Secrets of Invisibility*. Kim also republished the original Dante's *World's Deadliest Fighting Secrets*. Ashida no doubt used his heightened psychic awareness via ninjitsu to sense the work's public domain status.

While his treatises on mental manipulation were plenty provocative, his most boffo title had to be *X-Rated Dragon Lady*. The cover photo depicted a naked Asian woman mounted on a white guy. In this indispensable volume, Ashida claimed to show you "how to use having your clothes ripped off into an advantage."

Not to be outdone, however, was Kim's own sexual memoir titled *The Amorous Adventures of Ashida Kim*. The cover photo looked like it was taken during the same session as the cover for *X-Rated Dragon Lady*. The web copy boasted that the book was soon to be a major motion picture. If only.

I wrote back to Yoshi and was nice enough. Although having

Ashida Kim appear onstage with me was mighty tempting, the guy was just too weird to be entirely harmless.

Barely a week went by before Ashida Kim himself wrote me:

Most Honorable Count:

So very good to find your webpage and know that you are alive and well. Gee! We all thought you were dead, Ha! Of course, you are not the original Count Dante, the one I met in 1968 in Chicago, but, since we of the Black Dragon Fighting Society do strive to carry on his tradition, we are honored that you have chosen the paths of professional wrestling and music and wish you the best of luck in both of these endeavors. As Grandmaster, I have some other wrestling contacts in South Africa and Australia I could place at your disposal. We have put on several Kick-Punch-Throw, win by Pin-Submission- or Knockout, bouts here and overseas. Or, perhaps there are some other projects we might find to be mutually agreeable. If I may be of any service, please do not hesitate to ask.

I remain, Ashida Kim, the NINJA.

I continued my correspondence with Ashida Kim but remained non-committal. He wrote me back and used the word "HA!" a lot to punctuate his sentences. He claimed that he had fought side-by-side with Count Dante against the Chicago police force during the 1968 Democratic Convention. His ability to render himself invisible helped him survive although he was outnumbered and outgunned. He commended me on discovering the "value of rhythm in combat and entertainment." Kim also talked about Dusty Rhodes' epic feud with the ninja Kendo Nagasaki in the Florida wrestling circuit during the 1970s as if the fights were real. Ashida Kim was amazing. He was nuts.

"I also play guitar and tell witty stories, and never eat more than twice my share, Ha!," he said in the final paragraph of a particularly long e-mail. He closed the message with a string of sci-fi clichés for good measure: "Live long and prosper. The Force be with you. I remain, Ashida Kim."

Although he was a master ninja, I didn't take Ashida up on his repeated offers of assistance with my entertainment and wrestling careers. Having him manage me in ISW or letting him warm up the crowd by playing guitar and "telling witty stories" before my band went on could have been pretty amazing, but it seemed like more trouble than it was worth. Still, I was more than a little relieved that the current proprietor of the Black Dragon Fighting Society didn't want to cut my throat with a samurai sword.

More about the original Count Dante was revealed to me when Scotto LeBlotto, a friend of the Bar Feeders, gave me an old copy of *World's Deadliest Fighting Secrets*.

"I've always been a fan," LeBlotto said as he handed me the pamphlet-sized manual. LeBlotto then assured me that he had another copy of the book so I wasn't putting him out by taking it. "Thanks for bringing him back," he said.

Dante was in fact a curly haired, white Irish guy with blue eyes although his comic ads strove to make him look like he could be black. He dedicated the book to "The Good, The Bad and the Ugly." He claimed to be the "immediate descendant of European nobility." What was even crazier than all of the graphic depictions showing you the multiple ways in which you could rip someone's eyes out or the claw hold to the nuts called "monkey stealing a peach," was that Dante brazenly boasted about being a "World Famous hair stylist and beauty consultant."

Evidently, Count Dante's flair for fashion is what led him to study the martial arts. "As the director of a large wig and hairpiece firm," the book's introduction explained, "[Dante] has frequent opportunity to visit their factories in India, China, Indonesia, Korea and Japan and always finds the time to train in the various Oriental schools of fighting arts."

The book's pièce de résistance came on its final page. After several pages showing you every phase of Dante's dance of death (which if used correctly, could kill your opponent eight ways to Sunday) was a photo of the Count in full swinger mode standing over an alluring fashion model with a severely lacquered hairdo. "The ultimate paradox," the photo's caption proclaimed. "The same hands that crushed bricks on the preceding page designed this natural, but seductive, look in the coiffure and makeup of this top Chicago model and Playboy Club Bunny."

A web search unearthed even more about Dante. His name was John Keehan. He once stormed a competing dojo with some friends. One of them was stabbed to death in the ensuing melee. Dante was later arrested while drunkenly struggling to tie some sticks of dynamite to the door of another dojo. He had big-time Chi-town mob connections. A lot of Mafia hit men and leg breakers were among his karate students. He died from bleeding ulcers in 1975 — right after his biggest magazine marketing blitz, which had landed him in so many issues of *Howard the Duck*. The real Count Dante was far more insane than anything my mere imagination could have ever come up with.

It wasn't long before another faction of the Black Dragon Fighting Society e-mailed me. They weren't nearly as nice as Ashida Kim:

Subject: The Illegal Use Of The Name Count Dante
To Who Ever You Are!

I am writing this letter to inform you that you are using copywrited [sic] name. You must stop this illegal activity or the Black Dragon Fighting Society will be forced to take legal action against you. If you have any questions about the allegations, you may reach Grand Master Aguiar of the

Dan-Te system at:
Bill Aguiar's Self Defense Institute
281 South Main St
Fall River, MA 02720
(508) 679-8188

Marcus W.
Black Dragon Fighting Society Honorary Member

I wrote back to Black Dragon Fighting Society Honorary Member Marcus W. and politely explained to him that the web page was a parody and that parody was protected speech. Three days later, he wrote back:

Dear Mr. Dante?,

As you may know, the real Count Dante died in 1975. After his death, a close friend of mine and his, Bill Aguair, was given the write [sic] to carry on his name.  A name in which is copywrited [sic] through his school.  Grand Master Aguiar trained with the Count and became the one to carry on and teach the Count's sytle [sic] of fighting, Dan-Te. The Count and Grand Master Aguiar started the Black Dragon Fighting Society. They also puplished [sic] a book called "The Worlds Most Deadliest Fighting Secrets". Something else that is copywrited [sic], which you use. Also might I add that Master Aguiar has been aware of who you are for some time now. When I talked to him on Friday, after I saw your Web Page, he instructed me to inform you of what you are doing. Master Aguiar told me to inform you that you are to stop using the name or he will be forced to seek legal action.

Marcus W.

It struck me as odd that this Bill Aguiar, who was reportedly so tough that he could deflect arrows with his bare hands, delegated his dirty work to hapless karate students who were in severe need of a spell-check program. I decided to ignore them, but this only made them more pissed off. They wrote me again. This time they got even nastier:

> The Black Dragon Fighting Society located in Fall River MA and headed by Supreme Grand Master William V Aguiar, whom was just nominated to the martial arts hall of fame, is the only official and authorized BDFS.

> You are a liar and a thief. If you were here now Master Aguiar would rip the skin right off your face. His book Worlds deadliest fighting secrets is copyrighted and any proceeds you are making from it is [sic] illegal. Get a life instead of trying to steal someone else's. Master Aguiar is always accepting challengers for no holds barred death matches. Do you have the guts to accept his challenge? You can use the money you are stealing from him to pay for your plane fare and headstone in advance.

> TROY CITY Specialties & Gifts
> Your Gift Super-Store in a Catalog.
> www.gearworks.net/troycity
> troycityspecial@webtv.net

Now this was getting seriously stupid. Even dumber than all the lame third-party threats was the fact that it was signed "Troy City Specialties & Gifts: Your Gift Super-Store in a Catalog." I clicked on the link that they so conveniently included at the end of the e-mail and found that Troy Cities Specialties sold gaudy home decor, potpourri collections and Beanie Babies out of somebody's house in Maine. I wasn't all that menaced by any Black Dragon Fighting Society that also doubled as a dealer in crochet toilet paper covers.

I e-mailed them back to tell them just how stupid they were. "The next time that you go and threaten somebody with death and dismemberment," I wrote, "please remember not to include the link to your home mail-order gift store. You still have no idea who I am but I now know where you live and how you make your money." I wasn't going to drunkenly try to affix blasting caps to their front door or anything like that, but the level of sheer idiocy of whoever sent me that e-mail deserved a slap in the face.

I quickly received the following back pedaling reply:

Look, I do not want to be your enemy. In fact I wish all people including you the best of luck in their lives. I did not threaten you. I only stated what I believe Master Aguiar would do to you himself. I am not associated with the BDFS and really it is none of my business about what goes on as far as the BDFS but it upsets me greatly to see people ripping off someone who put their blood and guts on the line to achieve what Master Aguiar has only to have it stolen. Your page and act may be a parody but you do not state that on your page, and I am sure you are representing yourself as the genuine Count Dante whom has been dead for over 20 years. My words may have been harsh and for that I apologise [sic] but come on, do you not see my point. Master Aguiar has in the past put his life on the line fighting by the real counts [sic] side to achieve what he has. He doesn [sic] deserve to be ripped off. Ashida Kim has especially gone to [sic] far as he even is selling Copies of the worlds deadliest fighting secrets that he is not authorized to. Its [sic] just unjust.

He still included the link to Troy City Specialties and Gifts at the bottom of this e-mail.

The Fall River, Massachusetts, sect of the BDFS soon erected their own website. It was adorned with lame blinking text and twirling skulls. They promised that you could become a member of their BDFS by passing through a "trial by fire" in a "ritual of blood." They had a merchandise page that was decorated with clip art of balloons and clowns from which they sold stun guns, paint guns, swords, knives, $50 copies of *World's Deadliest Fighting Secrets* and something called the *Dead Book*. In short, the site looked as if was designed by a severely disturbed thirteen-year-old.

Ashida Kim and Bill Aguiar's crew were locked in a vicious dispute over who was the real heir apparent to the Dante legacy. Unlike in Dante's time, when dojos were stormed, lives were lost and arrests were made, the dojo wars of the postmodern era were fought exclusively in cyberspace. Ashida Kim and Bill Aguiar chose to settle their differences like the true followers of an ancient warrior code that they purported to be: they endlessly flamed each other's message boards.

As a staggering barrage of hypertext insults flew between Kim's and Aguiar's underlings, a letter from the man himself, William V. Aguiar, arrived at my band's post office box. The missive was composed on Black Dragon Fighting Society stationary that I would kill or die for. The original Black Dragon logo from Dante's comic book ads was centered on top of the page. In the upper left corner was Dante's unimaginative coat of arms from one of the opening pages of *The World's Deadliest Fighting Secrets*. Underneath the Dante family crest, small but bold text read: "House of Danté, WILLIAM V. AGUIAR, 2nd Patriarch." Aguiar considered himself to be more than just the inheritor of a forgotten fighting system. If his stationary was any indicator, he thought of himself as a regal heir.

In the letter, Aguiar informed me that he had obtained a federal trademark on the BDFS logo and its clip art dragon as well as the exclusive rights to teach something called "The Count Danté Fighting System." He even gave me the courtesy of supplying me with the registration numbers. The letter was a formal cease and desist order that didn't come from an attorney but from a man calling himself "Supreme Grandmaster of the Black Dragon Fighting Society."

That letter had the potential to deliver a financial death blow to my meager musical operations. I had invested a serious amount of time and energy into perfecting my version of the Count Dante persona. I thought of changing the name to Lord Dante or King Dante but nothing really had the same ring to it. Everything else just sounded incredibly lame. I wished that I had just called myself El Dante, which was what everyone seemed to call me for the first year or two I played around San Francisco. I wished that I had been endowed with the foresight to come up with a name that sounded vaguely like "Count Dante and the Black Dragon Fighting Society" when I first started out instead of opting to lift the name wholesale. I wished I had done those things, but I hadn't.

As the information economy advanced, intellectual property became the coin of the realm. Even the dimmest among us were aware of this new reality. During this time, it seemed as if every band in San Francisco was getting hit with cease and desist letters from somebody. This little hard rock band called Mack Truck was served with some especially nasty papers by the attorneys representing the Mack Truck corporation. I guess that this major freight vehicle manufacturer didn't want to risk being confused for a bunch of short guys with Gibson Les Pauls. One band called the Stitches sued another band called the Stitches. Band fliers for Stinky's seemed to be littered with disclaimers underneath the current names explaining what the bands were called before the legal papers came. It was getting out of hand.

Ashida Kim, William V. Aguiar and I were all set to play a legal game of chicken over what was in reality a piece of found art. None of us created the Count Dante name. None of us stormed the dojos or placed the comic book ads. We were all just pretenders to the throne and keepers of the flame at the same time. The hairdresser who transformed himself into Count Dante through sheer marketing genius and martial arts mastery was buried in Chicago in what I would later find out was an unmarked grave.

I kept on wrestling women and playing with the band. I didn't take the bait. I didn't flame anyone's chat room and figured that if I was going to navigate through this mess, then placing myself above the fray was the only way that I was going to do it. No matter what, I wasn't going to cave into some badly spelled e-mails. Aguiar was going to have to drop some money on a lawyer before I changed a thing.

# 11
# CHRISTIANS TO THE LIONS

TOM CORGAN HAD RECENTLY moved into my building. His studio apartment was upstairs from mine. It was a bit smaller than the room that I lived in, but due to the changing times, he paid $300 dollars more per month than I did for my spacious rent-controlled unit. His entire room was dominated by a queen-sized bed and a second-hand armoire from a hotel liquidation sale. The armoire housed his TV and VCR and its drawers were filled with hand labeled videotapes of pro wrestling and boxing matches. Corgan's bed, which he had bought brand new only a few months before, was noticeably sagging in the middle. Corgan was using his spring mattress as a practice mat. He drunkenly did backflips off his armoire in order to get the mechanics of his dragon moonsault and superplex down in case he should ever be allowed back into ISW. He also practiced choke-slamming his poor cats.

I sat in a rickety chair in the corner while a tape of hardcore legend Terry Funk's greatest Southern wrestling moments played in the background. It was by far Corgan's favorite of his mail ordered wrestling cassettes. Funk wrestled in a barbed wire death match in Japan while he was in his mid-fifties. Funk was pushing sixty when, while slugging it out with some guy in a stable during a broadcast of WCW *Nitro*, he got kicked square in the head by a horse. Funk got pushed out of balconies and set on fire. He had had scores of retirement matches but he never retired. Terry Funk could barely walk and had broken as many bones as Evel Knievel. Funk was Tom's idol. Corgan wanted to emulate every aspect of him right down to the aging redneck warrior's arthritic knees. For Tom that compilation tape of Terry Funk highlights wasn't just sports entertainment, it was an instruction manual and a self-help program.

As images of Southern fried carnage flickered in the background, I showed Tom printouts of some of the Internet death threats that I'd been getting.

"So where are these ninjas from?" Corgan asked as he opened a bottle of beer.

"Well, these aren't the ninjas," I explained. "The ninjas are from Florida and they seem okay with me for the most part. The jerkoffs sending me the second-hand death threats are from Fall River, Massachusetts."

"Oh," he said taking a swig of beer. "So you're dealing with a bunch of Massholes."

The term Massholes was pretty funny to me. I had lived in California my whole life while Corgan was from Baltimore. I had never been privy to all of the regional slurs and putdowns that East Coast types had for each other.

While my travails with Bill Aguiar's branch of the Black Dragon Fighting Society had some entertainment value, Corgan was mainly interested in my progress in Incredibly Strange Wrestling. I told him that Audra had gotten tired of cramming twenty-plus sweaty guys into her apartment so she no longer had those wrestling meetings. Now the upcoming shows were planned during late night bull sessions with Audra, Craig and me at this retro bar called Annie's, which was across the street from the criminal courthouse. Audra's boyfriend Spike drunkenly hosted ironic karaoke at the somewhat out of place watering hole on Tuesday nights so Audra held court at a table in one of the bar's dark corners. It was a lot easier planning the shows that way. We could finally strive for the cohesion that isw desperately needed and we could even start to map out a couple of shows in a row. We could build up to matches and skits on one show that would take place at a show somewhere down the line.

The news of this development instantly sobered Tom Corgan up despite the six or seven beers he'd just downed. "Bob, you're becoming the booker," he said with seriousness so intense that it was almost scary.

He stood up from the corner of his bed and loomed above me. I looked up at him but was still half paying attention to the TV. Terry Funk was bludgeoning perennial Andy Kaufman opponent Jerry "The King" Lawler in what appeared to be an empty stadium.

"Do you have any idea what this means, Bob?" Corgan asked, cutting off my view of the TV screen. "Bob, do you really know what that means?"

I cracked a smile in an attempt to alleviate the tension and said, "No, Tom, what does that mean?"

"The booker's the one who chooses who gets championship gold and who gets buried under an avalanche of humiliation, Bob," Corgan said explaining the significance of my new position within the ranks of isw. "If you're the booker you can bring me back in. I can be your best wrestler. You and me, we can be the clique. We can run the show. Me in the ring. You in the backroom. That's how it works. Triple H and Shawn Michaels run wwe. Hogan and Nash run wcw. Cliques run wrestling Bob. We can be the clique that runs isw."

Tom wanted back in the wrestling show more than anything. It was what he wanted to do his whole life and his lousy jobs working the cash register at the pizza by the slice joint didn't do much to keep his mind off the wrestling world he so desperately needed to be a part of. I had made my way towards ISW's star chamber. I wasn't really the booker, but I kind of was. I did want to bring Corgan back. I owed him that much.

"Look, Tom," I said looking him right in the eyes, "I want to bring you back. I am going to bring you back. You helped me get my start in this thing. I owe you, but I'm just getting my leg up here. Let me cement my position a bit more. Trust me here. I won't let you down."

Tom seemed a bit put off by that. He was impatient. He felt he had been wronged by a bunch of people who had been thrown out of the show. His pal, whom he had helped get into the show, had replaced them and Corgan didn't understand why he had to wait to get his spot back.

Corgan may not have understood why he had to wait, but he accepted it and spent the rest of the evening regaling me with the more lurid lore from the annals of pro wrestling history. They were stories from his videotapes or from years spent reading *The Wrestling Observer*. Tom told me how this menacing Tongan named Haku once scooped out a dude's eye during a barroom brawl. He told me about how Bruiser Brody was stabbed to death in a locker room shower during a nasty booking dispute in Puerto Rico. Despite several wrestlers at the scene, no one was ever convicted of the crime.

There was also the time that Sid Vicious (not the bassist from the Sex Pistols, but a muscle-bound redneck with a blond perm who wrestled for WCW) stabbed Ric Flair's right hand man Arn Anderson with a pair of scissors in an English hotel room. Sid also tried to attack Brian Pillman with a squeegee. Sid was big, but he was a pussy. Pillman was under six feet tall. Pillman died at the age of thirty-five with an enlarged heart that probably resulted from dosing with massive amounts of human growth hormone in a doomed attempt to be bigger.

For Tom, the appeal of pro wrestling came from its backstage backstabbing as much as from its in-ring violence. The backrooms were where reality and fantasy were irrevocably blurred. It was where those of us in the inner circle of even the most insignificant promotions could shape our own realities and create our more fantastic personas. It was where we could become the characters we created no matter how ludicrous they were. It was the flouting of the confines of reality that made pro wrestling so addictive.

On the TV, Terry Funk was in a cage now. His eyes had the far-away look of one driven to madness. Funk was good at that. "What you've seen is the final conflict," Funk said earnestly and ominously, pressing his face up against a chain-link barrier. "The conflict that ends it all. It's when there's no children left. It's when it all goes. It's when somebody presses the red button and it's been pressed many times before. Dusty Rhodes did it when he double-crossed me in the Bayfront Center and cost me the NWA title. Cost it to me . . ."

The "Christians to the Lions" match was going to be the most ambitious squared circle spectacle that Paul Van Dyne and I had yet attempted. It was the match that I had been inspired to do since the morning before my first bout with Tom Corgan. During those nervous hours before I left to run through my in-ring debut at the Transmission, I had killed time by watching cable TV — a tunic-clad Victor Mature grappled with a toothless and clawless tiger (held in place by a clearly visible chain for good measure).

With what Van Dyne and I had to work with, we were going to fall far short of the grandeur of a Cecil B. DeMille biblical epic, but we could at least attain the look and feel of a fire-and-brimstone Easter play put on by an Armageddon obsessed holy roller church. If we played our cards right, the only difference between our New Testament sports entertainment and any production of evangelical Grand Guignol would be provided by the audience reaction. We were counting on the Transmission Theatre crowd cheering on the lion and booing the Christian.

Van Dyne ponied up for the Caesar drag and a lion suit that conjured up a Disney chipmunk as much as it did the king of the jungle. Ruby made me a boat-necked slave's tunic out of canvas and burlap that was pretty impressive. What was even more impressive still was the three-dimensional cross that my guitarist Andy "The Beast" Davis made for me out of stapled balsa wood. Andy was always great with woodwork and cabinetry even though his guitars had the wiring hanging out of them and his amps all too frequently cut in and out at shows.

When I asked him to make me a cross for the Christians to the Lions match, I just expected him to quickly nail a couple of pieces of plywood together and call it a day. I would have been happy with that. When he showed me the finished crucifix, I was in awe of it. It stood at above seven feet and it looked like it was made from two interlocking 4" x 6" pieces of solid mahogany. At first glance, you would guess that it weighed at least 200 pounds, but it was hollow and light as a feather. After Andy put a couple of coats of wood stain on it, it looked like we had lifted it from a Catholic church somewhere. For the finishing touch, Andy splattered some dark red paint across it to make it a little more gruesome.

We tapped John Pierre to don the plastic laurel leaves and play the part of the gay as all hell Caesar character. We had some trouble coming up with a name for him and for a while he was just going to be called Bigus Dickus like in Monty Python's *Life of Brian*. This match was already borrowing pretty liberally from Python's "Scott of the Sahara" bit where Michael Palin fought off an oversized stuffed lion intercut with grainy nature stock footage. I had gotten into enough trouble appropriating the name Count Dante and I also didn't want to rip off Python any more than I had already. I racked my brains until something truly inspired popped into my head. Our nellie Nero would have a name. He would be called Flamius Caesar.

My Christian persona was just referred to as Christian Dante.

Later on he became Dante of Nazareth or Dante the Baptist. Audra came up with the name "Corpus Bloatus" but that was a little too much Latin for a post-Vatican II San Francisco to take.

The Christians to the Lions match took place at the Transmission on June 20, 1998, during the second set. As I made my way to the ring before the match I carried the cross on my back propped over my shoulder so the audience could plainly see what it was. I hunkered down and acted as if I were straining under the holy symbol's weight. When I finally got to the ring steps, this security guy named Gabriel took the cross from me and easily handled it as if it weighed less than ten pounds. So much for the art of illusion.

Allan Bolte seemed somewhat rattled by my characters' new sanctimonious direction. The usually golden voiced announcer stuttered and stammered as he asked, "What, what is this new... Explain it!"

"I will no longer participate in this barbaric spectacle," I answered. The audience responded with a fusillade of boos and groans. "I will no longer bring harm to my fellow man for I am a Christian! You are all sinners unless you find eternal salvation through Jesus Christ!"

I called the crowd idolaters, sodomites and adulterers. I ranted like a cross between Charlton Heston with a fake beard and a Bible-toting bum on a soapbox until Flamius Caesar finally made his grand entrance. The hedonistic wrestling fans cheered as the pagan emperor took to the stage. "If you will not fight, Christian, than you will DIE!" John Pierre exclaimed while giving the Roman thumbs down. "Release the lion!!!"

Paul Van Dyne, hampered by his costume's severe tunnel vision, lumbered out into the ring. As predicted, the crowd was on his side from the get-go. The match itself was an afterthought. It was pretty much the same match that Van Dyne and I had done before but with different costumes. The lion tackled me hard to the mat. We tried to do a gag where I stuck my arm in the lion's mouth and acted as if it was eating me. If we were a bit more on the ball we should have had blood packets set to spray out of the lion's mouth at that moment, but neither of us wanted to soak our new costumes with crimson karo syrup on the very first night that we used them.

While the match went on, Flamius attempted to engage Bolte in some dialogue from *Spartacus*.

"Tell me, Allan Bolte, is it immoral to like both oysters and snails?" John Pierre intoned with a voice that was far queerer sounding than any even he would dare use in a Castro District dance club. Allan was already flustered by our bit of religious pageantry and didn't really know how to respond or what Flamius was even talking about. Legendary wrestling announcers like Gordon Solie or Gorilla Monsoon never had to deal with this.

At the end of the match, Flamius and the Lion tied me up in the ring ropes in a crucifix position and then Flamius proceeded to whip me while stopping to give the crowd the "Hail Caesar" salute. I chomped down on the one blood capsule that we had but only the people pressed up against the ring apron saw the stream of bloody spittle spew out of my mouth.

My work wasn't over when Flamius and the Lion whipped me into submission. I still had my announcing chores. Audra and Allan insisted that I call a few matches. I had to stay in character and deliver my lines as the newly anointed Christian Dante. I was never forced to go to Bible camp as a kid so my ability to weave scripture and verse into my commentary was somewhat limited. The other Count Dante could say anything but Christian Dante had to keep bringing it back to God.

During a match that pitted a construction worker tag team (made up of those teen burnouts that the Steele family took in) against the combined queer might of El Homo Loco and the Cruiser, I kept yammering about how the hard hat wearing wrestlers were "artisans and craftsmen" and were "following in the footsteps of Christ the carpenter." Homo Loco and the Cruiser gave me a lot of anti-sodomite material as well but the straight lucha libre match that followed was pretty hard for me to convincingly call while wearing that tunic.

Luckily, I didn't have to stay in character when the show was over. Nobody made me drag a seven-foot cross on the mini bus while I made my way to work, and I wasn't expected to hold a prayer meeting while I emceed Stinky's Peep Show.

While I didn't have to maintain my Christian Dante character during my daily mundane existence, the cross had a life of its own beyond 1sw. I couldn't store the thing in my tiny apartment so it had to stay at the Transmission where it was often put to good use on goth dance nights.

After the last wrestling match of the night was over, Allan cornered me by the beer keg. "Dante, I don't like this new direction for you at all," he said. "I like the heel Dante, the heel!"

Allan didn't realize that the Christian *was* the heel.

# 12

# THE BIG-TIME POLITICS OF SMALL-TIME WRESTLING

TOM CORGAN HAD A NAME for it. He called it "The Big-time Politics of Small-time Wrestling." With this cute little catchphrase he was referring to the endless backbiting, deal making and jockeying for position that goes on in even the most rinky-dink backwaters of the pro wrestling industry. Slots on a pro wrestling card were not doled out due to performing well in qualifying heats. Championship belts were not won in the ring but in the backrooms where indie wrestlers performed acts of influence peddling and insider trading that would be the envy of any GOP congressman.

Wrestlers competed within a promotion for that much-coveted top spot which usually centered around belts that they had created for themselves. Promotions competed with each other through wars of words and ideas. These wars of words were fueled by the proliferation of the Internet and its message boards and chat rooms. Like the ongoing conflict between the two claimants to the legacy of the Black Dragon Fighting Society, aspiring pro wrestlers wired on cocktails of creatine and Red Bull spent most of their time putting down rival promotions on each other's message boards. Roland Alexander's All Pro Wrestling from the East Bay hated Sacramento's Supreme Pro Wrestling. They all ganged up on the South Bay's Big Time Wrestling. But all of the quarreling factions that made up the Northern California wrestling scene were united in their contempt for ISW.

As wrestling grew more and more popular while the '90s wore on, more small-time promotions sprang up in every backyard-laden suburb with a sizable population of young white males who were inspired by manufactured Nü Metal angst to drive staples into each other's foreheads in front of intimate crowds of friends and family members. With indie federations rapidly expanding and carving up smaller and smaller pieces of the pissed-off beta male pie, these little online turf wars became more common, confusing and meaningless.

Much of the ideological fodder for these conflicts stemmed from arguments over what pro wrestling was in the first place. "Our fake pro wrestling is more real than your fake pro wrestling," was Tom Corgan's way of summing up this common indie-worker refrain. It was an argument that made sense when it was used by grizzled Greco-Roman wrestling coaches to denounce all of pro wrestling as a sham. It made no sense coming from guys whose biggest athletic achievement was taking a dive for the Honky Tonk Man or Doink the Clown in front of a little over 100 people.

To the rest of the ramshackle independent wrestling world, Incredibly Strange Wrestling "wasn't wrestling." This was absurd. The very fabricated nature of pro wrestling made it whatever the fans wanted from it.

Sometimes pro wrestling was a vicious heel called the Sheik repeatedly stabbing Dusty Rhodes with a pencil for twenty minutes. Other times it was a muscle-bound, balding longhair named Hulk Hogan doing little more than leg drops. To some, pro wrestling was comprised of chubby dudes wrapping one another in barbed wire and cracking bamboo shafts over each other's skulls. There were other times when pro wrestling did achieve an undeniable athletic artistry however. There were the Ric Flair vs. Ricky "The Dragon" Steamboat matches, the ladder match between Shawn "The Heartbreak Kid" Michaels and Razor Ramon and the classic series in Japan between Tiger Mask and the Dynamite Kid. All of these matches pushed the wrestlers' levels of endurance to super-human levels and set new acrobatic standards for what pro wrestling could be.

In the case of ISW, wrestling was a flaming queer in a pink tutu shoving his crotch in his opponent's face and dry humping the referee. Wrestling was a guy in a chicken suit fighting a chef. Wrestling was a fat guy in a toga dragging a cross around and battling it out with a guy in an unconvincing lion costume. To the ISW fans, that was pro wrestling. They bought it and paid for it.

Still, Audra did use indie wrestlers to flesh out the top of her cards and to give ISW something more in the way of actual wrestling content to offer the fans than just the raunchy satire strung together with botched moves from her homegrown talent. When she brought the indie workers in, they brought their sniping ways and attitudes with them. They kissed her ass and sometimes even kissed up to me to get a slot on an ISW show with bigger crowds than they had ever wrestled in front of before, only to slam us afterwards on their message boards for not being "real" wrestling.

Shane Dynasty/Gran Fangorio, the ringleader of the ISW contingent of indie workers hired on from other promotions, referred to Chango Loco, the Cruiser, El Homo Loco and myself as "the untrained masses of ISW" in one of his exhaustive "California Independent Pro Wrestling Reports" which he regularly posted on the Usenet pro wrestling board. "These poor souls have a lot of heart, but no knowledge of the sport whatsoever," he wrote.

To remedy what he perceived as ISW's shortcomings, Shane recommended that ISW "phase out the non-trainee 'bitch fights' and bring in more real luchadores and American-style pro wrestlers." He urged that Audra bring in even more wrestlers from APW.

Of course if Shane was successful in implementing his roadmap for a better work rate in ISW, he would have destroyed what appeal the promotion had in the first place. Replacing El Homo Loco and the Poontangler with your garden-variety indie workers would have just made ISW run-of-the-mill. It would have patterned a show that regularly drew over a thousand people after shows that barely broke 100 paid attendance.

"The untrained masses," as Shane called them, were what brought in throngs of irony-seeking hipsters as well as the local and even national media. In early 1998, the Fox affiliate out of Los Angeles, ever hungry for important breaking news, sent a camera crew up to the Transmission to do a story on the feud between Chango Loco and El Pollo Diablo that never ended up happening in the ring. This was back when Fox was still nothing more than a joke of a network best known for producing the alien autopsies and nature snuff reels that served as the inspirational fodder for Paul Van Dyne's future wrestling matches. It was only a scant two years before the network had the power to declare presidential victors.

In Fox's ISW feature, I had to translate for the Devil Chicken because I guess that Count Dante, besides being well versed in the classics and ancient martial arts training manuals, can also understand the seemingly random clucks and crows that emanated from the cock from hell. "This chicken spreads pestilence! This chicken spreads famine!" I proclaimed on camera after Van Dyne made a series of high-pitched clucking sounds.

At the end of the piece, Chango and Jefferson Monroe double teamed me and stomped me into the ground while Van Dyne in his chicken suit prophetically did absolutely nothing. As I rolled around the concrete floor in mock agony, the cameraman shoved his lit-up steadicam into my face. I astutely muttered, "Tell the chicken he's fired." This little ad-libbed bit closed out the piece, which was deemed so important by the newsroom at KTTV Fox 11 Los Angeles, that they aired it twice. I thought for sure that the Hollywood agents would call. They didn't.

While ISW's lunatic luchadores continued to be in demand by the mass media, we ignored the need to improve our wrestling skills at our own peril. The visual gag of the guy in the chicken suit was quickly getting stale and the mere sight of El Pollo Diablo tromping into the ring didn't quite get the laughs it did the first couple of times around.

A seemingly easy solution would have been to have Paul Van Dyne, Cruiser Craig and I write scripts for the better-trained indie wrestlers to perform. While this sounds reasonable on paper, it would have been impossible in practice. There is an oft-repeated mantra in indie wrestling circles that states: "The booker is always right." It's also true that the wrestlers that invoke this directive most often are also the ones most likely to argue over every last detail concerning their portrayal in the ring. Wrestlers are jocks that get to debate over wins and losses and manipulate their athletic destinies. If you were to put on a production of Shakespeare's *Julius Caesar* using the roster of APW as its cast, then Michael Modest in the role of the bard's tragic conqueror would no-sell the stab wounds and proceed to slam Brutus and Cassius with a steel chair in order to "get his heat back" and maintain his position on the card.

The other solution (and the only one that had a ghost of a chance of being actualized) was for all of us weirdos and freaks ("the untrained masses") to improve our own damned wrestling skills. Missionary Man and Kid Anarchy had helped out in this regard as best they could the year before, but they had both moved back to Boston. Missionary Man was reportedly going to start a ska and wrestling promotion that Audra had mocked openly since she first heard of it. "Ska and wrestling?" she exclaimed with noticeable revulsion, "can you think of a more lame-assed, disgusting combination!?!"

Indie wrestlers who had handed over thousands of dollars to the likes of Roland Alexander in order to learn the wrestling trade in the hopes of someday making it into one of the big leagues weren't going to be much help either. All indie workers seemed to be agents for the wrestling schools they sprang from. I guess this was to justify the incredible amounts of cash that they spent learning their pratfalls.

The Cruiser and Count Dante could have enrolled in one of these wrestling schools but then we would have been subject to indie wrestling's sadisms and infected by its narrow mindset. We would have become indie workers and Audra had forbade such deeper forays into the mainstream wrestling world by her regulars. "Look, I know how fucking nuts these people are," Audra often said when the subject of being trained inevitably came up. "I've had to deal with these fucking assholes way more than you ever will."

Audra preferred shitty wrestling on her under-card to putting up with anything more than the bare minimum of indie workers needed to pull off her monthly shows.

What we could hope for was a defector — someone who had been through the indie wrestling assembly line and had learned its moves, but was no longer a part of it. We needed a bitter fuck who had given up on dreams of wcw or wwe glory. He had to be out there. Sooner or later, we'd find him or he would find us.

In the meantime, there were some in-house prospects for improving isw's in-ring presentation mostly provided by the hell-headed teens that the Steele family took in. These kids had to be getting sick of being beaten up by Dave at isw shows for the slightest domestic fuck-ups like guzzling all the milk or leaving potato chip crumbs by the PlayStation. I figured that little Josh Steele would jump at the chance to put on the lion suit or undertake any other seeming embarrassment in order to avoid being lovingly abused by his big brother in front of hundreds of drunks. Josh also looked like Jesus so we could definitely do something with that.

There was also this kid named Manny Franklin. He was only seventeen when he first wrestled for ISW and would have been tossed out of the Transmission if he had ever been carded by the doorman. He had Matt Damon good looks and was amazingly athletic. He could do spinning mid-air somersaults at the drop of a hat. It was easy to regard him as ISW's Shawn Michaels or Dynamite Kid, but with his curly blond hair, oversized blue eyes and ability to effortlessly launch into standing back flips, he was more like a Gen-Y Russ Tamblyn from *Seven Brides for Seven Brothers* or *West Side Story*.

Manny's first character was a masked El Homo Loco knock-off called the Castro Kid, but we quickly found that our roster was becoming too crowded with gay characters (as if such a thing were possible). The audience wasn't quite popping for El Homo Loco as much as it usually did when they had just seen another flamer take a twenty-foot dive from the club's rafters. We needed to protect El Homo Loco from any scene-stealing newcomer. We had to come up with some other part for Manny to play. With Manny's penchant for the exaggerated gestures and facial expressions that were the bread and butter of the pro wrestling school of acting and his obvious youth appeal, we required a concept that was both incredibly strange *and* didn't involve him wearing a mask. Getting Audra to agree to leave the mask off him was going to be the hard part with her staunch devotion to lucha libre aesthetics.

The other solution to shoring up the wrestling end of the show was to bring back Tom Corgan. Corgan wasn't trained. He was labeled as "backyard" by the indie workers, which was a description that Corgan clearly resented. "Backyard wrestlers just put each other through tables and jump off roofs," Corgan once angrily explained. "I know how to tell a story in the ring. I know how to put things together so that the fans care about the match."

Corgan was right about that. He was my go-to guy even when he was banished from ISW. His ideas for forwarding the action always made the standard five-minute Dante match with all of its bells and whistles make more sense to the audience. Every action that a wrestler took in the ring or on the microphone needed a plausible reason why that wrestler took that action. Corgan was an avid student of professional wrestling's rules of causality and spent hours studying them by reviewing his wrestling tape collection, reading the *Observer* cover-to-cover and draining twelve-packs.

You couldn't use a guy like Corgan and keep him swept under the rug forever. Bringing him back into the wrestling show was a debt that I felt I owed him. Getting Audra to agree to it wasn't going to be easy but the upcoming Christian vs. the Cruiser match held an opportunity to bring Corgan back in a limited role. For this match, Craig and I actually wanted to utilize a ref bump. We wanted the ref to be knocked out cold during a key moment of the match, which would allow the Lion and Flamius Caesar to run into the ring. Ref bumps were all too common in wrestling's major promotions but in ISW using the ref in such a dramatic fashion was unheard of. Bob, with his cigarette in one hand and his beer in the other, was still the model of Incredibly Strange officiating.

It was at Annie's during one of those late Tuesday night ISW planning sessions that I pitched the idea of Corgan's return to Audra. The bar was adorned with second-hand velvet paintings culled from the local St. Vincent de Paul store and screen-printed rock posters. Everything glowed reddish orange from the strings of li'l devil and jack-o'-lantern lights that hung over the bar. Hipsters croaked out karaoke tunes in the background in an endless contest to be more ironic than the neo-greaser who went on before them. Spike trumped them all by singing "Elvira" by the Oak Ridge Boys.

Audra looked over her yellow legal notepad. She tapped her pen on the table and said, "Okay, we have a show coming up in two weeks. What are we gonna do?"

I started to speak. Craig tensed up. He knew what I was about to suggest and we both braced a little for the potential downpour of expletives that Audra might unleash.

"Well, we're going to do the Christian vs. the Cruiser," I said, starting off slow. She knew this already. "But we want it to be really big. We're going to have the Lion and Flamius running in and we're going to need our own ref for this one."

Audra could tell from Craig's body language and my unusually hesitant speech that we were about to ask for something that she wouldn't like. "Why can't you use the refs we have already?" she asked while chewing her gum. She opened her eyes wider at the end of her question to signal that the floor was open for further comment.

"Well, Bob and the other ref are good at the typical ISW match," I said, being especially diplomatic, "but we need a regular ref for this match. Bob will miss his cue. He won't give a shit. That is his whole thing. He doesn't give a shit." I took a drink of my bourbon and Seven and sucked up my courage. "I was thinking we could bring Tom Corgan back for this match."

Audra sat back in her seat and surveyed both of us. I could have waited for Craig to chime in but he wasn't going to. I kept talking, hoping to head off the inevitable bitching out.

"Look, Corgan's good but he's disgraced," I continued, stepping up the pace of my words in order to get out every point that I had to make before being shut down. "We can forget about the Three Mile Baby or any of his other characters. He will be the ref as a tryout and if he doesn't fuck this up then he can wear the Sasquatch suit or go along with these other Van Dyne ideas. We need somebody who can wrestle in those things. They aren't working the way we do them now."

Audra let out a heavy sigh but the edges of her mouth were still curled up in a slight smiling position. Thank God she appeared to be in a good mood.

"Okay," she said, still smiling but asserting her authority. "Corgan can come back as a ref...."

I started to open my mouth again, not knowing to quit while I was ahead but Audra cut me off. "We can talk about him wearing the Sasquatch suit or anything else later. I don't want to hear any more about it right now."

That was good enough. I did it. I won.

The Christian vs. the Cruiser match graced the Transmission on July 19, 1998. An ugly but hard rocking outfit from the East Coast called Electric Frankenstein was the headlining band. The trucker punk band Crosstops squeezed themselves into denim skirts and tube tops, looking like some of the ugliest truck stop whores ever to grace the parking lot of a Flying J as they opened up the set next door in the Paradise Lounge. A band from Seattle called Redneck Girlfriend also played. Despite their name, they were all dudes, but with their fastidiously maintained pompadours and neatly pressed cowboy shirts, they were a whole lot prettier than the cross-dressing Crosstops.

Corgan was back as the referee but there were plenty of ground rules for his initial return to ISW. Corgan was already pushing thirty but Audra's laundry list of dos and don'ts must have made him feel like a little kid. Then again being treated like a kid seemed like a proper penance for trying to live out your adolescent fantasies.

He couldn't talk to Audra except to maybe say "hello" and "thank you." Even excessive groveling would only serve to piss Audra off so it was best that he stay out of her way as much as possible. She had a show to run and she was never the most pleasant person while she was doing it. The Three Mile Baby was dead and gone. He had to get over this. If he was going to wrestle again, it was most likely going to be in one of Van Dyne's animal suits. Half-assed atomic mutants with off the rack lucha masks were out. Fuzzy mascots were in. Under no circumstances could he pitch his ideas for future matches to any of the wrestlers. If he did, it would get back to Audra and she would can both of our asses. Lastly, he couldn't have any beer at this show no matter how much that pained him. Corgan needed to stay sober for a few hours. This was admittedly a bummer because beer was about the only payment any of us received for risking our necks, but that was a sacrifice Corgan had to make. Corgan had to do this show pro bono.

Our little passion play that pitted the sodomite against the sanctimonious was our most ambitious yet. Like the biblical epics that we were spoofing, Dante the Baptist vs. the Cruiser featured a proportionate cast of thousands. Flamius Caesar and the Lion made their return. There was our planted ref, Tom Corgan, and we also had the evil temptress Jezebel Delilah played by stripper/con-tortionist heartthrob Suzi Ming.

Suzi studied contortion and trapeze at a local circus school and she was able to regularly work the backroom peep show at Stinky's without having the usual prerequisite high body fat ratio. Slender, she had that all too rare combination of being as cute as a button and drop dead fine. She was a favorite of all those icky guys in San Francisco who were "really into Asian chicks," and her stunning good looks and showbiz skills accursed her with more than her fair share of stalkers.

At Stinky's I was her favorite backroom barker. We both made a little bit of cash on those shows. She even allowed me to help her stretch for the contortion routine once, figuring that I could handle it since I took jiu-jitsu. I was pretty nervous while I bent her lithe yet so vulnerable looking body into positions that would have crippled even my toughest sparring partners. With her athletic abilities and numerous charms, it was amazing that Audra was never able to get her to wrestle, but Suzi Ming guarded her good looks. They were her biggest source of income and she didn't want to risk them by doing anything more than a couple of low-risk spots in the ring. The role of our composite Old Testament femme fatale suited her well.

I couldn't say that the Christian vs. the Cruiser came off without a hitch, but Tom Corgan didn't fuck anything up — if anything he saved the match. I came into the ring brandishing two Styrofoam tablets that were spray-painted gray so they looked like they were carved from stone. One had the words "THOU SHALL NOT" stenciled across it and the other read, "THE WORD OF GOD." After I made my speech condemning the Sodom and Gomorrah that was San Francisco, I held the tablets aloft as if I were Moses or at least Heston coming down from Mount Sinai.

The Cruiser made his entrance to his abominably garish techo theme music and immediately snatched the microphone from Allan Bolte's hand.

"Listen, Christian Dante," he yelled, "You've been spouting your precious dogma all fucking night long!" He paused for a beat as the crowd cheered his every word. "You like to kneel? You like to kneel, baby? Why don't you kneel right here!" He commanded as he motioned to his crotch.

"I'm gonna show you that there's nothing wrong with fucking a man up the ass!"

After his opening challenge, I attempted to slam one of the tablets across his head as we had planned. The flimsy piece of foam frayed apart as I brought it down towards his head. Not a shard of that Styrofoam tablet actually touched his person as one piece of it snapped off and flew backwards over my head. The rest of it crumbled in my hands but the Cruiser sold the move and fell off the ring apron anyway as if he'd just been cudgeled by solid granite. The audience stood there confused, but we couldn't change gears and ad lib a match to save our lives. We followed our script as if we were doing live television in the '50s. We hoped that nobody noticed but everyone in that crowded hall seemed unusually astute at that moment. It was as if some otherworldly force had caused them all to sober up and stop tossing tortillas. At least they were paying attention.

Cruiser and I battled back and forth; I had the upper hand for most of the first two minutes of the match. Flamius Caesar joined Allan Bolte on color commentary and started a rousing chant of

"*Die, Christian, Die*" that faded in and out throughout the rest of the night. Drunks probably even chanted that at Electric Frankenstein. I body slammed the Cruiser and then did a big splash on him where he felt just a bit too much of my 290 pounds landing across his chest.

He tossed me into the corner and I landed on top of the top turnbuckle with my ass sticking up in just the right position for El Cruiser's most dreaded submission maneuver: the Rectal Wrecker. He held up his thumb to the crowd to build up the anticipation and then he plunged it right into my rectum. I always thought that Craig faked this bit of anal prodding and held his thumb harmlessly in his clenched fist while he performed this move, but I was wrong. Cruiser pried me open and burrowed his thumb as far up my poop chute as my burlap and canvas tunic would allow. I was in pain. I turned green and then white. I kept struggling to flail my arms and act like I was hurt even though all I really wanted to do was barf. Cruiser's invasive probe was a little too deep into the world of method acting for me.

Finally, Corgan, in his role as the busybody ref of wrestling tradition (the role he was chosen for) broke up the move and started shaking his admonishing finger in the Cruiser's face. Cruiser had to break the move because I was on the ropes. Plain and simple. Pro wrestling 101.

I revived myself and grabbed the other Styrofoam tablet, the one that said "THOU SHALT NOT." I tried to hit the Cruiser with it but he ducked out of the way. It broke into two pieces just as the other one had, but Tom Corgan leapt into the air like a star soccer player and butted the shard of gray foam with his own forehead. The Styrofoam broke into pieces right across his dome. It looked good. We couldn't have two props fail in the same match.

Corgan collapsed to the mat as if he were knocked out cold. I beat the Cruiser down during the confusion. Dante the Baptist was poised for victory. Most of the audience was about to go home disappointed. They had paid good money to see a leather fag kick some Christian ass. They didn't need to see the Christian win. That was too close to reality. That was Flamius' cue. He held up one hand and screeched, "*Release the Lion!*"

The audience had either forgotten or forgiven our earlier prop malfunction. They cheered wildly as Van Dyne in the lion suit stumbled his way into the ring. The lion speared me hard and then picked me up and delivered a face first DDT. Then the Cruiser, Flamius and the Lion restrained me facing the audience while Suzy Ming in a skin-tight devil girl outfit clipped my hair with a pair of scissors. We wanted an electric razor just to make things even more anachronistic but nobody seemed to have one. The people right in front of the ring grabbed handfuls of my hair and tried to shove it into my mouth while Suzy snipped off more of my locks. I spat gobs of hair back out onto the fans below.

After Suzy Ming clipped my hair, Dante the Baptist was robbed of the source of his Samson-like strength. Cruiser got the pin. The Christian was finished. The audience chanted "Die, Christian, Die" some more as Flamius gave his Roman salute to the crowd. After the hedonistic victors left the ring, I slowly rose to my feet and once again slung my oversized cross onto my back. I then took the microphone and muttered, "Father… Why have you forsaken me?"

Yes, I am going to hell.

It was the worst possible time to be without a venue, but that's exactly what happened. The July 1998 show was the last time that ISW brought its tortilla tossing madness to the Paradise Lounge and Transmission Theatre. There was a huge rift between Audra and some of the higher-ups at the conjoined nightclubs.

ISW still guaranteed a full house and had nothing but forward momentum, but this didn't matter to some of the head barkeeps and business managers of the venue where ISW got its start. They just wanted to be done with Audra. Audra counted the cash and acted like she owned the place. She screamed at the bartenders and cursed out the club's managers. She bitched out the people who were used to doing the bitching out and she did it in a louder and grosser way than they ever would. "You fucking assholes! How the fuck did you get so stupid!" she frequently hollered at people who didn't work for her.

Audra was a bitch. This made her a local media darling and got her plenty of ink in the late 1990s when tough broads held a certain feminist fascination. Audra's bitchiness enabled her to be a successful independent concert promoter while managing a wrestling show and dealing with psychotic strippers on a regular basis. Without being a bitch, Audra would have been nothing. But that same freight-train-plowing-into-a-battleship personality that propelled her forward could also chase away as much business as it brought in. Being bitched out by Audra, having to clean up piles of tortillas and mounds of honest-to-God wrestler shit in conjunction with that sinking feeling that isw was a lawsuit waiting to happen made the Paradise/Transmission decide that they would be better off without their top drawing punk rock wrestling show. Audra still had a few friends rattling around the place, but none where it counted. She didn't just burn her bridges; she dynamited their foundations so that they could never be built again. isw would have to find another venue.

While isw was without a home, the San Francisco live music scene was rapidly being bought out and paved over as the dot-com boom and a development frenzy had the City by the Bay cannibalizing its clubs and converting them into office space and trendy live-work lofts at an increasing pace.

The Club Cocodrie (formerly Morty's) was the first to go. It was the one club where any band that bothered to send them a demo package and give them a follow-up call could play. The scene needed places like that. Without them new bands never got a chance. Unfortunately, the closing of the Cocodrie was somewhat understandable for there were far too many nights where the only people who showed up to see shows were the bands on the bill. As an ominous forecast of things to come, the Cocodrie was transformed into yet another nondescript new media company.

The Chameleon in the Mission was next to fall. Its owner Karen Carney had failed to come up with several months of back rent. She had lived in the club's unsanitary downstairs basement for a time and then was reportedly making her home in a van parked out by the Golden Gate Park panhandle. One night a crusty punk band showed up to load in for a show that had been booked weeks earlier to find a chain with a big padlock on the door. One of the band members had a pair of bolt cutters and was able to cut through the lock and the show went on as planned, to the delight of several bike messengers and hopheads. Luckily, Karen had paid her power bill, but bass players with bolt cutters could only delay the inevitable. The Chameleon was soon gone.

The Nightbreak, the place where my band cut its teeth and Fast Mike first insisted that I join the ranks of ISW, went down around the same time. It reopened briefly as the incongruously named Thirsty Swede, but by then what was already a punk rock dive had seen a sharp decline even by its own standards. Bartenders served whatever bilge they could out of the one working tap the bar had left. Junkies from the park openly shot up in the back room by the Terminator 2 pinball machine that myself and just about every other musician in San Francisco fed full of quarters while waiting for a sound check.

At the last few shows booked there, people shattered their pint glasses on the ground as if they were at a Greek wedding. Shows at the Thirsty Swede had the feel of a regime on the brink of collapse. Finally shows stopped happening there and the club closed its doors. When they reopened again some months later, the room had been converted into a bright pastel colored Internet café. This was a real feat of renovation work because to look at the Nightbreak one would have thought that even a sandblaster could never strip away all the grime and nicotine stains. The Terminator 2 pinball machine in its corner remains as the sole remnant of what was once the Nightbreak.

The most galling change of all was when the owner of the Kilowatt realized that he could make more money keeping his club quiet so all the dot-com workers could talk over their business deals and count the imaginary cash in their stock options. The Kilowatt pulled the plug on live music on the hot corner of 16th and Valencia and it became just a bar. The chatter of the city's high tech nouveau riche was able to drown out so many electric guitars.

In the end, Audra's falling out with the Transmission didn't matter. Crazy Robin Reichert, owner of both the Paradise and Transmission, abruptly canceled the Transmission's bookings, closed the club and rented the space out to a web design firm. He couldn't beat 'em so he joined 'em. The nightclub's vast floorspace — big enough for our wrestling ring, a stage for the bands and enough room left over for nearly 1,000 hell heads — was divided into featureless gray cubicles. The hall where I wrestled lions, sasquatches and gutter sluts was populated by ergonomic workstations. A high volume photocopier right next to the mandatory espresso machine most likely occupied the spot where "Psycho" Johnny Pain had once squatted and left a steaming pile of Andro-laced man dung.

# 13

# UNCLE
# N.A.M.B.L.A.

CHANGO LOCO WAS FULL of rage. Chango Loco was at war with half of San Francisco. He kept a shit list. "Talking shit" got you on the shit list. In an insular scene like the one surrounding ISW and Stinky's, there was a lot of shit talking. Most of us just let that sort of thing roll off us. Chango wanted to condemn people to the ninth circle of some kind of Santerian hell over it. Chango openly bragged about the latest additions to his shit list to his closest friends, including Craig and myself. For a time, his outrageous put-downs of poseur goth DJs and the dumbest of the psychobilly scene were pretty fucking funny. After a while, it got too ugly.

When someone from the shit list haplessly walked into a club or taqueria and Chango happened to be there, sheer hatred radiated from his body. His eyes rolled into the back of his head, his muscles tensed like a tweaker who had just done a fat line cut with too much strychnine and you could hear the sound of his wooden tribal ear hoops slapping against the sides of his neck. It was pretty hard to finish your 2 A.M. al pastor plate at La Rondalla while sitting next to a 230-pound tattooed Mexican who was literally quaking with rage.

Pro wrestling sent Chango Loco plummeting off whatever edge of sanity he had been teetering on. Chango got way too into "Stone Cold" Steve Austin for a man in his late twenties. He started walking around Haight Street with Austin's overstated macho swagger. He tried to start a fight with Bob the Ref and some guy with neck tattoos named Lucky at the last ISW show at the Transmission. Lucky and Bob had evidently been "talking shit." Chango always wanted Craig and me to join him on some kind of holy crusade against the people on his shit list. A lot of times, the people on the shit list seemed like pretty cool individuals when you met them without Chango skulking around. The revenge fantasies that Chango concocted for the ring were starting to dominate his real life. Wrestling was no longer a social safety valve for him. If anything, it poured gasoline on his raging fire.

I got the bright idea to have Craig and Chango join my band for a show at Stinky's. My drummer Ed couldn't make the show and Andy the guitarist had quit in the hope of being in a band that wouldn't make him wear a karate suit. The show with Craig and Chango was an out-of-tune disaster that bordered on free jazz. After the show, Chango left his drum set at my practice space. Tigger's band, the Glamour Pussies, shared my space for a while and used Chango's kit a couple of times. This put Tigger LeTwang and a bunch of black-haired girls who played canoe paddle guitars on the shit list. Chango's drums stayed at my practice space. Ed and Andy rejoined the band. To make room for Ed's drums, we stacked the bulk of Chango's kit in the corner of the practice space and I stored Chango's bass drum in my apartment.

Chango's divided drum set stayed in my practice space and apartment for months. I should have driven it back to him, but we already weren't speaking. The drums that put Tigger and her band on his shit list put me on the shit list too for reasons that didn't make any sense. He could have just called me and arranged to pick it up but he never did.

Months went by. I forgot the drums were there for the most part. One afternoon, Chango got into my practice room. He must have still had a key. While collecting his gear, he somehow took the cymbals from a band that we split the space with called The Spinning Jennies. When he couldn't find his bass drum, he decided to hang onto those cymbals. It was one thing for him to lash out at me, but why did he have to drag a bunch of shaggy and sensitive alt-pop dudes into this?

He had those cymbals. I had his bass drum. It was my fault the Jennies got dragged into this whole mess. I had to get those cymbals back.

It was 11 o'clock on a weeknight. I went to Chango's lower Haight apartment to make the trade. I brought Ed and Andy with me, not that they were going to do anything. I might as well have been on my own. I rang Chango's apartment buzzer. I had his bass drum on his steps. He came down without the cymbals. He wasn't going to give them to me. I wasn't going to leave without them. Chango was standing two steps above me. He had the high ground. If anything happened, I was fucked. I had maybe one shot straight to his nuts. If it went physical, I would have had to punch him there as hard as I could to keep from eating concrete and getting rolled downhill. Like I said, Ed and Andy weren't going to be too much help.

Chango raged at me and accused me of stealing from him. With his shaved dome and big shoulders, he looked as scary as another human being could. A neighbor from across the street yelled that they had called the cops. Chango held tough for a few more seconds and then he started to plead with me. "Please, Count, just go," he said in a softer tone as his expression melted from anger to anguish. Chango and his girlfriend were having some kind of legal hassle at the time. Chango couldn't afford a run-in with the law. I wasn't going to leave, but every second I stayed there brought us closer to blows. He knew how to make me leave, yet he was hanging onto those cymbals that didn't belong to him out of spite. Spite was his reason for living.

Six squad cars clogged Chango's narrow, one-way street. My '63 Catalina was double-parked with Andy in his old Econoline double-parked behind me. Andy was stoned out of his mind. He knew the cops were coming. He knew he should get the hell out of there, but he was a little slow to react. After a minute, Andy's idling van was surrounded by the SFPD.

The cops broke things up as fists were about to fly. They didn't understand why Chango was so mad when he had gotten his bass drum back. They couldn't figure out the mess with the Spinning Jennies' cymbals. I couldn't figure it out either and I was a central figure in the whole thing. The cops told Chango and me that we needed to address it in civil court if we were going to pursue the matter any further. The cops always said that sort of thing. Chango had his drum but he still had those cymbals. With the cops standing around, I had to leave empty handed.

Ed and I got in my car and pulled away with flashing red and blue lights all around us. "You know, Count," Ed said as I turned onto Oak Street, "I think he can take you." He may have been right.

I told Audra what had happened — about the cops, the drum set, the Spinning Jennies, the whole Chango Loco quagmire. I expected her to axe me right then and there. I was prepared to leave the wrestling show but I didn't want to. Chango couldn't work with me, Craig, the Poontangler, Bob the Ref and a constantly expanding roster of Stinky's and ISW regulars. When you have problems with that many people, you're the problem. But still, Audra and Chango went way back. Audra even testified against one of her former boyfriends on behalf of Chango in some wrongful termination lawsuit. Audra's ex used to run another closed down South of Market nightclub. Both

Audra and Chango were on his payroll. The poor sap needed a better employee screening process.

Chango was her biggest star, but I had become the brains behind the operation. I was announcing every match except for the ones that I wrestled and I had a hand in organizing several other bouts as well. I put my stamp on more storylines than my own. On the other hand, Chango had the post punk/luchadore chic image that Audra wanted for her promotion. He had the charisma. Drunk dudes wanted to be him and there was no short supply of chicks that wanted to go home with him. If ısw wasn't too disorganized and lazy to have a championship belt, Chango would have been the champ.

Audra needed both of us. Audra still had pull with Chango. She may have been one of the only people in the world who could control him. She told him that everything had to end right then and there or he would be ass out of the wrestling show. Chango's entire sense of self was held together with ring ropes and turnbuckles. An uneasy truce was handed down from up high that kept us both in the show. Out of his strange sense of honor and the need to put forth a magnanimous public image to nerdy musicians who were already scared shitless of him, Chango returned the Spinning Jennies' cymbals.

Still, I knew that this wasn't going to be the end of it. Things were going to boil over in that backroom sooner or later. Luckily, Tom Corgan was back in the wrestling show. I didn't bullshit him and had gotten him back just like I promised. Tom was loyal and he knew how to break arms and knock people out for real. If Chango and a bunch of his creepy cronies tried to start anything, Corgan was there to back me up.

After the falling out with the Transmission, ısw became nomadic and Audra intended to keep it that way. She had these portable liquor licenses that allowed her to legally serve booze at any venue she could get a permit for. In case the city pulled one of her liquor licenses, she had a second one in reserve. Without an established nightclub to support the show, she was going to have to rent a hall, hire the sound crew, bouncers and bartenders. She'd get a cut of everything including the booze. But she had to organize the entire ground floor operations of a special event that was set to draw over 1,000 people as well as dealing with three rock bands and over twenty-five pro wrestlers.

The next isw show was held on October 24, 1998, at an ornate civic center ballroom at 50 Oak Street. The Phantom Surfers headlined the show and a New York glam band called the Toilet Boys played the middle slot. The Toilet Boys pushed the gender bending of '80s hair metal to its obvious extremes as they had a genuine chick with a dick fronting the band. They also packed as much pyro into tiny punk rock dives as Kiss used at the Oakland Coliseum. When they played Stinky's, I spent most of the show standing by the fire exit. Twelve-foot high pillars of flame shot up from the cw's cramped stage. When I first heard about the 2003 fire at a Great White show in Rhode Island that burned almost 100 people to death, I naturally assumed that it must have happened at a Toilet Boys gig.

Hours before the show began, Audra called all of the wrestlers into a carpeted reception room that was furnished with old couches. *"You don't get paid to work security,"* she screamed.

*"You don't get paid to have a good time,"* she followed.

*"You don't get paid to chase women."*

After the fifth or sixth "you don't get paid," I could no longer resist the urge to chime in.

"Hell, we don't get paid," I said, cutting in on Audra's big pre-show scolding. The room broke up into uncontrollable laughter. We didn't get paid. Audra had spent the better part of two years bragging to the press about how she didn't pay her wrestlers. What was she going to do? Withhold our non-existent paychecks? The ironic thing was that Audra started paying some of us after that show.

The 50 Oak show was the surrealistic mélange that I had always wanted ISW to be. Paul Van Dyne's entire menagerie of acrylic fur-covered beasties squared off against each other in the "When Animals Attack" match. Josh Steele wore the lion suit and I convinced Audra and Paul to let Tom be the Sasquatch. Tom injected some much-needed wrestling into the three-monster brawl and Van Dyne's satirical sight gags finally had entertainment value beyond their ring entrances.

There was also a chop socky death match that Jefferson Monroe did entirely to re-cut audio from Bruce Lee's badly dubbed revenge opus *The Chinese Connection*. Monroe's idea of having kung fu masters communicate through out-of-sync voiceovers was later utilized by Vince McMahon on *Smackdown!* when he couldn't figure out anything else to do with his very good Japanese wrestlers but to have them ape the basest stereotypes. Hell, it's pro wrestling — a medium that works in base stereotypes the way that painters use oils and watercolors.

To top it all off like an ornament on a wedding cake, El Homo Loco and the Cruiser tied the knot on that show years before San Francisco same-sex weddings were blamed for handing Bush the 2004 presidential election. That gay wedding gag also turned up some time later on WWE programming when Vince had Billy Gunn walk down the aisle with a grappler named Chucky. McMahon's gay wrestling wedding got a lot of press, even making it into the *Washington Post*. But at the height of the media storm, Gunn, who never seemed to object to showing his butt cheeks when he wrestled under the name of name of Mr. Ass, anxiously issued denials of homosexuality to a skeptical public.

But Vince McMahon still hasn't touched all of the simulated ass raping, ball grabbing and playacted pedophilia of the Uncle N.A.M.B.L.A. vs. Lil'Timmy match. Sure, Vince has come pretty close to this rock bottom of bad taste, but he has yet to introduce a child molester wrestler (although I would never put it past him). I was Uncle N.A.M.B.L.A. and I let it all hang out wearing nothing but some tight blue hot pants that didn't quite cover my ass and a really twisted clown-like lucha mask picked up from the isw merch booth. Manny Franklin was Lil' Timmy. He was so desperate to get away from being beaten up by Dave Steele that he was willing to be groped by an almost naked fat guy with stretch marks and sagging man boobs for seven minutes in front of more than a thousand people.

My big tagline for the match was *"Don't Tell Anyone Where I Touched You."* Lil' Timmy came into the ring wearing a school tie and short pants and skipping to GN'R's "Sweet Child O' Mine." I beat him down pretty quickly and felt him up from behind as if I hadn't grossed the audience out enough already. Manny could get vertical with ease. He rallied with a series of drop kicks. He did backflips off the ropes and turned around into a high cross body. The fans were with him. They started chanting "Timmy! Timmy!" A group of really pissed-off Samoans kept making like they were going to storm the ring. I was really worried about this. They would have massacred us if they had.

Finally, Timmy attempted a leg scissors take down, but I caught him and slammed him hard. I thought that I had dropped him on his neck, but he was fine. I then pulled a dirty rag out of my skin tight man panties and put it over Manny's face. "Oh my God! It's the chloroform!" Allan Bolte exclaimed right on cue. Manny went limp and acted as if he had passed out. The kid could act, or at least mime. I picked up his motionless body and dragged him into the backroom. "Little Timmy's getting an education into the facts of life right about now," Allan said as the crowd stared at the empty ring in shocked silence.

I was Count Dante. On the microphone at Stinky's and isw, I was funnier than half of the comedians working the comedy clubs. I had confronted the mighty Chango Loco and survived with all of my teeth intact. I wrestled the Poontangler and a Sasquatch and tempted fate in front of pissed-off Pacific Islanders. I was in demand. I was world famous — in two or three of the most trendy neighborhoods in San Francisco.

But when I wasn't the Count, I was just some big, fat nerd who worked temp jobs in libraries to make rent. To save some cash, I spent far too many months driving around without car insurance. Back then, you could get away with that because the SFPD wouldn't pull you over even if you were driving figure eights down Mission Street with your hood on fire.

I was still in school. I hung on month by month until the student loan checks came, but I was graduating soon so there went that revenue stream. I was smart enough to convince one of my professors to count my work with ISW for internship credit. I was already penning enough press releases for Audra without being paid for it. Why should I go and do even more volunteer PR for some radio station? It didn't make sense ISW was getting me media exposure. Your average broadcasting intern didn't get on TV. They just pushed papers or poured coffee. The lucky ones got to freeze their asses off while handing out station-ID key chains and condoms in front of the Rage Against the Machine concert. No station manager in their right mind wanted all 300 pounds of me to pass out prophylactics. Luckily, I was able to convince my prof that ISW was a multimedia firm and I earned those three units in the broadcasting program for basically being Uncle N.A.M.B.L.A.

Besides college credit, ISW landed me a string of one-night stands. There was something about the mass hysteria induced by all of that sweaty grappling while booze and tortillas flew in every direction. After shows, women jumped in my car. Club babes wanted to come back to my dirty-assed apartment with me after I had just spent ten minutes exchanging holds with El Homo Loco. "Dante, you're the guy that all of the girls talk about in the ladies' room," one of them told me as I made out with her in my parked car on the corner of Folsom and 11th.

"What are they saying about me?" I asked while coming up for air. I never got an answer.

Being talked about in the ladies' room didn't seem to be doing me any good in the romance department except when there was a wrestling show. When isw was at the Transmission, we did one show a month. After we left that nightspot, we did shows whenever Audra could book them. We never knew if there was even going to be another show, let alone when it was. If I waited on isw for all of my tail, I was going to be waiting a long time.

In the end, the one-nighters weren't all that they were cracked up to be. There were too many rocker chicks cheating on their boy-friends who wanted to move in with me after one guilty make out session. I also seemed to be far too many lesbians' last male partner before they came out of the closet for good and took up female bodybuilding or other butch pursuits. I don't know what made me a magnet for that sort of thing. Maybe it was my man boobs and my effeminate day job. Maybe those confused gals thought, "Hey, he has tits. He's a librarian. It won't upset my mom. I'll give Dante a try." While sex with lesbians might seem so crazy and wild, in reality it's just a lot of bad sex.

I got tired of the girls that I started to like always going back to their shitty boyfriends. I got tired of the noticeable look of dis-appointment that fell across rocker chicks' faces when they realized that I wasn't covered with the standard issue tattoos. What was it with nautical stars, flaming dice and little swallows anyway that made everyone want to permanently etch them on their bodies? It was easy for aimless scenesters to blow all their money on their ink addiction, but I had a band. I was burning through all my cash on bass strings, amp tubes and practice space rent. I didn't have any leftover dough for stamping a trail of vaguely Celtic squiggles around my bicep.

After a while, I just wanted a girlfriend.

I had too much unsupervised time during my rotating day jobs.

I had to stretch the hours just to get enough money to make rent every month. Everyone else with my skill set was getting outrageously high paying Internet jobs with big stock options. I applied for those jobs but I never got a call back. I had worked too many jobs that screamed "former union member" and I was too damned old. The Internet boom had turned the working world into some kind of reenactment of *Logan's Run* where you might as well just float around until you exploded on your 30th birthday. The engines of our economy were outwardly being run by T-shirt wearing twenty-four-year-olds with little weird beards. Behind the scenes, the same sharks in suits were still calling the shots and cooking the books at the venture capital firms.

With all of that free time at work while sitting in front of a wired Pentium, I started to browse through the Yahoo! personal ads. They were free back then. I felt like a loser at first. This was before Friendster and MySpace remade the web into a rollicking 24-hour fuckfest. Personal ads were previously the province of middle-aged spinsters and well-meaning widowers who owned isolated cattle ranches in old westerns. But I quickly realized that women in their early twenties didn't attach the same stigma to online dating that those of us pushing thirty did. To people five years younger than me, it was just another way to hook up.

I started dating the interchicks. Some of them were the wallflowers that I expected but none of them had the baggage of going out with me because they saw me wear hot pants and grope a teen-aged boy for five minutes in the ring. They were going out with Bob — not the Count. But the Count always intruded. I'd be on a date at a Market Street bar only to have a skater kid in baggy pants come up to me and say, "Man, that was great when you kicked El Homo Loco's ass!" That kind of thing made me look like I was some kind of arch-fag basher. My Internet dates tended to involve a lot of explaining.

Finally, there was Dana. She was a weird girl from Marin who lived with her two gay dads. Her biological father was in the s&m scene so she didn't have a problem with big hairy guys hitting each other for entertainment. We talked for hours on the phone. My voice was so loud that she often rested the phone about a foot away from her ear on her pillow. I was still ashamed of how we met. I told everyone that we met "at the Paradise Lounge." That was only half true. That was where we first hooked up for cocktails.

She found out about the wrestling show. To impress me, she even endured a really terrible episode of wcw *Nitro* where the heel Hulk Hogan repeatedly bashed his nephew's head with a chair. She was pretty broken up by Hogan's newfound villainy. I was officially smitten. Anyone who would watch such lousy wrestling for me was worth keeping.

Dana had long brown hair and was as cute as a button. Audra wanted to put her up on top of a pool table at Stinky's the first time she laid eyes on her. I convinced Dana not to do it. The girls in the bathroom thought it was because I was being some kind of overly possessive jerk. In reality, I just didn't want my woman to take the same kind of shit from Audra that I readily volunteered to put up with. I wanted Dana apart from all of that. In the end, shaking her ass until 2 A.M. for a bunch of college kids in trucker hats didn't hold that much appeal for her.

Soon, I gave Dana the keys to my apartment. A short while later, she found out that I had been lying about my age on my Yahoo! profile. I had flipped the nine in 29 into a six. She was mad about my deception for a few minutes, but by then it was already too late. She was hooked.

Running the whole shebang at the 50 Oak show proved to be a bit too much even for Audra. She never utilized those liquor licenses again. Five months passed until our next show but it was worth the wait. Audra booked us at the Fillmore in March 1999.

The Fillmore was San Francisco's most enduring rock and roll icon. It was the musical epicenter of the Summer of Love where Bill Graham figured out how to cash in on psychedelia. At the Fillmore I'd be announcing from the same stage where Hendrix, the Stones, the Dead, The Who and the Doors once kicked out the jams before the scene had died one of its many deaths.

For our brush with Bay Area rock and roll immortality, we shocked the Fillmore with matches where hippies were mauled by bears, Fartbreath Jones lightly smacked Señor Bueno with a chair that was wrapped with entirely too much barbed wire, and the Poontangler tangled with the Inbred Abomination. There was also something called "Doctor Loco's Alien Autopsy."The Bomboras and Satan's Pilgrims provided the rock and roll, which marked some-what of an end to San Francisco's decade long garage rock revival. Ironically, the whole country would get caught up in a garage rock resurgence a couple of years later with the Strokes and the White Stripes. For the rest of isw's run, upbeat happy punk replaced the sounds of surf and psychobilly.

For the Fillmore, I decided to focus on my announcing. I had gotten tired of wrestling my match and then announcing everyone else's. There were plenty of guys in isw who didn't know how to work a match. The show didn't need another one and announcing made me as big a star as wrestling ever did.

I knew that things were different from the Transmission days from the first moment that I stepped out onto the Fillmore's hal-lowed stage. There were faces as far back as I could see. The same lights that had recently shone on Santana and Johnny Cash were now pointed at me.

"*Are you ready for bloodshed?!*" I said and held the mic out towards the crowd to start the show. The unison cheers in that old ballroom were thunderous. I got chills. At that moment, I was a star.

"*Are you ready for carnage?!*" I stalked the stage and then finished with, "*Well then you must be ready for Incredibly… Strange… Wrestling!*" The cheers swelled to a crescendo. We had only been gone for a couple of months but the Fillmore felt like a successful comeback.

While I reveled in being the announcer along with Allan Bolte, I was never going to announce any of Chango's matches again. Any off the cuff remark that I made while he was out there had the potential to send him into a rage. For him, our wrestling roles and real selves were intertwined. What started at the show could finish after it. During Chango's match, I handed the mic over to Jello Biafra. Jello was managing Chango at the time. While it burned my ass to see my teen angst idol palling around with my new mortal enemy, it was the best thing for the show. Having Jello there as a "special commentator" allowed me to leave the stage for Chango's bout without dragging the fans into the drama.

The first Fillmore show was supposed to be a one-off, but ISW gave the concert hall its biggest bar tab of all time. Our ticket prices weren't as high as all that tired hippie bullshit like Bob Weir and Friends, but with the jacked-up prices that the Fillmore charged for cocktails, the pure profit from ISW was enormous. However, while our loyal boozehounds paved the way for our return, our follow up show wasn't for another five months. And wrestlers can go real crazy in five months.

It was the afternoon of August 20, 1999, during the hours leading up to our second Fillmore show. A local TV station wanted to do a cutesy human-interest story on ISW where some bubbly newscaster went record shopping with a couple of wrestlers at the Haight Street Amoeba. Audra chose Chango Loco and his opponent for the evening for the feature. I had helped set up the news feature by e-mailing the station, but Chango was who Audra was pushing. Audra wanted to let me know who was still running things.

I was later told that Chango strolled down Haight Street wearing his mask. He was playing it kayfabe all the way. Kayfabe is a piece of wrestler carnie jargon for constantly staying in character even when you aren't anywhere near a wrestling ring. It came from the days when wrestlers had to maintain that what they did was real.

It was pretty silly when you applied it to a show where a guy in a chicken suit wrestled Jesus. But Chango was living and breathing kayfabe.

He strutted down Haight Street and drew a lot of attention. He got into a tiff with those street kids that are always panhandling in front of the McDonald's. Things got out of hand. Chango spit on one of the kids and told him to go fuck himself. Chango didn't have any peripheral vision in his lucha mask. Before he knew it eight spindly crusty punks jumped him and started hitting him from all sides. He was stronger than any one of them but that didn't matter. He couldn't see where the blows were coming from.

He somehow got away from them and blood was streaming from underneath his mask. He was a mess. He made it into the record store and terrified the news crew. The story never aired.

Moments later, Dana picked me up only blocks away from Amoeba at my day job at St. Mary's Medical Center. We were going to drive straight to the Fillmore. Chango was walking down the other side of the street. He wasn't wearing his mask anymore but was wearing an oversized pair of shades. The blood had been wiped away. I didn't know about the two black eyes the homeless kids had given him. He stared straight at me. I stared back. He started to come towards me but the blonde retro babe that he was with stepped in front of him and convinced him to move along. He pointed at me and said something. I couldn't tell what it was. I kept staring at him until he got farther down the block.

That night, I had to step into the ring against El Homo Loco. The Poontangler was supposed to fight him, but Tigger had been badly burned in a kitchen accident. Tigger had already given herself a case of liver failure by insisting on making go-go gigs while she had a major case of mono. Tigger was going to wrestle the show anyway even though her arms were covered in second and third degree burns. In that filthy ring filled with beer soaked tortillas, she was bound to get a major infection. I agreed to sub for her so she could sit out her match.

El Homo Loco and I didn't have time to work anything out. I hadn't wrestled in several months. I was way out of shape. John Pierre was drunker than usual so he just pummeled my nuts for most of our match. I tried to manhandle him but it wasn't easy. He was slippery when sober. Shit-faced, he was impossible to get a hold of. James Hetfield of Metallica was standing at ringside. Before the show, everyone had been talking about how he was there. He kept yelling, "*Kill the fags!*" I was shocked. It was San Francisco, but Hetfield is so far to the right that he makes Ted Nugent look like Mahatma Gandhi.

Luckily my nut pounding only had to eat up about five minutes of ring time. John Pierre later apologized to Dana for it. After that, it was back to announcing. I didn't even get a five-minute break after a low blow like in boxing.

Chango Loco came out onto the stage for some other match. I wasn't expecting him and had really been avoiding putting myself in any situation where fantasy and reality could get crossed up anymore than they were already. I was a little uneasy. He pulled out a T-shirt that read "COUNT DANTE IS A PUSSY" in those Vato-gothic iron-on letters. He must have gone to some old school South San Jose T-shirt shop for that one. He started calling me out in front of the entire Fillmore. I had only seconds to react. I wanted to pummel him once and for all. I wanted to put him in some kind of hold and make him go to sleep with 1,500 people as witnesses, but I didn't. It was the Fillmore. It was the big time. A lot more was at stake than anyone's ego. I just let it go.

When Chango called me out, I still didn't know about the beating he'd taken on Haight Street. When he pulled off his mask backstage, both of his eyes looked as if they were nearly swollen shut. Drops of blood intermittently dribbled out of his nose. If I had decided to fight him, I would have won but I also could have accidentally committed manslaughter. He had to be suffering from a concussion. One stiff punch to a man in his condition could have been fatal. I'm not boasting here. Chango was in no shape to pick fights with anybody. He probably shouldn't have wrestled but he still managed to get through his match. I have to give that much to him.

The scene backstage was crazed. Chango had wrecked the TV shoot and now he was trying to inject his personal vendettas into our follow-up show at San Francisco's premiere music venue without any regard for ISW's potential future there. I didn't know if that whole thing with the T-shirt wasn't part of some fake wrestling angle that Chango was building up in his mind. I doubt if he knew either. Audra was pissed but she thanked me for keeping my head and staying professional. In the tug-of-war between Chango and me, I won by staying cool while he self-destructed.

Chango got the axe that night. Five days later, a picture of El Homo Loco dragging my face across the top rope ended up splashed across the front page of the *Contra Costa Times* in full color. It was just a suburban daily out of the East Bay, but it had a circulation of over 100,000. That afternoon, Audra left a message on my machine saying, "Count Dante, you're on the front page of the paper. You are now famous. Just thought you should know."

# 14

# HOT MAN ON MAN ACTION

WAS IT THREE TABLES or only two? Cruiser Craig didn't need to do this. He was part of the ISW brain trust. He was on the booking committee. He was funny and, on top of it all, he was a damned good graphic artist, but he was determined to go through that stack of tables even if it killed him. Cruiser had just spent the last fifteen minutes being pummeled by a 6' 5" black corrections officer who made his living keeping the peace at the San Francisco county jail. The jail guard's name was Wally. He had made some appearances in ISW before as a manager but he was built like a brick shithouse, brandished his billy club and looked damned impressive in his screw uniform so naturally the fans wanted to see the guy get in the ring. There is an unwritten rule in wrestling that you can't look freakish, weird or damned fucking big and not get in the ring. If you try to just stand there and wave to the fans, they are going to hate you for all the wrong reasons.

Craig keyed in on this so he decided to give the fans what they wanted and work a match with Wally. The problem was that Wally didn't know the first thing about wrestling. The only thing that Wally could do when he was faced with a standing room only crowd at the Fillmore was to beat the shit out of the Cruiser. He ripped hard punches into Cruiser's midsection and sent his oversized fists crashing into Craig's nose. When Wally sensed that Craig was about to go down, he held him up and whispered a simple "I'm sorry," in his ear and then started beating on him all over again.

The beating went on for over ten minutes. Wally's partner, another SF County hack who wrestled under the name of Dead Man Walking, had joined in the fun and was tossing Craig around like a ragamuffin. Soon it was time for the big finale where Dead Man was to push Craig through that stack of tables. They botched the first attempt at the table spot. Cruiser hit the tables all right but they didn't break. He slid off the tabletop and hit the hard floor at the Fillmore with a sickening thud that most of the audience couldn't see or hear. Wrestling fans love nothing more than the sight of recently broken particleboard. Craig had to try it again and make sure the tables broke in half this time.

Craig's gray-bearded, free spirit father had become ISW's semi-official photographer and was on the Fillmore's floor clicking away during his son's brutal match. Craig climbed back onto the stage wearing the Cruiser's leather mask and the denim cut-off shorts that often pulled to the side and revealed his scrotal sac. After the first botched table attempt, Craig had a large gash across his upper thigh. Blood was running down to his feet and soaking his socks.

Craig's dad put down his camera and looked his son square in the eye during a break in the action. "What are you doing?" he said, pleading with his son not to try the table spot again, but Craig didn't listen. Wally tossed Craig into the air a second time and the tables broke in half like they were supposed to. The crowd went wild and you could see their clenched fists shaking in the air in unison as they heard the crunch of so many folding picnic tables.

While Cruiser Craig had had to be seduced by pro wrestling's theatrical masochism, Tom Corgan was born with it in his blood. Since I had negotiated his return, Corgan as Macho Sasquatcho had teamed with Paul Van Dyne's El Pollo Diablo. Paul came up with the kooky concepts and Corgan had the ring psychology. It was a division of labor that paid creative dividends for over a year of shows.

There was the "When Animals Attack" match at 50 Oak and their first Fillmore match, where the Sasquatch and Van Dyne in a rented bear suit mauled a couple of hippies. This Man vs. Nature concept continued with the tag team of El Pollo Diablo and Macho Sasquatcho going against a pair of construction workers who (as my sterling commentary put it), "were tearing down old growth forests to build more yuppie lofts in South of Market." After taking down the construction workers, the Sasquatch and the Devil Chicken, natural enemies in the wild, started fighting each other. El Pollo Diablo eventually slammed a framed Robert Doisneau print over Sasquatcho's head.

Before the last isw show of the millennium, Corgan went to Van Dyne's parents' house to talk over the upcoming Christmas match, which would pit the animals against Santo Claus and his Crackhead Elves. Corgan had smoked a lot of grass and started going on about "wanting the pain."

"You have to want to feel the pain," he kept telling a terrified Van Dyne. Corgan wanted to emulate Terry Funk and Mick Foley. He wanted to wrestle on exploding pallets covered with barbed wire or to fall twenty feet from a steel cage onto stacks of tables. Van Dyne just wanted to do crazy shit in front of a drunken audience with as little risk-taking as possible.

Corgan's pot-induced pep talk about the glories of self-mutilation had Van Dyne not wanting to get into the ring with him ever again. The Santo Claus match that we had planned for the December 1999 show was in jeopardy. If Corgan's bloodlust had scuttled that match, I'd be up shit creek with Audra. Bringing Corgan back was still my bright idea. I had to call Corgan and make him understand that not everyone — particularly not Paul — shared the idea that getting crippled in the ring was a glorious thing. Corgan paid little attention, and kept arguing for some weird non-sequitur shit involving a run-in from the Easter Bunny. It wasn't going to be just any Easter Bunny, but a hardcore/extreme Easter Bunny. None of this made sense because nobody had a rabbit costume. I had to dig in and hold my turf. I had to remind him that he was back in the show on shaky ground and he was already stirring up shit and it had to stop.

After an hour of aneurysm inducing blather about hardcore Easter bunnies, Corgan finally calmed down and agreed to do the match the way that Paul wanted it. That was a good thing. Jose in the Santo Claus outfit was always a crowd pleaser and, as crack pipe toting Santa's helpers, Super Pulga and Rasputin the burnt-out midget went over big. Seeing the shoddy Christmas combo crushed by the animals went over even bigger. It was one of the better Van Dyne ideas.

For that holiday-themed ISW show, I brought back Dante the Baptist for an End-times match against the Whore of Babylon herself: the Poontangler. I was trying not to wrestle anymore but I had to do this match with all of that Y2K hysteria whipping all the end of the world types into a frenzy. Some ideas were just too good to pass up no matter how out of shape you were. This bout was the sprawling "Quo Vadis" of Dante matches. Its cast of thousands included the Poontangler, Dennis Erectus, Flamius Caesar and the Lion. I hurled a Styrofoam boulder at the lion and slammed the cross down on the Poontangler. I convinced one of the lighting guys at the Fillmore to kill the house lights and shine a single spotlight on me. It gave me the strength of God and allowed me to defeat the "Harlot of All Nations" that was the Poontangler. It was the only time that I ever beat the Poontangler and it took divine intervention to do it.

We had no way of knowing it at the time, but Tigger was barely two weeks pregnant with Craig's baby during that religious spectacle match. Nine months later, she gave birth to a beautiful daughter. During those months we tastelessly exploited her visible condition for a surreal series of paternity test skits that involved Count Dante, Dennis Erectus and the Sheik of Physique as the potential papas. After the kid was born, Rasputin the midget, swaddled in a bonnet and fuzzy jammies, played Poontangler's baby. In ISW, nothing was sacred.

But leading up to that Christmas show, I had to play the part of backroom dealmaker. I played both sides against the middle the way that I always had in ISW, only this time I wasn't undercutting competing scenesters that I didn't give a shit about. This time I was politicking with people who were my friends. Van Dyne would have rather gotten rid of Corgan right then and there, but the show needed both of them. Making matters worse, Corgan wasn't going to give up the Sasquatch suit. With his wild risk-taking, he was making Macho Sasquatcho more popular than ever. He pulled off top rope moves and dragon moonsaults. The fans started chanting for him because of his foolhardiness. Audra and I both agreed to keep Corgan in that suit with little regard for the ninety-nine bucks that Van Dyne had shelled out for it.

My friendship with Paul Van Dyne suffered after that. We were cordial to each other but things were never the same as when we used to slam down beers and thumb through raunchy porn rags on road trips. I had sacrificed a friendship to keep our flea circus together. That was getting to be a habit with me.

I walked out of the Mexican restaurant and found my '63 Catalina wrapped around a Mission Street telephone pole. In the time it took me to down a plate of chorizo enchiladas, some asshat in a '79 Grand Prix had done a hard U-turn into my parked car and pushed it onto the curb and into the pole. Unlike the Starfire, I had a half-decent policy on this baby. The insurance company gave me nearly $4,000 for my totaled four-door sedan with two-tone vinyl seats. It was finally time to put out my record.

*The Deadliest Man Alive* by Count Dante and the Black Dragon Fighting Society was recorded in a couple of days by Bart Thurber at House of Faith Recording Studios in Oakland. Bart is the Mother Theresa of rock bands with no money. His life's mission is to give the Bay Area's oddest bands that big analog sound on shoestring budgets. Craig Martins did the cover art. He made Ed, Andy and me all look like *Jonny Quest*–era Hanna Barbera cartoons. Suzy Ming posed with me on the back cover to make me look good.

Around this time, the Black Dragon Fighting Society of Fall River, Massachusetts, crawled out of the woodwork again. They had gotten a lawyer this time but they hadn't gone and filed anything in court yet. I had 1,000 discs spread out between my practice space and my mom's garage (which was a lot for me). I couldn't really turn around and change the name now. Fortunately, I had an attorney friend from one of my downtown temp jobs. She took on the case pro bono and sent some letters back and forth with the Massachusetts lawyer. We were locked in a legal game of chicken. It costs about $100,000 to pursue trademark cases in court and none of us had it. In the end, their attorney agreed with my attorney and thought that something could be worked out. I didn't hear from the Fall River Black Dragons for quite a while until I got the following e-mail…

From : <Officer80@aol.com>
Subject : YOU PHONEY BASTARD

I challenge you to fight to the death, hand to hand, I was a student of Count D'ante, second generation, You should have respect for the dead, FOR HE DIED IN THE 1970'S Name the place and time winner take all, And the name that

Count Dante calling the matches at the Fillmore.

The Count with the ever-fetching Suzy Ming.

Waving copies of *Dianetics*, Scientologist boy band
69 Degrees delivers the word of L. Ron to the masses.

Chango Loco slams
the Chicano Flame
with an X-factor in
a match that raised
1sw's work rate by
leaps and bounds at
the Fillmore in 1999.

Risa de Muerte and
Gran Fangorio double
team a member of
69 Degrees through
a table at Homomania
in October 2001.

ISW promoter Audra Morse demonstrates her unique managerial style at the Mission High School (San Francisco) benefit show on February 21, 1998.

69 Degrees always had their female fans despite consistently being booked as closet homosexual heels.

On a canvas covered with corn tortillas, leather daddy grappler the Cruiser shoves his barely covered crotch into the face of Dancin' Joey from 69 Degrees at the Fillmore on August 18, 2000.

After a hard fought battle with Dead Man Walking, the Cruiser gets put through a table onto the filthy floor of the Fillmore. Note the beer cups and tortilla debris.

ISW fans at ringside work themselves into a tortilla tossing frenzy.

Pelted by a hail of tortillas, San Jose shock jock Dennis Erectus slams Dante with a steel chair to prove that he is the father of the Poontangler's child.

Way up high! Super Pulga leaps off the top rope onto
Macho Sasquatcho on August 18, 2000, at the Fillmore.

Macho Sasquatcho makes his way into the ring.

Macho and Sassy Sasquatcho.

With costumes that were often as provocative as the wrestlers', the thrashy garage rock outfit The Demonics were a frequent ISW opening band.

LEFT: The Dickies (with singer Leonard Graves Phillips hiding his trademark phallic puppet behind his back) headlining ISW at the Fillmore on December 11, 1999.

BELOW: More highflying action as The Man from M.O.N.K. battles . . . The Man from M.O.N.K.

LEFT: The Poontangler at the Fillmore.

Being the Count has
its privileges.

During his debut match, the Devil Chicken gets jabbed in the beak by El Gourmexico at the Transmission Theatre in April 1998.

(Photo: Brandi Valenza)

## Rear Entry!

CLOCKWISE FROM TOP LEFT: El Homo Loco grabs an unwilling Dennis Erectus from behind. The Cock Fight: El Homo Loco vs. El Pollo Diablo at the Fillmore. The Cruiser demonstrates his unique take on Greco-Roman wrestling on Libido Gigante. El Homo Loco prances and poses on a tortilla covered mat. The Cruiser comes to the aid of his on-and-off-again lover, El Homo Loco (note the milk jug labeled "CUM").

The Oi Boy glares at
his audience.

The flier for one of ISW's Mission High
School benefit shows.

El Gran Fangorio stretches his opponent's neck with a hangman's noose during ISW's only barbed wire match on October 24, 1999.

L'Empereur slams U.S. Steele's head into the turnbuckle.

The Poontangler lapdances the ref.

Tortillas fly at the burning cross of the Ku Klux Klown.

After being hit with a steel chair, Count Dante starts
to regain consciousness.

The cross of Dante the Baptist pins the Poontangler
at the climax of the End of Times Match at the Fillmore.

In the upper left-hand corner of this pic, promoter Audra Morse beams with pride as she stands flanked by her show's odd assortment of flaming gays, gutter sluts, tunic clad Christians, inbred abominations and men in monkey suits.

ISW group shots taken on December 11, 1999.

doesn't belong to you, I'll prove it with my techniques

Sincerely: William E. Maine 3rd

William E. Maine 3$^{rd}$ really hated using periods, but he loved commas. I thought of copy-editing his hand-to-hand death match challenge and sending it back to him but I was just happy to be done with these guys.

I bought a 1977 Dodge van from a Santa Cruz indie rocker. Supposedly the Fucking Champs had used the thing once. It had two blown cylinders but it had the loft area built into it to hide our equipment. I booked a short run up to Oregon. Andy called me two days before we were going to leave claiming that he had broken his hand in a construction accident. Ed said that it was probably a self-inflicted wound to keep from going on the tour. Craig knew the songs already and he could get the time off work from his Sausalito web design job. He filled in on a moment's notice. With no time to practice, we hauled ass up to Oregon.

We played John Henry's in Eugene. Craig and I had good memories of the place from when isw did that show up there in 1997. That club looks a lot more packed when you have a wrestling ring taking up most of its floor space. After the show, the kid who booked us wanted to take us back to some house party. The kid kept asking us if we could "handle parties with real rock stars." Craig and I had already done shows at the Fillmore by this point. James Hetfield wanted me to kill the fags. Of course we could handle parties with real rock stars. We were real rock stars — kind of.

On the van ride over to the party, the guy kept talking about how Steve Perry was going to be there. He said it over and over again. Finally, after getting sick of hearing the guy's country-assed chatter, I pulled the van to the side of the road, looked him square in the eye and said, "You really fucking mean to tell me that Steve Perry from Journey is going to be at this place?"

The kid was crushed. I had rained hailstones the size of golf balls on his parade. He tried to play it off like I must've been joking, but I wasn't. In my book, there's only one Steve Perry that rates rock star status and that's the Steve Perry from Journey. It turned out that there was some guy from the Cherry Poppin' Daddies named Steve Perry. He was Eugene's closest thing to a local rock star. The kid thought we would be really impressed with this. We weren't.

The next day, I traded a copy of my CD for a cassette of *Journey's Greatest Hits* at a used record store before we left Eugene. We played the shit out of it as we drove through the Cascades. We joked about the Macho Man pulling over and bursting into tears while listening to "Faithfully." This floated our sleep-deprived boat for hours.

With Audra's help, I booked some shows in Southern California. We played Linda's Doll Hut in Anaheim. From the club's parking lot you could see the fireworks over Disneyland. Inside, the joint was crawling with Nazi skinheads whose bodies were covered in swastika tattoos and Wehrmacht eagles. Not that we wanted to please a bunch of psycho Orange County Nazi fucks, but they were all over the place. We wanted to get out of there alive and I had to take the stage in my fruity assed leopard skin kimono. We went on anyway. I ripped into my success seminar spiel. The racist skins went apeshit for us. They started hieling me and grunting like apes. Their fascist mindset had no end of respect for my fiery oratory. I sold a ton of CDs to them but later sent the money to the Anti-Defamation League.

I pushed CDs off on any independent record store that would take them. I received a pile of rejection letters from indie labels. Jello Biafra told me that he "liked some of it and hated some of it." I was also enough of an oddity to keep getting ink in the papers. That seemed to be all anything amounted to: ink in the papers. But I was a ham. I loved seeing my mug in print and those write-ups were more than enough to keep me banging my head against the wall.

I was putting my life on hold for my rock and wrestling dreams. It was hard to worry about some pissant career strapping yourself

HOT MAN ON MAN ACTION

into a cubicle after you had worked in front of a sold out crowd at the Fillmore. Those brushes with fame fuck with you. Billie Joe Armstrong of Green Day once walked up to me at a Fillmore show and talked to me for five solid minutes about how great ISW was. Green Day sold out the Fillmore just like ISW had done multiple times. But *Dookie* moved millions of records so Billie Joe didn't have to worry about things like filling out a job application or putting away for his retirement. I did, but chose not to.

I kept working temp jobs when I could get them. I never committed to anything because anything substantial might get in the way of the wrestling show, emceeing the peep shows or touring with the band. I didn't pass go. I didn't collect two hundred bucks. All too often, I desperately needed those rolls of chocolate covered one-dollar bills that had been crammed underneath Tigger LeTwang's tremendous tits that I'd received as payment for barking the peep shows. Those singles were sometimes the difference between boiling another potato or actually springing for a plate of greasy chow fun for lunch the next day.

In order to supplement my income as much as anything else, I started using my connections in the local entertainment scene to pitch articles to newspapers and magazines. I sold some stories, making anywhere from twenty-five bucks for trite little website concert previews to $500 for a feature on the desert rock scene that begat Queens of the Stone Age. Writing wasn't so much about those tiny little checks that took forever to come. It was something that I'd wanted to do ever since I was old enough to figure out who Stan Lee was. It became the first thing that I'd done outside of my square jobs that wasn't totally joined at the hip with the wrestling show.

I was a wrestler, writer and musician, but during my day-to-day existence I was kind of pathetic. This moved Dana to move in with me. She gave up living in her dad's million-dollar spread nestled on the hillside of Mount Tamalpais on the ritzy side of the Golden Gate Bridge to live in my rundown studio apartment. She worked a whole hell of a lot more consistently than I did, so it saved my ass. She also took my rattrap of a room and made it look like somewhere you'd actually want to sit down in. Amazing.

Still, she had trouble keeping jobs as she was bounced around by the dot-coms. The dot-com days were the era of enforced fun. Every new media company prided itself on its kooky rooms with beanbag chairs and ping-pong tables, only they weren't so kooky when every company had them. The atmosphere at these offices started to be more cult-like, where employees were pressured into going to ever growing numbers of work parties and movie nights. If you had a real life outside of your Internet job, your co-workers reacted to it like something out of *The Crucible* or *Invasion of the Body Snatchers*. Not attending the weekly Friday night happy hour get together with the same Gap-clad clones that you had been looking at all day was tantamount to heresy. Dana actually lost a job once for not joining her dot-com's bowling team. She "didn't fit into the corporate culture," she was told. Some of that was my fault. I was working the peep shows and the wrestling shows. I had a life of my own and couldn't go to all this happy bullshit that her soon-to-be-gone startup had mandated.

I still lived in somewhat elective poverty, but by 2000 the streets of San Francisco were no longer paved with gold. The inevitable bust had happened. The people who were running around town flashing their plastic claiming to be "new millionaires" a few months earlier were now having their BMWs repoed, selling off their high end stereo systems and moving back with their moms in the Midwest. The clubs that had been closed to make way for the extra office space were still closed. Now they were just empty offices instead of shut down rock clubs. The lofts that couldn't be built fast enough only months before now mostly sat empty.

During the boom, I had tried to convince Audra to put together a business proposal in order to secure a line of venture capital. All we would have had to say is that we were going to "put wrestling on the... Internet." We could've secured seven figures that way. Dumber things were attracting that kind of dough even as late as 1999, but ISW was too lame to even have a website. Psychotic teenagers who belted each other with tackboards in Tracy, California, had the technical ingenuity to create Geocities pages for their backyard wrestling federations, but ISW, with a roster that included web animators and professional journalists, couldn't manage this. At least we still had the Fillmore.

Everyone hated Rasputin the midget. Nobody hated him more than the Mexicans. Rasputin was a Haight Ashbury burnout with coarse gray hair and tangled strands of a scraggly white beard dotting his chin. But Rasputin was valuable because midgets were hard to come by. The hardcore wrestling midgets who put staples through each others' heads and threw themselves onto mats covered with thumbtacks wanted at least a thousand bucks just for getting anywhere near a wrestling ring. The more traditional midget wrestlers wanted nothing to do with our tortilla throwing bullshit. Rasputin was the only midget that ISW could find and ISW needed a midget.

The Mexicans hated him because he drank all the beer and said really lewd shit to Paul Van Dyne's sister. He also had the habit of telling people to fuck off for no reason. Anytime Rasputin got into the ring with Jose or Boris, they beat the living shit out of him. Rasputin had to wrestle Jose and Boris a lot. The Mexicans always wanted matches with Rasputin so they could pummel him for ten solid minutes. Poor Rasputin didn't have another foul-mouthed midget that he could be paired with. The Mexicans specialized in tossing tiny Rasputin over the top rope as hard as they could. They aimed for gaps in the crowd so Rasputin would be sure to hit hardwood.

Rasputin must have had bones like a rat. His skeletal structure expanded and contracted but it never broke. You know how midgets and dwarves always have super strength for some unexplained reason in old horror movies? Well, it's true. Any average-sized man would have been put in the hospital from any one of the beatings that the Mexicans dished out to isw's lone little person.

It was an afternoon show at Shoreline Amphitheatre, forty miles south of San Francisco in the strip mall saturated suburbs of Mountain View. The concert was sponsored by underperforming modern rock station Live 105 and it featured a murderer's row of excruciating MTV friendly alternative acts on the main stage such as Limp Bizkit, Stone Temple Pilots, Moby, Offspring and Third Eye Blind.

As a forecast of isw's future place in the entertainment world, we were a fairway sideshow. The ring was tucked between some extreme sports bullshit and a Howard Stern booth with Hank the bitter drunken dwarf (another overpriced midget if ever there was one) and Crackhead Bob. Other sections of the side stage area were clogged with tables staffed by the remnants of dying dot-coms who were hoping to secure another line of venture capital by gathering as much marketing info on the emerging tween demographic as possible. Lanyards and other cheap crap made by Chinese prison labor were handed out to kids who took the time to fill out questionnaires. Rock and roll was now nothing more than a marketing tool. Concerts increasingly resembled trade shows.

As the ring was being set up, Boris picked up Rasputin by the feet and dragged him face first through a mud puddle for no reason whatsoever. When Rasputin held his head up and gasped, "You fucking asshole," Boris just picked him up over his meaty shoulder and slammed Rasputin down in the mud.

Before the show, Pauly Shore was walking around. I had no idea what he was selling. Wasn't Mr. T available? Talk about sub-has-been status. As the ring started to come together it called to Fred Durst of Limp Bizkit like a white trash bug light. He strutted around the squared circle with his entourage wearing his trademark red baseball cap turned backwards. He wanted to get into our ring really bad. It was like the Banjo Minnow fishing system. He was compelled to strike. One of his security guys used to wrestle for Jerry Lawler out of Memphis. Shane agreed to work out a match with the guy and have Durst come in at the end and lay Shane out with one punch. It was paint-by-numbers pro-wrestling celebrity ass-kissing.

Durst's roadie was nearly seven feet of solid muscle by the name of Tom A. Hawk. He later wrestled in the WWE under the name Tyson Tomko. During their match, he tossed Shane around as if he were the midget, but Shane was enough of a pro to be able to handle it — barely. Needless to say, Shane didn't get to mount much offense.

When the one-sided match ended, Shane was supposed to complain about a quick count like a crybaby. Then Durst was supposed to get into the ring and do that one punch knockout but Fred had the attention span of a rap metal rock star or a mayfly on meth. First he wanted to get into the ring and now he didn't. I had nothing to do but chide him on the microphone, expecting him to show us all up by getting into the ring. "Come on, Fred, let's see your cred! Your mama shops at K-Mart!!!" I said. I ran through a laundry list of every fourth grade playground put-down that I could think of. I even uncorked the timeless gem: "You're moded, corroded and your booty exploded."

Fred hightailed it back to the celebrity lounge and left me there ripping on him for five solid minutes in front of a cluster of his ass-licking hangers on. It was easily 90 degrees out there in the South Bay but Durst's crew all wore big black Raiders jackets because they thought that made them look cool. One of them pulled the mic out of my hands and started yelling at me with tears in his eyes. Our wiseassed security guy Gabriel remarked that the surprised look on my face made it look like the guy had yanked off my dick. The wrestlers fell in behind me. Luckily that Tom A. Hawk guy had left with his boss. We were only facing the bullshitters who spent Durst's money so nothing was exchanged but swear words.

Later on, the unbroken cycle of humiliation and brutalization of little Rasputin continued, as he had to climb into the ring wearing a kid's Pokémon Halloween costume to square off against Dead Man Walking. Dead Man hated Rasputin even more than the rest of the Mexicans. For the next fifteen impossible to watch minutes the action in the ring wasn't staged. It wasn't a work. It was a very large jailhouse hack pummeling a diminutive and mostly helpless hippie. Dead Man's fists were as big as canned hams and he sent them crashing into Rasputin's pliable skull. Dead Man effortlessly folded Rasputin and his bright yellow Pikachu suit into painfully disjointed positions and then power slammed the midget into the mat for good measure. Dead Man put every last ounce of his 260-pound frame into every blow and body slam.

Finally, the beating came to a close. There were other matches still to come and we had a schedule to keep. A red-faced Rasputin pulled off his cute costume and yelled, "Fuck you" at Dead Man as he exited the ring.

Audra was understandably pissed while Jose and Boris chuckled in the background. "Big man," she said as Dead Man pushed his way through the ring ropes, "Big man."

When Dead Man put that beating on Rasputin he thought that it would make the little man leave the wrestling show for good, but nobody ever left the wrestling show. Chango Loco couldn't even leave the wrestling show behind when he was tossed out of it. Before ISW, Chango really didn't care for pro wrestling or lucha libre any more than he did for the rest of the pop culture waste that cluttered his consciousness. After three years in that rundown ring, he lived and breathed lucha libre like some kind of cocaine addicted lab rat from a really heinous Stanford mind control experiment.

After his banishment from ISW, there was nothing left for him to do but start his own promotion. It was called SF Lucha Libre (SFLL for short) and his driving goal was to show how phony and "un-lucha" ISW really was. He denounced ISW at every turn. He got Johnny Legend to emcee his first show at this cumbia joint on Mission Street just to needle Audra a little bit further. He even called up a *San Francisco Chronicle* reporter who had just written a piece about one of our Fillmore shows and spent a half hour badgering the guy about how ISW "wasn't really wrestling." The reporter told Chango to write a letter to the editor. Chango never did.

But Chango did put on some pretty good lucha shows for a while there. From a pure lucha libre standpoint, they were the real deal and ISW wasn't. Chango somehow hooked up with Rey Mysterio Sr. and got top-shelf Mexican talent like Hijo De Santo, Blue Panther and even Mil Mascaras to work his shows. The best South of the Border worker that Audra had ever wrangled was a Tijuana transvestite named Ruby Gardeña. She wasn't as much a crowd pleaser in the ring as she was backstage where she tried to go for the pin or the submission on young Manny Franklin. Manny summoned up some broken Spanish to try to hold the lascivious luchadore at bay. "No, no, *mi novia, mi amor*," he said desperately. Franklin, being quick on his feet, managed to get away from Gardeña, who was later seen necking with a member of the band Bottles+Skulls who either didn't know about the extra appendage that the wrestling queen was carrying or didn't much care.

For some reason Chango's attempts to expose ISW got to Audra. Part of it was that Chango Loco was one crazy motherfucker who was probably cooking up Santeria curses on all of us all of the time, but another part of it was that Audra was never the total carnival huckster that she needed to be. She still cared too much about being cool in those narrow 1990s parameters. Being exposed for not "being lucha" actually hurt her.

ISW didn't need the high and mighty work rate required of lucha libre to keep our fans coming back for more. As long as Tom Corgan and Cruiser Craig were willing to put their asses through tables and Manny Franklin and Super Pulga could pull off some high-flying moves here and there, we had just enough wrestling to justify our haphazard existence. Also, by the time that the Fillmore shows really got cooking, we had a much needed defector from the ranks of the indie-wrestling scene.

His name was Timothy Newhall. He was the top-rated sales-man of aftermarket German auto parts in the Northern California region. During his off hours, he pranced around the wrestling ring in full Napoleonic garb as the vile, anti-American heel known as L'Empereur. His Bonaparte drag came complete with gold braiding on his wrestling boots, epaulets on his 17th century General's jacket, tri-color shorty-shorts and sideways hat with the proper plumage. He spoke with an atrocious French accent and didn't even know enough of the language to pepper his wrestling speeches with it. Of course not knowing a shred of a language that you are supposed to speak fluently is an American wrestling tradition that harkens back to the French-Canadians who were impressed into service by ruth-less promoters as evil Soviets, or the hulking Hawaiian-Chinese guys who had to play the part of shifty salt-throwing Japs during wrestling's race-baiting past.

L'Empereur was a total fitness nut who moonlighted as a personal trainer at a really steroid-heavy bayside gym that wasn't all that far from Victor Conte's BALCO HQ in those days before Congressional steroid investigations. L'Empereur kept himself on a rigidly enforced regimen of ten "baby meals" a day in order to kick-start his metabolism, and he got downright cranky if he missed his "nappie." He used to wrestle for Roland Alexander's APW and he could regale us with tales of their ineptly run workouts, which were monitored by obese wrestling wannabes who spent more time munching taquitos than they did hitting the gym.

L'Empereur had thought he'd had left wrestling behind him, but his little Napoleon suit still hung in his closet and he still had a stack of 8" x 10" promo pics on his desk. The allure of working an ISW show in front of over a thousand people proved to be too much for him to resist. In order to secure his slot on our shows, he volunteered to whip our sorry asses into shape.

L'Empereur convinced Audra to allow him to set up the ISW ring at his gym in the weeks leading up to another Fillmore show. We had regular practices, which I mostly avoided because I'd been even more bloated and out of shape than I was three years earlier and I honestly never planned on getting back into the ring again. Sure, I'd eat a chair shot every now and then because the fans wanted to see me abused, but I didn't have the drive that Craig and Corgan seemed to have to jump off ladders.

At the training sessions I did attend, L'Empereur could never get me to do a forward somersault. I would do the shoulder roll version that I learned in martial arts because your head was never in any danger of touching the mat, but doing the classic forward roll was out for me. Yes, I was a pussy. Dead Man Walking also refused to do the forward roll for much the same reason. There was something about being fat and in your thirties that just made you not want to do that move anymore. I could at least show some guys how to do an armlock or neckcrank and make it look real. The one time that Jefferson Monroe showed one of the wrestlers a triangle choke, he actually knocked the guy totally unconscious with it, sending L'Empereur into a tizzy.

Paul Van Dyne excelled at the training but, oddly, chose not to utilize any of it in the ring. He had developed a growing disdain for wrestling in general and believed that he could just go out there in those strange suits of his and wave to the fans like he was on a float in a parade. Paul's new motionless approach to wrestling violated hard and fast rules of squared circle performance. The visual power of the chicken suit kept Paul from having to go through tables or set himself on fire to get the fans behind him, but he at least had to do some ridiculous rooster strut en route to slamming his opponents. The costume couldn't do all of the work for him.

L'Empereur taught us how pro wrestling was basically a complex system of hand signals. If you grabbed your opponent a certain way, it meant that you were going to do a certain move. Pro wrestling was more developed than any of us could have ever gleaned from the way that we had previously gone about things. All of us got better because of L'Empereur. Even the ponderous Mexican Viking was endowed with the ability to get through a five-minute 1980s WWE style match. That was the style that L'Empereur taught us. He didn't teach us lucha or ECW extreme wrestling. He just taught us this well-grounded, old school method that probably kept some guys from breaking their necks. As a result of the grappling Bonaparte's labors, those days of ISW wrestlers standing there not knowing what to do next were largely over.

The only problem was that L'Empereur drove Audra up the wall. He sent her multi-paged faxes outlining his plans for the show. On the day of a show he stupidly painted the ring posts without asking for her permission and they were still wet when the doors opened. He was a busybody and a fuss-budget and this made Audra decide to humiliate him whenever an opportunity presented itself while getting as much out of him as she possibly could. She dressed him down in public and had other wrestlers interfere in his matches without him knowing about it beforehand. She made sure that he lost every match that he worked in ISW and he always had to work harder than the rest of us to pry his fifty bucks from Audra. Sometimes he never got paid at all.

For the last training session that L'Empereur ran he couldn't secure a space big enough to set up the ring so we had to make do with tumbling around the floors of my Mission District dojo. The mats were crowded as incredibly strange wrestlers lined up to do drills before they paired off to work on the finer points of their upcoming matches as best they could without the benefit of ring ropes. About twenty minutes into the session, Audra burst through the doors and proceeded to curse out everyone for no reason whatsoever.

"You people need to fucking practice," she bellowed to a room full of wrestlers who were already practicing. "I am not putting up with any more shitty wrestling," she huffed at such a high volume that even the shoppers at the Safeway next door probably heard it. After laying down laws that didn't need to be laid down to a bunch of guys who were giving up their Wednesday night to make her show just a little bit better, she left as quickly as she had stormed in. Her outburst pretty much killed the spirit of cooperation for the evening.

One of my senseis was hanging out in the dojo to make sure that the big bad fake wrestlers didn't drink all the beer he kept in a mini fridge under the front counter. "Why do you guys put up with that?" he asked.

"That's Audra," I answered. "That's just Audra."

Like the rest of San Francisco, Craig Martins lost his web design job. He was one of the luckier ones though. He had an offer to go and work for a fledging videogame cable network that was starting up on the Disney lot in Burbank. He and Tigger had a daughter. They had to go where the money was and there wasn't a whole lot of money for cartoonists and 2-D animators in the Bay Area after the dot bomb. But even with Hollywood dreams being waved in his face, Craig couldn't leave the ring behind — partially because of the addiction that we all suffered from and because Audra wouldn't allow him and Tigger to escape. The Poontangler was right up there with El Homo Loco as far as the fans went. Losing her would have been a big blow to the show. Both the Cruiser and the Poontangler were valuable enough for Audra to part with the dough to fly their asses up to SF for the all-important Fillmore shows. Audra had deals on the table. She couldn't go futzing with her cast now.

On their way out of town, Craig and Tigger somehow swung Dana and I the rental on their house on the Southern outskirts of San Francisco. Their landlord was a low-level Tony Robbins–inspired property monger so he was financed to the gills and couldn't afford to lose even one month's rent. He let us move right in.

The house was tiny and would be called a railroad shack if there were only train tracks close by. But it was a palace compared to our downtown studio apartment and besides, downtown had changed. The dot-coms were closed but the gentrification continued. The Giants' new ballpark had been built and was open for business. At first it was called Pac Bell Park, but its corporate benefactor has since changed names three times and the big sign hanging over the park's front entrance has come down with each new branding direction.

Living close to the ballpark started to suck. Before and after the ballgames, Third Street was clogged with fair-weather yuppie fans who filled the stadium to talk on their cellphones while they ignored the game that some biotech firm had paid for. With the new ballpark in town, the meter maids were ruthless in towing cars for the most minor infractions. Living downtown was starting to cost us an extra 200 bucks a month in parking tickets and towing fees. The desolation speckled with sleaze that had drawn me to South of Market was now all but gone. It was time to leave.

Our new house had a driveway and a sloping backyard that was filled with waist-high weeds and feral cats. There were no fences between us and four of our neighbors. The Chicano kids to one side of us had barbeques every weekend and used so much lighter fluid in their Smokey Joe that they almost burned down half the block as they incinerated their Costco pre-pressed burger patties. To the right of us was an extended family of migrant Mexicans who grew corn in their section of the backyard but still hucked beer cans and other trash into their crops. The Nation of Islam delivered bean pies to our door and always seemed surprised that a cracker-ass like me wanted to buy them. They left *The Final Call* sticking out of our mailbox each week, which helped keep the Jehovah's Witnesses and Mormons away. Even the most ardent evangelical proselytizer didn't want to deal with white people crazy enough to read Farrakhan's fish wrap. We started collecting cats. The cats knew us for suckers so they started flocking around our front doorsteps for a handout. We ended up with three cats that way.

We still didn't know who our president was. Was it Al Gore or that little beady-eyed Texican from New England? A lot of my friends voted for Ralph Nader as a way of protesting our increasingly one party system, but I just couldn't do it. It wasn't just any Republicans. It was *those* Republicans. Bush and Cheney represented the most megalomaniacal wing of a party that strove to create an American serf class under the best of circumstances. If bloodthirsty sociopaths like Bush and Cheney won the White House, they were probably going to put the Red Skull in charge of the Justice Department and make the Heat Miser Secretary of the Interior. And that's just what they did.

I had landed a job at the Worst Newspaper in the World so naturally I was in a media blackout during the biggest constitutional crisis since Watergate. The Worst Newspaper in the World wasn't always so bad, but the staunchly nationalist Chinese family who had recently acquired it from Charles Foster Kane didn't understand why a room full of reporters might need to access something like CNN from time to time. They wouldn't even foot the bill for basic cable let alone a boob tube to watch it on.

I had stayed up late the night before glued to Dan Rather's on-air meltdown as Gore had dared to throw a wrench in the works of GW's Fox News guaranteed coronation. Rather rambled on about frogs with side pockets and chewing shards of glass while Ed Bradley occasionally woke up and added something equally incoherent. But in the newsroom where I worked, I had no idea what was going on. Our Internet service worked only intermittently and the connection to the AP feed didn't work at all. There was a rather large black lady security guard with a pile of indestructible banana curls on her head who brought her own TV so she could watch crappy court shows and *Oprah* while she was on the job. Reporters looked at her portable set longingly but you didn't dare get between that woman and her *Oprah*.

TWNITW made me their head archivist as well as their only music reporter. It was a very odd combination of duties to be sure, but one that I was dumb enough to think I could handle. At first, the editors told me that I'd only have to spend a couple of hours a day archiving articles online and I could spend the rest of my time covering concerts and reviewing records. The editors were wrong. When the Chinese family took over the paper, they were also given the largest continuous archive ever amassed by Kane Enterprises. The collection comprised over 150 years of clippings files, photo files, microfilm, microfiche and hardcopy. It was divided up and warehoused in numerous spare Kane buildings throughout downtown San Francisco. When I informed the Chinatown matriarch about the enormity of the collection they had acquired, she and her handlers acted like I could just load it into the back of a mini-truck and drive it over on my lunch break.

When the first edition of TWNITW published by the new ownership hit the stands just before Thanksgiving weekend in 2000, its front page was littered with badly depixelated pictures, numerous typos and sentences that neither began nor ended. They didn't even get the day's date right. Soon just how horrible TWNITW was became a featured topic on NBC's *The Today Show*. Of course nobody in the newsroom knew about this because we still didn't have a television.

In editorial meetings, I overstepped my bounds and advocated turning TWNITW into San Francisco's version of the *New York Post*. The only way to salvage being an industry laughingstock was to become a sleazy tabloid. With San Francisco's collection of crooks and crazies calling the shots, the material for a good sleaze rag was definitely there. But nobody listened. My superiors clung to their delusions of becoming a respectable daily despite our paper's incredible quality deficit.

Paychecks got held up for weeks. When I needed paperclips or staples, my editors told me to buy them myself and expense it back to the paper. The problem was that I hadn't been paid in a month. I had no money. I couldn't even buy a cup of coffee with what was rattling around in my bank account, let alone a digital mini recorder.

Things started out weird at the TWNITW and kept getting weirder. Weeks went by. We still couldn't get paperclips. The CFO from the Chinatown office put up a horrendous fight every time anyone attempted to order writing pads or copier paper. We finally had Internet access but the off-brand page design software that the Chinese family had signed up for had the nasty habit of unexpectedly expunging all punctuation from submitted copy as it went to press. The paper was also plagued by delivery problems. We lost thirty percent of our subscribers during our first week of operation. At that rate, we'd lose all of our subscribers in less than a month. To add injury to insult, one of the paper's delivery trucks was involved in a fatal car crash in Salinas. "What the fuck is one of our trucks doing all the way down in goddamned Salinas when you can't even find the paper on Market Street?" the paper's managing editor quipped as he walked past my desk.

TWNITW was taking in water and rapidly sinking. Middle-aged editors almost came to blows in the hallways and the shouting got so loud that even the medicinal marijuana clinic downstairs started to complain. (Yes, TWNITW shared a building with a medical marijuana clinic, which does go a long way in explaining things.) Some reporters contemplated unionizing in the hopes that a newspaper guild contract would somehow force the paper to run more smoothly. Others braved the humiliation of begging for their old jobs at *Contra Costa Times* back.

For me, there was a shitstorm gathering over those archives that I was in charge of. By the time that a newshound from CBS called me about doing a story on the archives for *60 Minutes*, I decided that it was time to cut short my foray into inane journalism or risk becoming the public face of incompetence being grilled by Mike Wallace on early prime time network TV. My blood pressure probably went down by several points after I left the paper, but I was out of work again.

During the Fillmore years, ISW went from a monthly occurrence to a sporadic spectacle. We did maybe four shows a year there plus other random gigs like the one at Shoreline or a Mexican art show opening at the swank Yerba Buena Center for the Arts. Still, the Fillmore shows were all sellouts and the bar tabs were huge. The overall match quality had improved drastically and it was then that Craig and I were at our creative peak as the men who came up with the matches.

We had a boy band tag team with the throwaway name of 69 Degrees. Manny Franklin was Bad Boy Corey and a door guy at the cw was Dancin' Joey. They wore baggy camouflage pants and oversized shades and converted silly dance moves from old Kid 'N Play videos into leg drops and elbow smashes. When WWE and WCW trotted out their boy band parodies, Craig and I converted 69 to Scientology. Manny had been a Pentecostal youth pastor at one time and he put all of his evangelical skills to work preaching the word of L. Ron. 69 pelted their opponents with paperback copies of *Dianetics* that Audra had brazenly purchased from the downtown SF Scientology center. Manny delved deeply into *Dianetics* with a born-again's attention to chapter and verse, to the point where people believed that 69 really were Scientologists. When fans heckled them, Manny often retorted, "You people all have to free yourself from the reactive mind where fear and negative feelings are stored!"

ISW shows were fewer and farther between but ISW was enough of an oddity to land some impressive media coverage. 69 Degrees received a photo feature in the pages of *Teen People* of all things. A local TV station started doing news segments on the tortilla throwing wrestling, which were almost more of a headache than they were worth. After those puff pieces aired, legions of frat boys started showing up to ISW shows with garbage bags filled with Mi

Casa corn tortillas. In the Transmission Theatre days, a smattering of cornmeal wafers made its way into the ring. By late 2000, the air of the Fillmore was filled with corn dust and Bolte and I felt like we were announcing a wrestling card held during a sandstorm. We did a show with NOFX where you could barely see the ring from the stage as maize particles filled the air. By the second match of that show, the ring floor was ankle deep in a southwestern slush of masa harina and spilled *cerveza*.

This pissed the Fillmore people off to no end. They had to clean up that mess and were worried about stray tortillas taking out their newly restored chandeliers. Audra handled their concerns with her usual finesse, often treating the brass at the old Bill Graham wing of Clear Channel to the same kinds of tirades that her wrestlers had to put up with. I was the closest thing that ISW had to a second in command so I often found myself caught in the crossfire. Some middle managers from the Fillmore asked me how to deal with the tortillas and, more important, how to deal with Audra. I suggested that they have security confiscate the really egregious loads of tortillas that the Stanford jocks were bringing in. They needed to think of managing the tortillas rather than eliminating them. You had to have the tortillas. They were ISW's trademark.

My suggestions fell on deaf ears. Audra claimed it would be "un-punk rock" to do anything about the tortillas. The problem with that logic was that ISW stopped being punk the moment it set foot in the Fillmore. Like so much previously underground culture, our weird wrestling show had crossed over into the mainstream — at least locally. Hell, punk rock wasn't even punk anymore and we were on the verge of finding out firsthand just how un-punk punk had become.

# 15

# WARPED

AUDRA'S WINNING WAYS killed as many opportunities as she created but that woman could still deal. In early 2001, she landed us a slot on Vans Warped Tour that summer. Warped's marketing motif for that year centered around cartoon images of a flabby luchadore crushing skinny skater kids so we were brought along as the tour's mascots. ISW was there to add a touch of buffoonery to the extreme sports side of the traveling festival. Our ring was going to be sandwiched in between the skateboarders' half-pipe and the smattering of small stages that had become mandatory for the postmodern rock tour.

Warped was going to last nearly two months with ISW performing forty-five shows including several two week stretches without a day off. Audra swung us a fully loaded tour bus and $100 a day plus $20 per diems and meals. The tour was going to start in Phoenix, wrap around the West Coast, cut down through the Midwest, and come up through the South into the Northeast and Canada with our final date in Detroit. Peoples' pain thresholds were going to be pushed past their limits, but we were all still chasing the dream.

Warped's combination of third generation punk, skateboarding, mass marketing and earnest activism was the brainchild of Kevin Lyman, a longtime music business insider who worked his way up from the clubs to command one of rock's most bankable road shows. Lyman was a meek, bespectacled man who looked more like a programmer for Apple than a millionaire concert mogul. He often mused during press interviews that he'd rather be a schoolteacher and he even taught a music business course at Claremont College in southern California as a penance for his profits.

While other summer festival tours such as Lollapalooza and Gathering of the Tribes had come and gone, Warped was the closest thing to perennial in the business. Lyman attributed Warped's success to holding the ticket prices down — first at $14.95 and later to $25. Instead of gouging vendors to sell shirts and posters, Lyman invited the representatives from the smaller record labels and the bands themselves to do it with more reasonable markups. The tour also provided a slew of smaller stages for unsigned acts. Young bands followed the tour in broken-down vans in the hopes of getting a shot at those lower tier stages and landing that elusive record deal. This more open approach allowed Lyman to keep his finger on the pulse of his audience and promote new acts in the process. If superstardom for brain-dead bubblegum like Good Charlotte resulted, it was because that's what the kids wanted.

At its best, Warped was a postmodern return to vaudeville with bands, skaters and other risk-taking roustabouts barnstorming across the country on a shoestring budget. At its worst, it was a marketing fuckfest where Target, Pontiac and Powerade used the show's openness to make so many ruthless corporations look cool to kids. Marketing was Lyman's Faustian bargain. No matter how heartless the scum sucking bastards of corporate America got, it was reasoned that the merger of teen rebellion and Wall Street would do little to harm rock and roll.

"The kids love marketing," one of the vendors told me during a late night Warped Tour bullshit session.

"The '60s ain't coming back," he explained, "the kids just love getting free swag too much. We all do."

For the two months that Incredibly Strange Wrestling was on the Vans Warped Tour our home was a Prevost bus conversion, all polished chrome and aluminum and trimmed with purple steel. It slept eighteen people but only barely. Wrestlers and crew were crammed into tiny berths and at night legs and arms jutted out into the aisle from behind beige curtains.

Due to my expanding waistline, I got to take the back lounge area for my bunk. It was easily converted into a bed. While it gave me extra sleeping space, I often found my bed cluttered with joysticks, videogame cartridges, other peoples' socks, wrestling boots and empty beer bottles. It was the flotsam and jetsam of a rock and wrestling tour, and I had to sleep with it.

Larry was our bus driver and spirit guide for our journey across George Bush's newly minted America. He was a lanky, gray-haired born-again from southern Alabama. He kept Christian broadcasting cranked up in the drivers' compartment as he moved us from venue to venue in the dead of night. He often took his hands off the wheel to give that horizontal palm, most-high Jesus freak salute during key moments of whatever regional preacher's sermon we happened to be passing through. Larry had a picture of a weeping Jesus on his business cards and a "Jesus Saves" license plate. He also had an assortment of psalms and other biblical verses hand stenciled onto the various T-shirts he'd gotten from driving for previous tours. The Pennywise shirt he often wore with little bits of ironed-on scripture looked pretty fucking strange.

During our nightly interstate journeys, Larry kept his pedal to the metal and drove by brail, pushing his oversized coach to speeds past 90 mph whether on crooked mountain roads or flat plains highways. If Larry took unnecessary risks with our lives it was because he knew that he was going to a better place if he wrecked. The rest of us weren't so sure. We just wanted to get to Cleveland in one piece. The other bus drivers nicknamed Larry "Rocket Man," and he got us to each venue at least an hour before anyone else arrived.

Getting to an arena early had advantages that were worth risking our lives over. The showers were still in working order before the hundreds of semi-pro skateboarders, extreme athletes, roadies and happy punk bands that were part and parcel of the Warped Tour rendered them inoperable. Sometimes, no matter how dirty you were, you took one look at those showers and decided that you'd only get dirtier if you actually tried to wash yourself. Being the first one into those stalls was key. Also, getting there early allowed you the luxury of taking a shit before thousands of fourteen-year-old skater punks squirted piss and diarrhea all over them. Finding a clean place to take a crap became a daily issue. I got really excited when a venue was walking distance from a public library because that meant free Internet access, clean toilets and most of all, quiet.

The mania for finding secure and secluded commodes grew even more acute after our slick-haired security guy, Gabriel, went to take a leak at the Flying J and found a bearded trucker jerking off in the men's room. Gabriel came back to the bus shell-shocked and looking like he'd just gotten back from an extended tour of duty in Baghdad. Wrestlers entered truck stop shitters very carefully after that.

I spent the early morning hours of the first working day of the tour hunched over the elongated toilet bowl in my room at the Phoenix Ramada. I hurled about a half gallon of whiskey and followed that up with a salvo of partially digested refried beans and two pork chimichangas that felt as if they had somehow reformed into their original shapes in my stomach. Those refried beans and their accompanying layer of lard had failed to hold my boozy barf at bay. I fumbled for my toothbrush to chase the taste of upchuck out of my mouth and tried to figure out why my greasy safety measures had failed me.

"The blunts," I thought. "It had to be the blunts."

Manny Franklin had rolled them out of cheap shake weed and even cheaper cherry-soaked King Edward Cigars as we all partied down in Tom Corgan's hotel room the night before. "Why are you smoking that weed that way?" Gino, our longhaired Brooklynite tour manager, asked as he watched Manny form the turd-like spleefs.

"It's ghetto weed," Manny answered, "so you've gotta smoke it ghetto style."

Gino, a veteran of many rock tours, was stunned into a rare silence by Manny's cogent philosophy. Manny's retort was a ringing endorsement for smoking those godawful things. We all toked heavily off them and drank with a fury born of success and recognition. Even as a sideshow, we'd hit the big time. From a tiny dark room at the Transmission Theatre, we were now embarking on one of the biggest tours of the summer concert season. And as a sideshow, we stood out. Twenty or thirty bands tended to blend together, but there was only one wrestling show, and it was us. Who knew where it might lead?

Everyone was getting along. The indie workers got along with the ISW amateurs. Shane, the wrestler that we once collectively feared, was now our best friend because we were all going to be in the same boat, or at least the same bus. We bullshitted about the inner torment of Ric Flair and the Macho Man as we pounded beers, slammed shots and smoked Manny's giant-sized joints until early the next morning.

It was those blunts. I should have never touched those things.

After scrubbing my teeth and taking a shower, I poked my head out of the bathroom to wake up Craig, but my barrage of barf had already done that.

"It sounded like a shotgun going off in there," he muttered as he held a pillow over half of his head.

Craig was my perpetual roommate on those few days that we were fortunate enough to have a hotel room. This arrangement only exacerbated Dana's fears back home that I was going to come out of the closet and start shacking up with Craig. This dread was justified by the fact that her father had done just that to her mother many years before. It was furthered by the bi-curious nature of the whole pro wrestling enterprise where its standard bearer "Stone Cold" Steve Austin, always clad in his black shorts and little leather vest, was woefully unaware of how gay he looked even though he would have fit right into the bondage float on any pride parade.

"You're going to start butt humping Craig," she said the night before I left for the tour.

"What would you rather me do," I joked, "butt fuck Tom instead?"

That didn't go over very well, but there was little I could do but comfort her with my claims of undiluted heterosexuality, which just made me sound even more like a clueless "Stone Cold."

On that first working day of Warped, we had to wake up at an ungodly hour to be shuttled off to a Scottsdale sports complex for a kind of pre-show dress rehearsal. Outside our air-conditioned room, the temperature in Phoenix was already approaching the high-80s with promises that it would top 100 degrees by noon. After we arrived at the arena, which the San Diego Padres and the Toronto Blue Jays shared for spring training, we sat in a narrowing slice of shaded concrete and waited for the ring to be set up. None of the indoor areas were unlocked so we just huddled in the shade to avoid the scorching Arizona sun.

My hangover couldn't be denied. With nothing to do but sit around, I passed out on the concrete. Oversized desert ants crawled across my midriff as I nodded in and out of consciousness.

"Hey, Dante looks like a bum," Dancin' Joey of 69 Degrees said, pointing at me and laughing. I drifted back to sleep.

"Is he always like this?" an indie worker asked as I neared my second hour of semi-consciousness.

Finally, the bathrooms opened and I could go and splash water in my face. I took a wiz and realized that it was probably the same urinal that hall of famer Tony Gwynn had pissed in — my brush with athletic immortality.

Hours passed. Nothing happened and the ring never got set up. It was nearly 115 degrees in the sun. Walking on the pavement practically melted the soles of our shoes. Finally, after spending half the day like the Desert Rats holed up in Tobruk, the buses were ordered to take us back to the hotel.

Conditions didn't improve the next day, but at least the show went on. The black ring ropes were so hot that they left grill marks across the wrestlers' backs. The corn tortillas Audra handed out for the fans to throw baked into brittle husks as soon as they landed on the ground. Corgan and Van Dyne had to wrestle in furry animal suits in that heat. There was the chance that their brains could cook in their skulls while they wore those outfits. But the show had to go on no matter how much the wrestling sucked or how indifferent the kids were as our set dragged on.

The wrestling came to a merciful conclusion. It was day one and there were no major injuries. Nobody died. Only forty-four more shows to go.

I made my way back to our air-conditioned bus through a fairway crowded with merch tables, display booths and competing smaller stages presenting different bands that all played the same three chords. In the middle of everything a Marine recruiting tent sported an oversized inflatable drill sergeant looming over the entire vendor area. Young jarheads in red T-shirts and cammies hustled even younger punks into considering a career in the Corps. Now that was really punk rock. I tried to take a shortcut through the main stage and bumped into Lee Ving of Fear. He was leaning up against a banister for support. Inhuman amounts of sweat gushed out of every withered pore on his body. He became even more leathery by the minute in that heat. Some people just weren't meant to be seen in the daylight.

The 21st century tour bus came complete with 500 channels of satellite TV, a DVD player and a VCR. Every pay channel, basic cable network and medium choice just gave the eighteen wrestlers and support staff more to argue over. We would've been better served with an old black and white Zenith with a crumpled tinfoil antennae. The limitations of UHF signals and fine-tuning would have helped us to agree on something to watch.

Gino had brought along these sleazy swinger tapes and he beamed with pride whenever he loaded them into the VCR. Sometimes he left those tapes running while the bus driver kept his radio tuned to Christian broadcasting. The sounds of middle-aged moans of ecstasy and the exaltations of the Lord battled it out for the souls of ISW assembled.

Shane quipped that watching Tony's swinger porn vids was like "watching your parents fuck." Shane countered by bringing aboard his *Girls Gone Wild* collection. Volume One started out innocuously enough with all of the drunken babes baring their breasts like the infomercials promised. By Volume Four the series degenerated into hardcore amateur footage of an army of jocks gangbanging an unenthused sorority girl on a motorboat in Lake Havasu. Arizona was behind us but we could never quite get away.

Audra had banned watching wrestling while she was on the bus. Of course wrestling was the one thing that we needed to watch because our shows started out shitty and got progressively worse as the tour rolled on. We sucked in L.A. and we sucked in San Diego. L'Empereur drove down to Fresno on his own dime. His being there gave a break to the guys who were wrestling two matches a day but

Audra didn't want to pay him after the show. Tony ended up giving him twenty bucks that probably came out of his own pocket. "I'm sorry, guy, but this is the best I can do," he said as he handed the French dictator the lone folded bill.

Audra banned a lot of things. There was no fucking on the bus. This was actually a good thing because A) half of us were married, B) nobody wanted to fuck most of us anyway and C) I was glad that I never had to walk in on Manny and Jefferson Monroe having a three-way with a pink haired piece of jailbait.

There was no shitting on the bus either but the reasons for that were primarily economic. It cost $500 to clean out the mobile septic tank if there was any solid matter in it.

Flatulence would have been banned from the bus if such a ban were actually enforceable. Farting was the one activity that everyone seemed to engage in, although not always equally. El Homo Loco dubbed the back area where Craig, Van Dyne and I bunked "the gas chamber." While the denizens of the gas chamber passed plenty of gas, nobody caught more hell for it than Manny. Manny had terrible, lingering gas and often let go in public acts of passive aggressive defiance. One time Gino chased him out of the bus for farting. "You little fucker, you trailed it!" Gino exclaimed as he tore off after him through the bus doors and into the parking lot.

But Audra overstepped even her considerable boundaries when she tried to ban Bengay. "No fucking Bengay on the bus," she hollered down the hallway as her battered cast tried to self-medicate their voluminous injuries.

"Audra, they're killing themselves out there," I said, daring a real ass reaming, "It stinks. It makes us want to die, but the wrestlers need their Bengay."

Audra rolled her eyes at me and went back to poring over a pile of receipts.

We were another Mexican wrestling tour with a decided lack of actual Mexicans. It was an ISW touring tradition to bring only one Mexican on the road but then claim that the whole kit and caboodle originated south of the border. We did have a Tijuana trained indie worker from the San Gabriel Valley named Frankie Dee, but he often claimed to be at least half Mongolian thus diluting our Latino flavor to dangerously low levels. Our solution to this desperate and improbable lack of Mexicans was to take a Hawaiian kid named Supes Ohana and make him into a crazed Mexican raver character called Mextacy. Supes bitched about having to play a Mexican because it would upset his grandmother (a direct descendant of King Kamehameha no less), but once given the role, he was damned good at it. He spent a good portion of his matches trying to hug his opponent and staring at his hand while he got pummeled. His finishing move was the candy flip, but he never got to use it. He'd usually lost by that time.

As the tour trundled up the West Coast, it became painfully apparent that half of our cast couldn't wrestle even after L'Empereur's training sessions, or at least needed some work. Some of these guys worked in offices. They pushed paper or made movies with computers. Now they were thrust into taking taxing physical abuse every day and traveling by night. The shortcomings that were easily compensated for while only putting on occasional shows were quickly laid bare during the day-to-day grind of touring. The wounds were never given a chance to heal.

Mextacy had barely worked a match before that tour, but was brought along because Boris didn't show up for bus call. We got the bright idea to have Shane run some morning training sessions to remedy this situation. He started off with a grueling regimen of bump drills and rapid-fire tumbling exercises. The wrestlers got halfway through their first session before Mextacy's spine was shaken and he had to walk around holding his head at an uncomfortable angle as he muttered faintly about how much pain he was in.

That was the end of Shane's impromptu crash course, and sadly it was also the end of Mextacy for that tour. He was the first one to be sent home, which was a shame because he had started to pick up some heat against Tom Corgan's racist skinhead character, the Oi Boy. Mextacy even got to win a match by taking some pills from a Ziploc baggie, thus endowing him with the MDMA-charged strength needed to defeat fascism once and for all.

For the Oi Boy, Audra gave Corgan advice on how to lace his boots and wear his suspenders so he would come off as an authentic racist skin. (Audra seemed to have an unsettling depth of knowledge where skinhead fashion etiquette was concerned.) She had Gabriel dig up a bootleg CD of the racist U.K. band Screwdriver so he could use their anthem "White Power" as entrance music. Somebody also gave Corgan a copy of *Mein Kampf* and he often began those matches by clubbing his opponents with it. Beating people with doctrinal literature was becoming commonplace in ISW for we also had 69 Degrees using copies of *Dianetics* as weapons. Audra did come up with the best put-down for the Oi Boy. "Only in ISW do you get to see a skinhead fight one on one," she often told the press while describing the character.

The Oi Boy inflamed audiences with speeches about "spics" and "mud people" as he entered the ring. Corgan started to revel in pro wrestling's darker side. He talked about the coming "racial holy war" or RAHOWA as the white supremacists call it, and he liberally lifted lines from his well-watched Terry Funk tape and twisted Funk's phrases to fit the Oi Boy's message.

An anti-racist skinhead kid in Idaho freaked out at the sight of Tom as the Oi Boy and started trying to scale these really tall barricades that surrounded the ring that day. The venue was an old rodeo palace and the barriers they had were meant to keep in cattle. Corgan taunted the kid by holding the ring ropes open for him. The kid ran around the ring like a cat with tape on its paws and tried to get in from every side. Gabriel repulsed him, but it took some doing.

Nobody really wanted to toss the kid out of the show because Idaho (a bastion of white supremacists under the best of circumstances) could use all the anti-racist kids it could get. There was just no way to pull the kid aside and let him know that it was just a show. He was too aggro.

Still, we worried about what we might have been unleashing as we unveiled the Oi Boy across the country. What about those really weird kids that kept coming up to us wanting to see the Ku Klux Klown? Did they think the Klown was a funny idea or did they want to run off and join some kind of segregated circus with him? It was decided that the Oi Boy should lose every match he fought. The last thing we wanted was the Oi Boy looking strong and becoming an idol to some of those fucked up kids. The Oi Boy usually jobbed to Frankie Dee, our only Mexican. After each match I'd announce: "Frankie Dee is a credit to his race — the human race." Nobody got the Joe Louis reference but Audra, who begged me to stop saying it after hearing it every day for three weeks.

The Cruiser also became controversial again. In San Francisco, he was just everyone's favorite leather fag but in red state America, he was hated. Buffed out football jocks and little mallternative skater punks just stood there with their jaws agape at the sight of the Cruiser as he alternately pranced and stomped into the ring. Those looks of shock quickly turned to rage. They shouted, "*Fag! Faggot!*" Interestingly, all of the girls laughed while Cruiser got on the mic and threatened every dude in the audience: "I am going to bend you over and open you up like a piece of warm San Francisco sourdough bread."

In Salt Lake City a gang of straight edge Mormon kids started a rousing chant of "*You suck dick*" at the Cruiser. He grabbed the mic and held onto it for several seconds and then said, "*Damn right I do!*" The whole audience burst out laughing at that one and the fag chants died almost immediately.

As the Salt Lake City show drew to a close, we were confronted with the unbreakable table. Macho and Sassy Sasquatcho (the husband and wife team played by Corgan and Craig) sprawled Dancin' Joey across it and proceeded to pounce on him four times from the top rope to deliver the broken particle board that the fans craved, but the table didn't even buckle. After taking so much abuse Joey rolled off and Manny adeptly staggered onto the table for a fifth try. Corgan went ass first but it damaged Manny's midsection more than the portable furniture. After the match we found out that the folding table wasn't formed from sawdust mulch but was composed of solid Formica. We feared those Formica tables after that. They might be lurking in an unassuming Home Depot somewhere. Waiting for wrestlers to attempt to break them.

At the Race City Speedway in Calgary, a dust storm powerful enough to lift 300-pound roadies two feet off the ground almost destroyed the ring. We all hustled to get the ring loaded onto the truck before it became more damaged than it already was. Miniature funnel clouds tore through the beer garden area and Manny was pressed into service by some Mounties to keep several yards of chain-link fence from crashing down on hundreds of drunken Canadians. We loaded up the ring and thought the rest of the show was going to be canceled, but the storm blew over almost as suddenly as it had come. Concert-goers resembling refugees from the dust bowl started filtering back onto the tarmac while Kool Keith took the stage as if nothing had happened.

"Naughty girls you learn your lesson/Spanked, whipped, or Smith & Wessoned," the man who doubled as Doctor Octagon rapped as confused Canucks disjointedly swayed to the beat. "Feel your breasts, bite your chest and/Shit on ya shirt, pee on ya dress and tossin' salad."

Walking around the backstage area at a Warped show, people over thirty instinctively gravitated to each other. Jerry Only of the Misfits always seemed so damned happy to see me. I'd never met him before. Maybe he had me confused with some other fat guy in a leopard print karate suit. Maybe we were the two largest, most ridiculous looking guys there. Only always seemed a tad disappointed that none of the wrestlers wanted to pump iron with him. "The wrestlers are hurtin' man," I explained. Only nodded with a half-frown and seemed to understand.

Only's band was a makeshift amalgam of punk rock's past. He had Marky Ramone on drums so they did "The KKK Took My Baby Away." On guitar he had Dez Cadena of Black Flag so they did a couple of Black Flag tunes as well. But when Only belted out the lines, "I've got something to say/I killed your baby today," hundreds of little kids sporting Only's signature devil lock hairdo (no doubt combed into place by their aging punker moms) popped out of the woodwork to sing along. It was unnerving.

There was still that problem with Paul Van Dyne's lack of movement in the ring. El Pollo Diablo's statue-like performances were compounded by the good job that Audra's paid publicist did of getting press coverage for the horned cock. Almost every city that we showed up in had a picture of the Devil Chicken splashed across the front page of their daily newspaper's entertainment section. Sometimes the Chicken even rated a small pic above the masthead previewing the story about the fighting poultry inside. But even those with the lowest expectations went away disappointed after catching El Pollo Diablo's act as all they were treated to was Paul lumbering around the ring and occasionally mustering a slow-mo series of missed clotheslines.

Craig and I tried to remedy the situation through the booking. We teamed him up with the Sasquatch and also had him fight the Sasquatch, but nothing seemed to click. We even went all the way back to the mid-1990s and had the Chicken go up against Jefferson Monroe in his old El Gourmexico getup. Gourmexico peppered the chicken with a nonstick frying pan and clubbed him with a very real bowling pin, but the crowds were still unimpressed. Our biggest star was, pardon the pun, laying an egg and Paul didn't seem to care.

But that was the least of our problems. Jefferson Monroe hurt wrestlers on day one and kept right on doing it. Audra and I both begged him not to hurt Mextacy during an early match in San Francisco so the first thing Monroe went and did after the opening bell was to slam a real bowling pin square into Mextacy's nuts. In pro wrestling you're going to take some pain, but you have to save it for when the crowd's paying attention. Fat, mullet-headed kids in Rob Van Dam T-shirts weren't striking up a chant of *"You're hard-core"* when Monroe nutted Mextacy. For the most part, they couldn't see the blow being delivered well enough to appreciate its realism. Also, a simple shot to the balls wasn't the kind of gore-drenched action that anyone got hot and bothered over. Instead, all the fans got to see was Mextacy doubling over in extreme agony as we carried him out of the ring. I guess you couldn't trust someone else's safety to a guy who went around twisting his own nut sac into knots for the amusement of others. To the other wrestlers, pain was an occupational hazard. To Monroe it was a turn-on.

We had forty-five shows to get through in a little less than two months. There was a stretch of thirteen shows in a row through the South without a day off. This tour was going to grind the wrestlers into bloody hunks of hair. As a booker, I had to make sure that the show was violently entertaining while also keeping the cast from getting killed. Both goals were definitely at cross-purposes, but they could be pulled off by relying on as much illusion as possible. Punches had to be pulled and blows had to be gimmicked. The fans' favorite thing was to see a wrestler go through a table: loud noise and shit breaks in half. There is both catharsis and closure in the table shot. It's what the money shot is to porn. But the trick is that the table actually cushions the blow if it's done right. It's all smoke and mirrors. Sleight of hand.

Craig and I got the bright idea to match Monroe up against Dave Steele, figuring that Steele was tough enough to handle it. It was a pretty stupid calculus to use any way you looked at it, but we were stuck. Audra had already had to ask the tour for more money to ship Mextacy out after that botched training session. She couldn't request more plane tickets to make replacements anytime soon.

At the close of their match, a trusting U.S. Steele lay sprawled out on one of those familiar tables waiting for Monroe to finish the move. The table shot was supposed to be easy but Monroe landed with nothing but knees. Steele was briefly knocked out and slid off the table at a bad angle. His arm bent the wrong way when he landed. Steele was our workhorse. He was our go-to guy. We expected him to last and now he had to sit out at least a week while his arm was in a sling. That also meant that everyone had to work more matches under different masks to take up the slack — including Jefferson Monroe.

The simple solution would have been to bring along more indie workers, but that approach had its pitfalls. It was the indie workers who bailed on the '97 tour after only one night while the ISW amateurs endured the whole odyssey. Indie workers were the ones most likely to be backstage basket cases with bloated egos. We had all experienced it.

For the first half of that tour, we had a top-notch indie wrestler with sad eyes and a small but muscular physique called Tech-9. *The Wrestling Observer* consistently praised him as one of the best acrobatic wrestlers working the West Coast. He wrestled a legit four-star match against Shane that we could have rolled out every day if their bodies had held up. But Tech-9 couldn't hack being on the bus. Every night, he got so loaded that he swayed back and forth like the bus was chugging over a bumpy road when it wasn't even moving. He ate an entire jar of Audra's peanut butter in one sitting and then did it again the next night after Audra had replaced it. He broke glasses, yelled at the women on the production bus who worked for the tour and generally fucked things up. When Tech-9 missed a match in Colorado because he was passed out in his bunk, it was time for him to go.

"Can't we keep him around another week until El Homo Loco flies in?" I asked during the next morning's booking meeting in Kansas City. We had fresh wrestlers flying in as replacements for the last leg of the tour. We had planned it this way from the beginning because some guys couldn't take two months off from work to go wrestle around the country. I feared that handing Tech-9 his walking papers would open up a gap in the roster that would have the rest of the guys killing themselves to make do.

But Tech-9 had eaten Audra's peanut butter and now he was missing matches. There was no saving him. Audra and Gino gave him his last day's pay and had him get his luggage off the bus. He walked up to Craig and me, shook our hands and thanked us. Then he was gone.

Luckily Shane agreed to delay his departure from the tour for a couple of days to keep guys from getting killed. Some of the wrestlers couldn't have survived without him. After his final match on his final day in St. Louis, Shane ripped off his mask, got on the microphone and said: "I'm leaving this fucked up, stupid assed Warped Tour and I'm gonna go home and I'm gonna *fuck my wife!*"

We couldn't help but envy him at that moment. Not because we wanted to fuck his wife, but, well, you know.

An enterprising skater punk band called Madcap hauled a large kettledrum barbeque behind their van on a trailer hitch. They bought meat in the morning, played one of the small stages in the afternoon and then sold burgers and dogs to make their gas money to get to the next town and do it all over again. They were smart. They had a captive market. Warped played the suburbs and the sticks and a lot of the amphitheaters we rolled into were walking distance from nothing but cul-de-sacs and gas stations. We were trapped in those parking lots with nothing to do but guzzle beer, eat those burgers and wait for bus call.

Sometimes the venues were close to a shopping mall or 7-Eleven and sometimes there was a strip club nearby. I didn't care much for strip joints when I was at home, but on the road for weeks on end, it was hard to escape their allure. It might have been Cleveland or it could have been Charlotte, but I was in this wiggle joint by myself drinking bourbon and disinterestedly placing dollar bills on the stage so as not to be a dick. Then this long-legged brunette glided out onto the stage and started sexily sashaying to Journey's "Lights" — their power ballad about San Francisco.

I struggled to hold back the tears that were welling up in my eyes as the dancer straddled the pole and the recorded voice of Steve Perry soulfully sang about wanting to get back to his city by the bay. When the bridge kicked in with the thunder of those Neal Schon power chords, I lost it. "It's sad, oh there's been mornings out on the road without you, without your charms," Perry wailed, his velvety voice hitting operatic highs. The dancer's top was off and horny old letches held up $5 bills to get her attention. I was reduced to a hulking mass of tears as Schon's skillful solo built to its crescendo.

I couldn't take it anymore. I had to get out of there. I left a twenty spot on the stage and made my way out of the club past a maze of neon Miller Lite signs and Molson Golden mirrors.

I stumbled into the street. I had to find a payphone. I had to call Dana and tell her how much I missed her, how much I loved her. I finally found a phone in working order. I didn't have any change. I had to call collect, but she wasn't home. I couldn't even leave a message before the operator disconnected the call.

# 16
# LIQUID
# GOLD

WAS IT THE Verizon Wireless Amphitheater? It probably was. We played about eight or nine Verizon Wireless Amphitheaters on that tour. Rod Serling wrote *Twilight Zone* scripts about things like that, about people trapped in a monotonous homogeneity created by unexplained rifts in the fabric of time and space. But our continuous sense of déjà vu was made by nothing more supernatural than corporate buyouts.

With the exception of the occasional off-season racetrack or the converted cattle stockyards, Warped mostly played those cheaply constructed Quick Crete outdoor amphitheatres. Called "sheds" by the roadies and stagehands who worked the circuit, they were about as picturesque as that little sheet metal shack where your dad kept his gardening tools. To cut costs and keep ticket prices down, Warped brought in its own stages, which were set up in the venues' expansive concourses or in fenced off portions of parking lots. That main amphitheatre, which rented out at a premium, was left empty.

Audra, Craig and I sat on an otherwise empty bus and hashed out the possibilities for the day's match-ups. It was our morning booking meeting. The tour was already at the halfway mark, but we still struggled to connect with the kids. We had Josh Steele on the road with us for a while. Josh looked just like Jesus so we teamed him with Jefferson's Buddhist monk character and had them go up against the Scientologist 69 Degrees in a battle of religious faiths. The wrestling was topsy-turvy during those matches but no matter what city we were in, the kids really loved chanting, "*Fuck 'em up, Jesus, fuck 'em up!*" Sometimes they alternated with, "*Fuck 'em up, Buddha, fuck 'em up!*" Without fail, the fans always sided with the traditional world religions over the sci-fi cult.

Audra ran her day-to-day operations through a trio of walkie-talkies. Gabriel had one while he scouted the venue for a good spot to set up the ring and Gino kept another with him as he headed off to the production tent to haggle over the day's set times. Audra made decisions and barked out orders through the third. The sound of Gino' and Gabriel's voices broadcasting from the tiny speaker of Audra's handheld unit were a constant but necessary interruption during our early morning booking meetings.

"You'll never believe this," Gabriel's voice said, crackling over the airwaves, "but this chick just squatted down right in front of me and took a piss all over the pavement."

Audra picked up her walkie-talkie as if to reply. As she momentarily paused to think of something to say, Gino's voice abruptly cut in on the conversation. "*Liquid gold!*" he exclaimed, his Johnny Guido accent adding an extra pinch of perversion to every lustily drawn-out syllable.

Audra sat there utterly mortified, her jaw hanging wide open. Craig and I soon doubled over with laughter. "Liquid gold," Craig panted as he tried to suck in breaths of air in between involuntary guffaws, "liquidddd goooolllld." We laughed until we both slid out of our seats onto the bus's carpeted floor. Audra finally joined in but we couldn't tell if she was laughing at Gino or laughing at us laughing at Gino. Although she was the purveyor of Incredibly Strange Wrestling and Stinky's Peep Show, Audra had an out-of-place puritanical streak to her.

We finally wiped away the tears and tried to carry on with the booking meeting. A few minutes went by and Gino walked onto the bus. Craig and I started laughing again. Audra did a spit take. "Liquid gold," Craig and I blurted in unrehearsed unison.

Gino looked completely confused. "That's what it's called," he calmly explained. "Liquid gold."

It could have been hotter that day in Houston, but it was still the morning and it was still Texas. It was another booking meeting — our twenty-sixth of the tour. Wrestlers were becoming a rapidly dwindling natural resource. Booking matches stopped being about coming up with crazy concepts and started being about getting the most out of everybody without fucking them up for the rest of the tour. Could we possibly get three matches out of Corgan or the Cruiser that day? Was Monroe going to gleefully kneecap someone and send them back home following a brief trip to the local county hospital for X-rays? There was also that stupid bungee jumping trip that Manny took on a day that he claimed that he was too injured to wrestle. Should we strip him naked and make him sit on a steel folding chair in the middle of the parking lot while wearing a dunce cap and drinking a bottle of Yoo-hoo? Did we risk letting U.S. Steele beat the shit out of him in the ring for real?

I used to be a comedian and a performance artist. Now I felt more like the manager of a last-place minor league baseball team who was under increasing pressure from the owners to "make something happen." The wrestling was so lousy for the first leg of the tour that there had been a betting pool going around the buses that isw would bail before leaving California. That no confidence vote galvanized us into sticking around. By the time we got to Texas, we had at least killed the rumors of our imminent departure.

At the Houston booking meeting, Craig sat sprawled out across the leatherette bench seat that extended along the side of the bus's front lounge area. I sat across the table from Audra as she scribbled the names of available wrestling characters on the back of an old Stinky's flier.

"Canadian MTV, you know MuchMusic or whatever it's called, wants us to do something with Sum 41 today," Audra announced, hoping that Craig and I would start bouncing around ideas.

"What the fuck's a Sum 41?" I asked. I really didn't know. It sounded like a band, but it could have been an energy drink or a math school.

"They're, like, the biggest band in Canada right now," Audra replied.

What was it with 21st century bands and their word-number combinations? Sum 41? Blink 182? It was like someone took all of those monosyllabic 1990s band names like Bush or Blur and ran them through a random number generator.

"Bigger than Rush?" Craig chimed in jokingly, "They can't be bigger than Rush."

"Well, no, of course not," a flustered Audra replied, "but they are the biggest Canadian band on this tour so we've gotta do something with 'em."

"Going into this, we should assume that these kids don't know jack shit about wrestling," I said. "They might watch it on TV but we don't wanna give them that much to do out there. I say we just keep it simple and have them manage the Chicken during that arm wrestling match."

The arm-wrestling match was a concoction of Craig's that made the Chicken more than passably entertaining, thus salvaging ISW's most talked-about attraction. Craig performed the match as his proto wigga rapper character Señor Bueno. He entered the ring wearing a second-hand sombrero and some ill-fitting Zubaz pants that usually slid halfway down his ass when the action got too intense. Sometimes he emerged from the ISW changing tent with a stream of toilet paper trailing from his pants for that extra something special.

"Shouldn't we have them do a little more than that?" Craig asked skeptically.

"Naw, man," I said. "We've been through this with rock stars before. They all think they can ad lib like they're Ric Flair or something and then end up freezing like a deer in the headlights and making things look shittier than they are already. Keep it simple. They manage the Chicken and shout words of encouragement from ringside. You get in their face a little then the Chicken puts your ass through a table. This Sum 89 gets in the ring to raise the Chicken's arm up in victory and we have Gino spin 'We Are the Champions' or something. It'll be easy."

Nobody had any better ideas so Sum 41 just had to stand on the sidelines and play it pissed off when Bueno got the upper hand on the satanic bird.

The arm-wrestling match was a piece of genius. It was the one bout that we could put on every day and have it go over every time. It got the fans really pumped up while delivering as little actual wrestling as possible. For starters, the bout began with the ref setting up a table and two chairs. The anticipation of chair shots and broken tables kept the fans from strolling off to check out the half-pipe or choke down some cheese curds. Then Craig worked that crowd like the second coming of Andy Kaufman. He came out rapping about cereal, locusts and minerals. The kids booed right away. He ran down AFI, 311, Good Charlotte and all of the other bands that they had paid to see. "You don't deserve to hear real music," he chided. "You don't deserve to hear my rhymes! You don't deserve to see me! You don't deserve to see me!"

The match itself involved ample amounts of hemming and

hawing from Bueno and every variety of stalling imaginable. Bueno refused to lock up. Bueno falsely accused the Chicken of cheating, took a powder outside of the ring and berated the fans some more before the ref threatened to disqualify him. Finally, a frustrated El Pollo Diablo chased the jiggling Bueno around the ring, earning a pop from the fans for almost nothing and allowing that dastardly Bueno to pick up a chair and slam it across Pollo's back.

Van Dyne complained about the chair shots every day. "Hey, Craig," he asked before each match, "Can you go a little easier with that chair?"

Craig responded by going out there and belting the Chicken harder and more often with that folding chair than he had the day before. Van Dyne's snide smirk and sense of privilege had already earned him the enmity of most of the wrestlers. By the time he was overheard saying, "I can think of better things to do than work two matches," at a particularly gnarly show in Arkansas, he was done. They hated him. Craig knew that we couldn't afford to lose the Chicken, but he had no problem with making sure that Paul went back to the bus more than just a little sore every night. The rest of the wrestlers envied Craig for earning 100 bucks a day to bash Paul with a chair. Many of them would have paid to do it.

After the chair shots, Macho Sasquatcho ran in to make the save. This got the fans oohing and aahing. Sasquatcho punched Bueno several times, then laid him out across the table. The Devil Chicken recovered, climbed to the second rope, then jumped onto Bueno sending both colorfully costumed grapplers through the splintering particleboard. After pinning Bueno's arm for the three-count, the Chicken was declared the victor and the fans went nuts.

"There you have it, folks," I announced. "That burning question of science that has plagued the questing mind of man down through the ages is finally answered: Devil Chickens really are stronger than white rappers."

Before the arm-wrestling match with Sum 41, I went into the

tent to go over the match with them. They were fresh faced, spiky-haired kids who didn't stand an inch over 5' 5" and couldn't have been a day over seventeen. They were dressed in matching terry-cloth robes with their band's logo stitched across the back. It must have been some new prizefighting-inspired fashion direction that their management had them try for about five minutes. I told them that all they had to do was cheer the Chicken and get pissed off at the masked rapper. It turned out that they even fucked that up a little. When Bueno hit the bird with the chair, everyone in Sum 41 uncontrollably applauded giving that Pavlovian response to the sound of corrugated aluminum smacking meat.

After meeting Sum 41, I realized that they were the band that tormented me almost every day by playing the opening riff to Iron Maiden's Crimean War metal epic "The Trooper." Sum 41 were playing the song mockingly with still present Clinton-era irony, making fun of something that was recorded before they or their audience were even born. It would have been really punk for Sum 41 to take a swipe at Good Charlotte but that would have been career suicide. Popular Warped Tour bands were quickly lionized by bored teens' ceaseless hunger for pop idols. Kids took it personally when you made fun of their favorite musicians, the way that they had since Sinatra or Elvis.

Just once, upon hearing Sum 41 mock the metal gods that were beyond their mortal ken, I wished that Maiden's Bruce Dickinson and Steve Harris would rush the stage flanked by an inflatable mummified twelve-foot tall Eddie the undead mascot and seize control of the tour. I really needed to hear metal. I needed to hear the minor keys and different time signatures. I craved long-assed guitar wanking delivered without a care of whether it was "punk" or not. The label of punk had become a confining sarcophagus that entombed all creativity. By 2001, Warped had developed its own sound that all of the bands on its multiple stages struggled to perfect. As punk entered its third decade, it morphed into nothing more threatening than pop tunes of suburban teen romance laden with wordy vocal phrasing and straight time rhythms. Except for Kool Keith and a couple of other acts, Warped was a cacophony of different bands all playing the same song over and over again with differing levels of proficiency.

It got to the point where even Tori Amos sounded good when I heard her playing in the background at a small Pittsburgh bookstore. Amos was still the same overly acclaimed chanteuse that she always was, but her music had haunting melodies and modulating scales. It was more than the straight-ahead strumming limited to those happy major keys that had been pounded into my head for over a month. At that moment, Tori Amos' mournful wails and dark piano melodies sounded like the most vibrant and alive music I had ever heard.

There was some salvation on the smaller stages where there were still bands that either hadn't yet bought into the myth of making it or never cared about it in the first place. One of these was a hard-driving party rock outfit called the Angry Amputees. Dalty, their bassist, was missing both of his legs and several of his fingers, but he played his instrument better than half of the other bass guitarists on that tour. He was the band's only amputee and, despite having his medical insurance carrier drop him on the eve of a needed heart operation, he wasn't particularly angry. Their CD was released by I'm Stumped Records.

However, the best act on the entire 2001 Warped Tour had to be this band of burnouts called the Desperation Squad. They were pals of Kevin Lyman's who all either worked at Claremont College or were perpetual students there. They played absurd heavy rock anthems with infectious choruses like "I'm an Asshole (for Rock and Roll)" and "(We Ain't Getting) No Pussy Tonight." Their magnum opus was "Taco Truck," which went: "Taco truck, taco truck/ It's not a restaurant/It's just a taco truck/If all you've got's a buck/ Taco truck/You've got your choice of *cabeza, lengua,* and *sesos* filled tacos..." That was classic. Lyman adeptly scheduled them to go on right after 1SW on stages that were adjacent to the ring and they rapidly became the wrestlers' favorite band. At the end of each Desperation Squad set, the singer put on an oversized panda mask, stripped down to nothing but that mask and a G-string, and covered himself in Hershey's syrup while he writhed around on the stage.

But Warped was always fraught with sinking revelations about the state of the music industry, punk rock and pop culture. I was on the main stage mooching free booze from Me First and the Gimme Gimmes. Fat Mike always had an open tiki bar set up while they played as a way of cementing his image as the post punk version of Bill Murray or Rodney Dangerfield from some 1980s slobs vs. snobs comedy. I was more than willing to oblige Mike by playing the part of a rowdy extra at his onstage party if it meant getting a shot of Cuervo Gold. I had very little shame, if any at all, at that point.

During that late afternoon drinking fest, as Spike howled through some Barry Manilow song and I sipped off a makeshift margarita of green Powerade and lemons snatched from the catering truck, I realized that the 10,000 kids that were singing along with him had absolutely no idea that the song was a cover. A lot of those kids were born in the late 1980s. They came into consciousness a full decade after Celine Dion had displaced James Taylor and Jim Croce on easy listening station playlists. To those kids, "I Am a Rock" or "Fire and Rain" were Me First and the Gimme Gimme originals! The subtle cultural parody that had floated them in the first place had been rendered irrelevant leaving behind just another pop band.

Alien Ant Farm joined the postmodern cover cavalcade as well. They were the tour's token nü metal band and their version of Michael Jackson's "Smooth Criminal" had been steadily climbing the charts that summer. They started on Warped's smaller stages but kept getting bumped up to bigger stages as the tour progressed, finally landing the main stage by the road show's final dates. Audra bitched ad-nauseum about them covering the Michael Jackson hit.

"Where do they fucking get off covering 'Smooth Criminal'?" she angrily mused as if ruining anything from the *Bad* album was even a remote possibility. It wasn't like they were doing something from *Off the Wall*. The irony that Audra was practically married to Spike, who made a career out of murdering old pop songs both classic and kitschy with the Gimme Gimmes, was completely lost on her.

I probably would have found a reason to bitch about Alien Ant Farm as well, but they were the nicest guys on that tour, plus they were way into the wrestling. You have to be careful whom you meet in this world. I met David Carradine once at the Dragonfest martial arts convention in Glendale and he was a total dick to me. He wouldn't even stop doing his newspaper crossword puzzle long enough to shine my ass into buying an autographed 8" x 10" glossy of Kwai Chang Caine and I was always a big fan of his. Alien Ant Farm were nothing but friendly and they openly dished the dirt on the music business. They had a Top Ten single but they were so in hock to their record company that they didn't have a dime to call their own. They still lived with their grandparents in San Diego. After meeting them, I found myself actually liking their curious brand of digestible math metal. If I had never crossed paths with them, I'd most likely be berating them from afar for not playing the balls-out metal about dragons and destruction that I personally think is cool. I guess it pays to be nice.

As I walked through the Warped Tour stages, both large and small, I realized that I had long since traded my bass guitar for a pair of wrestling boots. Cracking wise through a Homo Loco/Poontangler bout had got me into the Fillmore and on the Warped Tour but it never quite opened to door for my band as I had originally intended back when I was guzzling beer day after day at the Nightbreak. People seemed more interested in seeing Count Dante wrestle, or announce wrestling, than they were in my music. Worse things could have happened. I got to tour like a rock band, but had to enter the squared circle to get there.

At one of the venues, I can't remember which, there was a room set up with a bunch of amps and instruments for people to jam on. Craig and I couldn't resist, so we headed over there in between wrestling sets. Craig had left my band when he moved to L.A. but we still found ourselves chugging our way through the Dante repertoire. We warmed up with "Redwood City Rock City" and "Speed Queen." By the time that Bad Boy Corey and a small crowd had gathered in the jam room to watch, we started playing this stompin' travel tune called "Indie Worker" that was inspired largely by working with L'Empereur. After a few aborted attempts at playing it where I had to jar Craig's memory about the chord progression, we finally got cooking on it. "Spendin' every dime that I get just to try to make it into the show," I sang, shooting knowing glances to the other wrestlers in the room. I then hit the turnaround on an A-note and continued with the song's sad refrain: "Fat man makes me keep a secret that every mark already knows/Fake, real or make believe/The twisted dreams that we conceive/The only one who thinks it's real is me."

The Church of Scientology finally caught wind of us. Newspapers in Dallas, Denver, Calgary, Kansas City and Orlando all ran stories on Warped Tour's wacky wrestling that mentioned 69 Degrees, the Scientologist boy band tag team. Several papers also published pictures of Dancin' Joey and Bad Boy Corey striking poses and clutching copies of *Dianetics*. There was also the Internet. There had been postings on anti-Scientology message boards about 69 since their Fillmore debut. Many of these postings pondered whether or not the Dianetics duo was a gag or a genuine Scientology stunt to gain converts. By the time that Warped had completed over a month's worth of shows, accounts of the battling boy band started cropping up on both punk rock and pro wrestling websites.

Our first encounter with Hubbard acolytes came in Milwaukee. A gaggle of preteen Scientologist girls accosted 69 as they made their way to the bar. They asked Joey and Corey what they read and where they got tested. Corey/Manny responded with the evangelical fervor that he had learned from his Pentecostal upbringing. He quoted passages of *Dianetics* from memory and preached a sermon based on Hubbard's psuedo-scientific screed complete with personal flourishes about how *Dianetics* saved him from a life plagued by thetans. It was the kind of passionate presentation that was most likely unheard of behind the Church of Scientology's closed doors. The girls clapped wildly and asked for autographs.

We didn't hear from any practicing Scientologists again until Warped made its way through the South. They somehow stayed away from us in Orlando even though they owned the half of that town that wasn't owned by Disney. But Orlando is a scary place and the fans that gathered around the ring looked way more 'roided out than anybody who wrestled for ISW. Some fucker tagged me with an unopened 20-ounce bottle of Pepsi there. Luckily, it hit me in the meaty part of my flabby back and not on my head. Greater Orlando is probably a little rough for your average Scientologist, despite their strong presence there.

The next time we ran into Scientologists was in Virginia Beach. I'd just gotten through announcing our last set of wrestling when this strangely dressed 400-pound sci-fi nerd with a beard and a strikingly short tie came up to me and asked to talk to ISW's promoter. He looked like what would happen if Doctor Who had a Hometown Buffet franchise added to the vast interior of his TARDIS. Due to the guy's size and strange look, I figured him for another indie wrestler looking to work a match so I pointed Audra out to him. I was wrong. He was from the Washington D.C. Church of Scientology and he wanted to meet with 69 Degrees. Audra found Dancin' Joey and Bad Boy Corey in the changing tent. They talked to the overgrown geek for several minutes. He invited 69 to be tested for engrams at Scientology's capital complex, and then left on friendly, but slightly ominous terms.

When 69 didn't show up for their free auditing session in down-town D.C., the Scientologists started playing hardball. They flamed the recently launched ISW message board (ISW finally had an official site by 2001). They made the same kinds of baseless crybaby claims that they have more recently with the whole spat over Isaac Hayes and *South Park* or *Scary Movie 4*. They said that Incredibly Strange Wrestling was bigoted towards the burgeoning Scientologist popu-lation and compared us to the Nazis. They also wrote that we only discriminated against Scientologists and never went after other religions. They must have never heard of those Dante the Baptist matches where I dragged a cross around and fought Flamius Caesar and the Lion. What about Super Kwanzaa and Matzo Mama?

We responded in the only way that we knew how; we continued to mock them and their Hollywood heavyweight spokespeople. 69 kept on being butt-rammed and manhandled by El Homo Loco and the Cruiser, their matches always ending with a homoerotic four-way submission that I dubbed "the wagon train." This was fol-lowed by a table spot for the grand finale and was usually punctuated by my trademark cry of, *"Hot man on man action!"*

By this time the Cruiser had added a particularly revolting move to his repertoire: he got behind Dancin' Joey and then spread Joey's legs apart. Cruiser drew out the tension while Joey begged for mercy. Then Cruiser buried his face deep into his opponent's crack. "It's the San Francisco Mudslide!" I announced to a nauseated audi-ence. "The stimulation to Dancin' Joey's anus must be so intense that not even Dianetics can keep him in the closet!"

Our next series of confrontations with the cult was hardly more than a minor annoyance. One guy showed up to pester us in sev-eral different cities. He claimed to be the head of their New York operation, but he never brought anyone else with him. This led us to question the Church of Scientology's claims of membership in the millions. If we had gone and pissed off the Church of Jesus Christ of Latter-day Saints then they would have definitely sent some

Mormon muscle to shut us down. It was simple enough just to have security eject the single Scientologist when he cropped up.

After their pathetic attempts at intimidation failed, the phone calls started coming from Scientology's lawyers to Audra's ISW business line. Their main bone of contention was over 69's use of paperback copies of *Dianetics* during their matches. It turns out that the look and logo of Scientology's holy book are trademarked money-makers. The church gets to maintain its tax-exempt status despite its pay-to-play attitude. Although we had the protections afforded parody on our side, L. Ron's advocates were notorious for tying up Scientology's critics in costly court battles. The Scientologists had all of Tom Cruise's and John Travolta's money to go after us with. There was no real way that Audra could fight them, but she did have her attorney draw up a letter pointing out that it was San Francisco's Scientology Center that stupidly sold her the box of books in the first place. The time it took for legal letters to go back and forth would allow us to finish out Warped (and possibly the rest of the year) with our Scientologist boy band tag team intact.

At that moment, ISW was still on its way up. We all believed that we'd only be doing more shows and tours after finishing Warped. 69 Degrees was one of the most dead-on concepts on which Craig and I had collaborated since we had been allowed to inflict our odd-ball ideas on ISW. That tag team allowed us to send up boy bands and *Battlefield Earth* at the same time. From our opening shows it was the one idea that clicked with the kids who came to see us on Warped and now we were being bullied into dropping it by a clique of nutjobs who worship multi-tentacled monsters from outer space. Hopefully, by 2002 I'd think of something as rich for Corey and Joey to do.

"Cheer up, Dante," Bad Boy Corey said to me as I mulled over our uninspiring options, "maybe I can become the Enrique Iglesias of Baha'i."

In pro wrestling there is a multiplicity of moves, all with millions of personalized variations. There's the German suplex, gutwrench suplex, belly-to-back suplex, back-to-back suplex, not to mention the full nelson, half nelson, chicken wing, pump handle, brain buster and hammerlock varieties. There's the frog splash, corkscrew splash, centon splash, springboard splash, the splash suicida, and your garden-variety off the top rope splash also known as the "Superfly" Snuka divebomb splash. The last is best delivered from the top of a steel cage. Positioning your or your opponent's foot, leg, arm, head or ass slightly differently could alter the character of the move entirely. On top of that, wresters were always adding double underhooks or front facelocks to powerslams or neck cranks in the quest for a finisher that they could call their own. As an announcer, keeping track of this endless catalog of squared circle maneuvers got to be a major bitch.

For most of the tour, I referred to every splash that Frankie Dee delivered as a frog splash whether it was or not. He started giving me shit about this. "Dante over here calls every move I do a frog splash," he said one night on the bus to rib me.

"I think that is the only move he knows," he added to a chorus of laughs from the rest of the wrestlers.

The next day, during his match with the Oi Boy, I really did call every move that Frankie did a frog splash. He did a simple clothesline and I called it a frog splash. He whipped someone into the ropes and I said, "Oh, what a tremendous frog splash!" They traded blows back and forth and I said, "The Oi Boy's delivering vicious chops while Frankie Dee counters with a blistering array of frog splashes." Frankie actually blew a move or two as he struggled to keep from laughing through the whole thing. After that, I started calling him "The Master of the Frog Splash," and he added that move to his repertoire just to shut me up.

I may have miscalled a few moves here and there, but it hardly mattered outside the bus. I still had skater kids, band members and roadies stroking my ego by telling me that I should be on television. I had subversion and satire on my side and my banter grew decidedly more barbed as we plunged deeper into red state America. When the fans in Houston counted the number of times that Macho Sasquatcho hit Señor Bueno over the head I jibed, "I'm surprised that you Texans can count after so many years of George Bush's educational plan!" When another creative crowd in Atlanta started yelling, "*You suck dick,*" at El Homo Loco, I responded with a lecture on Dixie homosexuality. "The South has a tremendous tradition of homosexuals," I opined, "Truman Capote, Tennessee Williams. Billy Ray Cyrus — another great Southern homosexual. Reba McEntire, one of the great lesbians of the South." They actually chuckled for the Billy Ray and Reba cracks.

Other times I fell back on taking tried and true wrestling announcing clichés and making them more blatantly gay than they were already. "Say what you will about El Homo's limp wristed, schlong eating, cum gargling lifestyle, this fairy sure can wrestle," I said after the rainbow warrior pulled off a series of snap suplexes.

But I saved my most caustic commentary for Warped's corporate sponsors. I ran them down at the beginning of each set. "The Vans Warped Tour is brought to you by Powerade," I said in my best traditional sportscaster voice, "Powerade, America's leading cause of type 2 diabetes!" Target, which had shelled out generously to have its logo included at the top of every Warped program and poster wasn't spared either: "Warped, sponsored by Target! Target, finding new and creative ways to deny their employees medical coverage since 1985!"

ISW's most unsavory characters modeled the sponsors' product as well. The Oi Boy drank from a cloudy, almost cum-like flavor of Powerade that I announced by saying: "After a full day of beating down ethnic minorities, the Oi Boy likes to refresh himself with an ice-cold bottle of White Powerade!" Mextacy also rehydrated with Powerade "after a hard night of rollin' on E," and Cruiser guzzled

Yoo-Hoo because "it's brown." I announced that the copies of *Mein Kampf* that the Oi Boy slammed over his opponents' heads were available at "Target Stores everywhere."

"Target," I elaborated, "your leading provider of hate literature!" I always wondered if there wasn't an increase in psychotic teens showing up at Target looking for Nazi literature after that.

My announcing job got easier as the wrestling improved, and ISW definitely turned a corner as we made our way towards the East Coast. Unprepared bodies that were more accustomed to the chair bound safety of office work adapted to daily pain. Our ideas got better too as we discovered what worked and discarded what didn't. The Señor Bueno arm-wrestling extravaganza compensated for the Chicken's lack of movement. When El Homo Loco joined the tour for a two-week stretch we immediately paired him with the Cruiser and finally had compelling opponents for 69 Degrees. When Homo left to return to his high-paying job at a pharmaceutical firm, Super Pulga and the Mexican Viking flew in, giving us another team that shined with 69. There was the race baiting of the Oi Boy vs. Frankie Dee bout that got the crowd heated and angry. Heated and angry was good. Heated and angry was what pro wrestling was all about.

There was also a fast-paced match between Macho Sasquatcho and a lanky indie worker called the Ladies' Man that started off every show for the last half of the tour. The match was geared towards short attention spans and showed the crowd that the guys in ISW could really work. Corgan and Ladies' Man delivered the same sequence of moves every day and never varied it. After their twelfth performance of this tussle, I knew the match so well that I had to keep from calling a move before it happened in the ring. I could have called it blindfolded.

The Ladies' Man had a body that was better suited for basketball than for wrestling and he was so tall that his feet didn't fit in his bunk. His real name was John Hannah and he made his living by managing his mother's cut-rate L.A. strip club. Stripping was a family business and wrestling was a sideline, and his sexist Ladies' Man persona emerged from the confluence of both worlds. Several of Hannah's best friends had made the jump from wrestling's middle tier into its big leagues. At the time of the tour, Hannah's pal Rob Van Dam was enjoying rising fame with the WWE. The Ladies' Man had been good friends with WCW wrestler Louie Spicolli, who had died after chasing twenty-six Somas with wine only days after his twenty-seventh birthday in 1998. Hannah was the one who discovered Spicolli's bloated body lying face first in a pool of his own vomit. Witnessing one of pro wrestling's grimmest statistics firsthand made the Ladies' Man oddly content with corralling exotic dancers and wrestling Sasquatches instead of pursuing his own piece of pay-per-view glory.

Since Ladies' Man worked in the adult entertainment industry, he knew all of its code words, carnie lingo and secret handshakes. This endowed him with the uncanny ability to get info out of strippers that most of us could only wonder about. At the Clermont Lounge in Atlanta, Ladies' Man found out this one blonde would perform a ménage à trois for the low, introductory price of 60 bucks. Ladies' Man had gotten married only two weeks before leaving for Warped so he had no intention on taking her up on her offer, but any darker impulses he may have had were headed off by the appearance of her privates. "She showed me her pussy," he confessed with a grimace, "and it was all bruised and nasty. It looked like somebody had punched it a couple of times."

The Clermont Lounge was on the bottom floor of a dilapidated hotel. When the taxi dropped us off, the cabbie glibly said, "Strip club downstairs, hotel upstairs. You know what to do." The Clermont proudly proclaimed it was "The Bible belt's Oldest Strip Club," and within its grimy walls danced some of the Bible Belt's oldest strippers. There was one stripper who looked like Ronald Reagan. Her pregnant daughter also worked the joint and the dancer who resembled our grandfatherly 40th president told us that she hoped to see the day when three generations of her family were shaking it at the Clermont. That meant that this woman, who was already ancient, planned on pole dancing for at least another eighteen years.

But the star of the Clermont was a middle-aged black woman named Blondie who had bleached all of her bodily hairs to justify her namesake. She made a show of crushing empty beer cans between her two titanic tits and she also passed out booklets of her poetry like she was at an espresso house Lit reading.

The cheap booze flowed freely at the Clermont and the Ladies' Man put in a standing order with one of the waitresses to keep the rounds coming. I also kept withdrawing twenties from the club's ATM and bought more drinks still. In the Clermont, liquid courage couldn't come fast enough. Finally, we all got brave and bought Craig a private dance from Blondie, but Blondie's dances were no bump-and-grind-cream-in-your-jeans trifles. She straddled Craig and then beat him with her mammaries, knocking his dome to and fro.

"Hey, go easy on him," I slurred, "he's gotta wrestle three matches tomorrow." The wrestlers in the room busted out laughing while Blondie tried to put Craig's eyes out with her pancake-sized nipples.

Audra showed up with Spike in tow and she soon insisted on subjecting her beau to Blondie's bludgeoning boobs. Besides gigging with the Gimme Gimmes, Spike also played bass for the Swingin' Utters and Blondie's personalized act gave that band's name a whole new meaning. The next day, Spike sang his set with a shiner from being brutalized by Blondie's breasts.

Things got really desperate as the tour headed into its final two weeks. Dave Steele had racked up so many concussions since that collision in Calgary that he was found wandering around the showers in Tampa, with a towel around his waist, still dripping and asking where he was and why he was there. If Dave kept on wrestling with what had to be multiple brain injuries, he risked becoming a mental vegetable. Since the thought of the patriotic parachute pants wearing Steele having to be spoon fed and sponged off for the rest of his life wasn't a pretty one, Audra sent him home. She replaced him with an indie wrestler called Libido Gigante. Gigante was an ardent libertarian with a Master's in economics who trained in lucha libre at Ultimo Dragon's Toryumon Gym in Mexico City. He fit right in on that bus, but he was only one man. We needed so many more.

Jefferson Monroe was moved to the referee spot after Bob the Ref bolted from the tour citing that his cat had died several days before. While having Monroe officiate matches instead of wrestling them probably kept a lot of wrestlers out of the hospital, it left us short one grappler. Making matters worse still, Audra also replaced a mostly healthy Dancin' Joey with her hairdresser. When Audra's stylist first hit the ring on a July afternoon in Florida, she turned a curious shade of purple and almost collapsed from heat stroke. Out of concerns for the woman's health, the hairdresser was limited to clipping and coloring Audra's hair and managing the Mexican Viking. This had us down by two wrestlers at a time when everyone was stretched past their mental and physical limits.

Craig and Corgan took up the slack by wrestling as many as three matches a day. In a delirium borne of continuous grappling, both men became hell-bent on slashing their own foreheads with tiny razor blades in a display of Southern style carnage. The practice of cutting yourself (usually on the forehead or upper arm) to simulate damage delivered by blows was referred to as "blading" in the backrooms. Flair and Dusty were the undisputed masters of this theatrical self-mutilation and they both bore the scar tissue across their foreheads to prove it. Tom and Craig justified this mutual masochism by firmly holding to the belief that strutting around the ring and bleeding from self-inflicted wounds was a whole lot easier than taking hard falls or getting hit with a steel chair.

"It'll be old school, like Dusty vs. Abdullah the Butcher," Corgan enthused one night as he pitched the idea to Craig and me in another nondescript parking lot. "We'll cut ourselves, bleed all over the place and just walk around hitting each other. It'll be like *I Like to Hurt People*."

*I Like to Hurt People* was required viewing for Tom's inner circle. It was a surreal wrestling documentary that contained the most extensive catalog of bloody wrestler footage ever assembled for one film. It featured a blood-drenched Dusty, a busted open Terry Funk and a crimson Ox Baker. It also had an interview with Bobo Brazil where he looked so out of his fucking mind that the movie could scare you if you watched it by yourself late at night. Those insane eyes of Bobo's — after six straight weeks of wrestling, Tom Corgan had developed that same disturbing gaze.

When Corgan came up with the idea of the blood match he sounded like he had just discovered a cure for cancer. His hysterical enthusiasm was contagious and Craig caught it in a big way. Craig was so damned excited about the razor blade fest that he even told Tigger about it on the phone later that night. Tigger freaked and begged him not to do it. Tigger was staying with their newborn daughter at Craig's folks' house in Humboldt while ISW was on the road. As Tigger got more and more exasperated by trying to talk her husband out of maiming himself, Craig's gray bearded dad got on the line.

"Craig, don't do it," Craig's father pleaded, "You have a family now. Think of your daughter!"

"I am thinking of my family," Craig zealously fired back. "I am thinking of my daughter! I'm doing this for her!"

The blood match between the Oi Boy and the Cruiser took place on a narrow fairway in Asbury Park, New Jersey. The ring was crowded between a collection of hotdog carts and cotton candy stands and an inappropriate number of young children had gathered to watch the wrestling that day.

Craig was the first to draw his own blood. He sliced his shoulder with an X-acto blade after the Oi Boy had whipped him into the ring post. An unsatisfactory small trickle of blood seeped out. It wasn't enough for Corgan so he started pounding on Craig's shoulder with a fork. A minuscule pool of blood started to form. It still wasn't enough. Corgan hit him more viciously. Craig's thespian screams became more and more real with every blow. The shoulder still wasn't bleeding enough. Corgan dragged the fork across the cut creating small tributaries of hemoglobin until the wound was finally pried open and red stuff started rushing down Craig's arm.

Parents didn't even bother to shield their children's eyes once the blood started to flow. Nobody left either. They just stood there and watched as the Nazi pummeled the bloody gay man. The whole point of the match was to let the blood provide the spectacle so Tom and Craig wouldn't have to do any high-risk moves. They did them anyway. They slammed each other on the pavement and did somersaults off the top rope. It was as if their bodies were now pro-grammed to take as much punishment as possible. Corgan finally made himself into a grisly mess by lacerating his own forehead after Cruiser hit him with a chair. Droplets of both men's blood commin-gled on ISW's sun bleached canvas making for a gruesome mosaic.

As more gore gushed out of her two hardest working wrestlers, Audra became visibly despondent over the match. She wouldn't even comment on it except to forbid her cast from ever again attempting such a thing. In a pro wrestling industry where hardcore violence was increasingly becoming standard operating procedure, Audra was probably the only promoter in North America to willfully ban blading. It wasn't as if safety was the issue for her, because she had no problem allowing wrestlers to risk snapping their necks by tak-ing twenty-foot dives off balconies. Blunt trauma and broken bones didn't make her nervous, but she couldn't stand the sight of blood.

Audra wasn't the only one. A year earlier a New Jersey state government that shared Audra's sensibilities had made the blood match illegal with the passage of Assembly Bill 2304. The legislation effectively banned blading and levied heavy fines for extreme wrestling promoters who sold tickets to minors for their squared circle blood feasts. However, the bill also contained very specific language exempting the WWE, WCW and ECW (the big three promoters of the time). By the language of the law the big three were considered unregulated "professional wrestling" rather than the heavily regulated "extreme wrestling," even though all three major leagues gleefully utilized blading by 2000. The "E" in ECW even stood for "Extreme." It was ECW's popularity that had so many Garden State kids hacking up each other's foreheads in the first place, but ECW was unexplainably held unaccountable. When the Oi Boy and the Cruiser bled all over the ring in front of a cluster of kiddies in Asbury Park, they were actually committing a crime.

State regulations aside, there was just something in the air in Jersey that made people want to see blood. Eminem pals D12 beat down rival rapper Esham with bottles and chains at the Warped show in Camden. After the beating, D12 tried to get their bus driver to crash through some barricades to get them out of the parking lot before the cops came. The driver just sat there and pulled his keys. Soon cop cars surrounded the bus and D12 were taken into custody. D12 were booted from the tour squelching any chance that Eminem would make an appearance at the Detroit Warped date, and Esham was sent to a Philadelphia hospital with a ruptured eyeball, hearing damage and a concussion. Later that night, I walked by Kevin Lyman as he frantically talked on his tiny cellphone. "I know Eminem is upset," he said impatiently, "but I don't really give a shit right now." Esham has been a one-eyed rapper ever since.

Jersey had enough bad feelings to go around, but it was positively electric the next day in the Big Apple. Over 1,000 hell heads surrounded the ring in New York that afternoon and from the looks of them, they had showed up just to see ISW. These were urban hicks from outer boroughs like Brooklyn and the Bronx. They were the people that made the barbed wire ultra violence of ECW a national cult phenomenon. Twenty years earlier, they'd provided the strong home base that allowed Vince McMahon to launch his global conquest of the wrestling industry. Wrestling may have been a staple in the South, but New York City had the best wrestling fans in the world — and the scariest. We didn't want to leave those dirtbags disappointed as they headed for home on the subway.

The show was held on a dirt-covered rock in the East River called Randall's Island, which the wrestlers both accidentally and jokingly referred to as Riker's Island. It had threatened to rain that afternoon so Gabriel had covered the ring with a tarp. When it was time for the show to begin, the crowd erupted into cheers as the tarp was removed. When I got on the mic, I felt like I was about to pitch game seven of the World Series. I got chills. We pulled out all the stops that day but stuck to the tried-and-true match-ups that we knew would work. Garbage and other debris was lovingly tossed into the ring. Fans broke through the barricades during Libido Gigante's match but were quickly pushed back by Gabriel and some of the wrestlers. By the end of the show, the Ladies' Man had to do a curtain call even though he'd lost to Macho Sasquatcho. Fans wanted me to pose for pictures with them. They wanted everyone's autograph — even Señor Bueno's.

That night, we had a few hours in the big city before bus call. Had I known that the World Trade Center was going to be wiped off the face of the Earth in little more than a month, I would have gone there or at least scanned the city's skyline for the Twin Towers. Instead, I got lit up on overpriced cocktails at the WWE's Times Square theme bar with a mob of unruly wrestlers. Then we headed down 42nd Street and barged into the Church of Scientology's NY HQ and heckled them until this schoolmarm in an admiral's outfit at the front desk threatened to call the cops. Harassing the Dianetics center was probably the dumbest thing I've ever done, but it seemed like a righteous idea at the time.

New York had reduced even the most urbanized San Franciscans into little more than gawking yokels with nowhere to go. Craig, the

Mexican Viking and I ended up at a Soviet themed art bar while Bad Boy Corey and the Ladies' Man got chased around Harlem by a transvestite hooker with a switchblade. "You couldn't really call it a cross dresser," Ladies' Man recounted back on the bus, "It was more like a drunk black dude with a wig."

The next day, Kevin Lyman went out of his way to walk up to me. "You know, I had my doubts about the wrestling the first couple of weeks of this tour," he confessed, "but now you guys are doing really good. I mean you're really kicking ass out there."

The Tuesday after that, *New York Times* music critic Ann Powers wrote: "[ISW] revived the backlot spirit of old-style bouts, keeping the act fresh, fleshy and theatrical," and, "the blend of satire aimed at the music business and plain old slapstick gave Incredibly Strange Wrestling the spark of old school punk." It was pretty lofty praise from the national paper of record. There was a moment there where we all felt that ISW was on its way. We were going to do more tours, maybe get on television, get a decent ring to practice in and finally earn a living from the damned thing. The only limits were our imaginations. As Warped headed into its final handful of dates, there was no holding us back.

# 17

# HOMOMANIA

NEW YORK WAS our pinnacle but the Toronto SkyDome was the prize. The SkyDome was hallowed ground to any pro wrestler under forty. It was the site of WrestleMania vi, where Hulk Hogan, who was never what you'd call a great ring technician, accomplished the impossible by dragging a memorable match out of the even more physically limited Ultimate Warrior. The faceoff between the two oiled up musclemen went down in the annals of the then World Wrestling Federation as one of the greatest championship bouts of all time mostly because Hogan allowed himself to lose.

Due to the arena's lofty mantle in pro wrestling history, the cast of 1SW had eagerly anticipated our show there ever since the finalized Warped Tour schedules had been handed out. Better still, the show was guaranteed to take place in the SkyDome and not in its parking lot, as had been the case with the Thomas & Mack Center in Vegas. As we crossed the border into Canada, the wrestlers were absolutely giddy over the possibility that our shopworn squared circle would be assembled over the same patch of cement where the Hulkster and Ultie once flexed their biceps and jiggled their boobs at each other.

Like Fred Durst before them, Lars Frederiksen and Tim Armstrong of Rancid couldn't resist the wrestling ring's allure. They'd been stopping by the ring every day for a while to catch some matches and they wanted to do something with the wrestling in Toronto. Unlike the other bands that had a major wrestling fetish, Rancid had more to offer us than just their rock star status. They had Vampiro.

Vampiro was a Canadian named Ian Hodgkinson who grew up wanting to be a rock star but became a pro wrestler instead. With a character culled from Anne Rice, Vampiro became a lucha libre sensation in Mexico and was even considered for a south of the border soap opera until the Latino TV producers found that Hodgkinson barely spoke any Spanish. By the late 1990s, Vampiro was signed by wcw. His gothy image — a face painted white and framed by natty dreads — won him a cult following that the Georgia based wrestling promotion never knew how to capitalize on. Vampiro started publicly airing his dirty laundry, complaining to several online wrestling scandal sheets about being held back by wcw's old guard of aging pros, including Kevin Nash and Hogan. He was soon ostracized by an industry that held its own code of *omertà* in highest esteem.

Only months earlier, Vampiro was a regular on one of cable's highest rated programs. By the time we met up with him, he was just another fame whore who got off on hanging out with rock bands and hoped that an appearance at the SkyDome in front of 20,000 prime members of pro wrestling's target audience would land him back on TV. Vampiro, the wrestler who wanted to be a rock star, was adept at befriending all of the rock stars that wanted to be wrestlers. Rancid were the latest to fall under Vampiro's charismatic spell.

Vampiro had agreed to work a match with one of our guys in Toronto, but Tim and Lars also wanted to do something with him onstage during Rancid's set. Rancid had a few teary-eyed ballads about skinheads so we figured we'd have the Oi Boy disrupt their set and spew some vile hate speech until Vampiro showed up to put the neo-Nazi through a table. Our skinhead heel was something that Rancid's fans could relate to.

On the morning of the SkyDome show, I took a walk around the retractable-domed arena's asphalt floor. For Blue Jays games the space was made into a baseball diamond with foam rubber and fake grass. For Warped, it was stripped of its Astroturf. The area that usually served as the outfield was dotted with a criss-crossing collective of half assembled merch tents and secondary stages that looked like a shantytown when contrasted with row after row of the SkyDome's perfectly symmetrical blue plastic seats. The teams of worn out roadies who positioned PA speakers and pushed around plywood resembled refugees from some 1980s Italian post-apocalyptic *Road Warrior* rip-off. I'd been in major league ballparks before but I was still in awe of how massive the SkyDome was.

As I wandered around the expansive main floor Tim Armstrong ran up to me. The bony punk veteran almost bowled me over with his sheer enthusiasm. He had been completely engulfed by the temp-to-perm insanity that came with staging violence. Hopefully for him, he'd get it all out of his system before it developed into a chronic condition. The wrestling bug could bite anybody.

"I can't wait 'til today man, I can't wait," he said, thrusting his fist in the air as if to channel his nearly uncontainable energy.

I could hardly wait too, but right then was my only chance to give Armstrong some ground rules. "Hey Tim," I said with a hint of hesitation, "When you're up there, you know, play to the crowd. Act pissed off when the Oi Boy takes the mic from you, but don't try to hit him. Don't try to kick him."

Armstrong nodded rapidly and I continued: "A lot of guys, they get in the ring or they get up onstage with a wrestler and they get excited and think they can ad lib something. The problem is that they don't know what they're doing and it could look bad to the audience. You know, let Vampiro and Oi Boy do all the work. That's what they're there for."

Armstrong seemed to agree with me.

"They know what they're doing," I added.

Well, at least Vampiro knew what he was doing. The night before in Montreal, Tom Corgan had consumed nearly a case of beer before Lars, Tim and Vampiro stopped by our bus to talk over Toronto. It could have been a bad situation. I tried to run some interference between Vampiro and Corgan to make sure that Vampiro didn't pull out of the deal thinking that we were a bunch of jackasses. Vampiro had packed on an unnatural thirty pounds of solid muscle since I'd last seen him on television. He was no doubt vying for the attention of the brawn obsessed Vince McMahon in hopes of getting signed by the WWE. Despite my best attempts to do the talking, Corgan kept drunkenly pulling at Vampiro and then acting out his grandiose plans for their little passion play by careening around an uneven patch of grass. Vampiro seemed unimpressed. I grew more nervous with every minute of face time that Corgan had with Vampiro.

Audra had already made us all miserable only a few days earlier in Buffalo by going on a fruitless witch-hunt after she claimed that somebody had eaten her Italian sandwich. In order to smoke out the culprit, Audra prohibited us from drinking beer or watching TV. "I will find out which one of you little shits ate my sandwich if I have to call all your parents," Audra announced repeatedly like a power mad yard duty. She had gone bonkers enough to believe that calling our parents was going to strike fear into a bunch of men in their thirties. It was something straight out *The Caine Mutiny* with Audra taking on Bogart's role as the paranoid Commander Queeg on his bogus quest for missing strawberries.

Being deprived of their medicinal Budweiser made the wrestlers crazier than they were already. Audra caved in after only a couple of days without getting a confession. In order to save face, she blamed Gino for the missing hoagie even though he was the one who brought it onboard in the first place. Audra just seemed to like heaping blame on Gino with scant provocation. Still, we all shuddered to think what Audra's reaction would be if a sloshed Tom Corgan managed to screw the pooch with the newly sober Rancid. Luckily, a bunch of wrestlers crammed into a tour bus for two months were given plenty of leeway by both the band and Vampiro. Everything was still on.

On the afternoon of August 11, 2001, Rancid's set went on like it always had — only this had to be the biggest crowd of the entire tour. The band hadn't enjoyed regular MTV rotation since the success of 1995's "...And Out Come the Wolves," but the East Bay punks had found a home on Warped as a kind of 1990s nostalgia act. For every new crop of tweens with safety pins stuck to their stenciled motorcycle jackets, singing along to "Ruby Soho" at Warped had become a right of passage.

Vampiro was already onstage, presumably to check out his friends' band. Right before Rancid went on, Tim Armstrong had the Oi Boy and Vampiro gather around in a circle with the band and hold hands for a moment of quiet contemplation. "It's something we like to do before every show," Armstrong earnestly explained, "It's called 'hands.'" In a tour filled with out of place images, the sight of Vampiro wearing corpse paint, Lars with his two foot tall multicolored mohawk and Corgan accessorized by boots and braces all huddled up for a team prayer before the rock concert had to take the cake.

I was on the side of the stage waiting to snap a picture at just the right moment. Warped was casual that way. If you had an all access pass you could hang out onstage as long as you didn't go and unplug somebody's guitar.

It was near the end of Rancid's set. Lars started strumming the opening chords to "The Ballad of Jimmy and Johnny." With his raspy singing voice he characteristically mumbled the tune's first phrase: "Jimmy and Johnny two friends of mine, skinheads what they claim."

That was Corgan's cue. The Oi Boy goose-stepped out onstage giving the seig heil salute. He ripped a microphone off its stand and started yelling, "No more Rancid! No more Rancid!"

Tim Armstrong had forgotten everything I had told him earlier that morning about not hitting the wrestlers. He immediately tried to brain the neo-Nazi with his solid-body Gibson Les Paul. Armstrong realized what he was doing and veered his instrument away just as the heaviest part of it was about to cave in Corgan's skull. Armstrong settled for repeatedly trying to kick the Oi Boy instead. Somehow Corgan persevered and a pair of guitar techs inconspicuously managed to set up a table in front of the drum riser.

"You nigger loving punks make me sick," Corgan's skinhead character raged as he had to straight-arm Tim and Lars. The fans started to get ugly. At least half the crowd seemed to believe that the Oi Boy was an honest-to-Adolf skinhead who'd found his way onstage. Several of those kids with stenciled motorcycle jackets tried to climb over the barricades, but nervous SkyDome security guards were pretty good at pushing them back. Those kids wanted to string the Oi Boy's battered corpse from the SkyDome's rafters like a recently deposed Mussolini. What was going to happen when that sea of youthful humanity surged forward like an unstoppable teenaged tidal wave?

A red-faced Oi Boy started chanting, "*You're a disgrace to the white race! You're a disgrace to the white race!*" Finally Vampiro stood up and grabbed Oi Boy by the throat. He held Corgan in place as he turned to the crowd. Like a real pro, Vampiro waited until every kid in the coliseum was hollering their lungs out. With his massive tattooed arm, Vampiro hoisted our racist wrestler way above his head. Corgan jumped a little to assist with the move, but from the looks of things, he hardly had to. As quickly as Corgan went up in the air, he came crashing down through the table. Every hand in the place shot up at just that moment ironically making the show look like a Fascist rally.

Corgan crawled and then rolled off the stage as if he were devastated. Vampiro took his bows and worked the crowd some more while Lars got back on the mic and yelled, "Fuck that Nazi bullshit!" The kids cheered again.

Craig and I accompanied Corgan back to the bus along with a couple of security guys. There were almost 20,000 kids who wanted to kick Tom's ass and it was agreed that he couldn't show his face in the arena for the rest of the show. For the next set of wrestling, he had to wear his Sasquatch suit the whole time.

Our SkyDome show closed with Vampiro headlining against Libido Gigante. Knowing firsthand how mercilessly sadistic even a lower tier pro could be towards someone who they felt was an amateur, we decided to have one of our better trained guys go against the former wcw star. Frankie Dee and Ladies' Man refused to get in the ring with Vampiro so that honor fell to Libido.

Libido didn't get much offense during his big match but he did eke out a two-count at one point. "I knew he was going to give me nothing," Libido later said on the bus, "so when I had that shot at that two-count, I applied a little leverage and I took it from him."

Gigante's big moment was short-lived however, and Vampiro quickly demolished him. After laying out Libido, the hulking Vampiro turned on referee Jefferson Monroe. Vampiro effortlessly pressed Monroe's small but dangerous body above his head and then sent the ref down headfirst into the mat with Vampiro's own vicious variation of the piledriver called The Nail in the Coffin. Monroe's body was folded into a heap in the corner.

Vampiro still wasn't done. He jumped out of the ring and grabbed me by my black belt and the collar of my gi and tossed me into the ring. I didn't want to go up for that finishing move of his. My only defense was to lie there like a beached whale. I tipped the scales at a hefty 350 pounds by that point. I gambled that even with his imposing muscle mass, Vampiro couldn't lift me if I didn't make it easy on him. Instead he split my legs apart while I begged for mercy and kneed me in the nuts. Vampiro pulled the blow like the pro that he was, but I definitely felt his tremendous knee hit my fragile family jewels. My pain was real, but I still sucked it up enough to get a couple of snapshots of me posing with Vampiro and Tim Armstrong after the match. We all looked like pirates.

Later that night, I strolled the mostly empty streets of Toronto until I found a 24-hour Kinko's Copies. Kinko's were like gold on tour. Wi-Fi connections were few and far between back then and Kinko's was one of the only places where we could check our e-mail. I hoped for a message from Dana or anybody else back home. I was mostly met with spam. While I still had some time left on the Kinko's computer, I checked the Warped Tour message board. There was already a raging debate among Rancid fans about whether the stunt with Oi Boy and Vampiro was faked or not. The majority of fans wrote that it had to be real because Tim and Lars would never do that sort of thing. If the twenty or so kids who bothered to post about it online thought it was real, then there could be hundreds or even thousands of others who felt the same way. Pro wrestling still had the power to put one over on people.

It was August 12th. We'd finally made it to the last day of the tour and nobody had died. There was one show left in Detroit and we were done.

I'd promised everyone that I'd bring back Uncle N.A.M.B.L.A. for our very final match. I had the hot pants and the weird sequined clown mask topped with eerie fake hair. Tom Corgan had purposely shaved his head to leave some randomly placed patches so he could play the part of a terminal cancer patient called the Chemo Kid. Chemo's last wish was to meet a real live pro wrestler.

There's an old comedy adage that cancer is never funny. ISW did nothing to change that. The match began with N.A.M.B.L.A.

groping the Chemo Kid. Chemo stood there and cried like a lost little child. The crowd around the ring stood slack jawed. I heard people in the audience say, "Somebody help that kid — please!"

I turned to the fans to taunt them. I was going to shout something really tasteful like, "I'm gonna fuck you 'til your bones crack!" But then I saw them. There were several kids no older than nine watching the wrestling. I looked at them and froze. It was a rare moment where I was speechless. I went back to dry humping and body slamming Chemo Kid as if that was somehow going to comfort those kids.

Quitting wrestling and switching to announcing kept me from breaking my neck, but left me in the worst shape of my life. As I labored to move around the springy surface of the ring, I could feel the trans-fatty acids slowly flowing through my hardening arteries. I was nearly naked as N.A.M.B.L.A., and my glowing white skin sizzled in the summer sun. "Look at the scarred flesh of Uncle N.A.M.B.L.A.," Craig said as he covered for me on the mic, adding an extra dose of gross-out to an exhibition that hardly needed it. "It looks like the surface of Mars!"

The Chemo Kid started to rally. He whipped N.A.M.B.L.A. into the corner. The fans chanted, "*Chemo! Chemo!*" After landing only a few blows, Chemo started coughing uncontrollably and collapsed in the middle of the ring from exhaustion. Sensing the bleak finality of the bout, little boys with tears streaming down their faces begged our merch guy to let them return the lucha masks they'd bought before the show. He refused, saddling the tykes with the stuff of nightmares.

It was time for the molesting uncle's big finisher. I pulled that chloroform-soaked rag out of my skintight shorts and placed it over Chemo's face. Corgan went limp. The shell-shocked audience stood silently as I slowly dragged him back into the changing tent.

I didn't know it at the time, but that was my very last match in an ISW ring. I spent the next two years with the troupe emceeing the action onstage and booking the matches behind the scenes. Craig's closing comments could have summed up my entire wrestling career. "This is probably the worst match that I've ever seen in my life," he announced as people fled our squared circle, "and I'm really glad that isw gets to go out on the Warped Tour on this kind of note."

I was home. I was with Dana. She smiled at me and smelled nice. My sheets were clean and my bed didn't have anyone's boots in it. I didn't have to fight with 12 angry wrestlers over what to watch on television. I could drift off to sleep without hearing the intermittent sound of oversized tires grinding over roadside rumble strips.

After two or three days of being home, I never wanted to tour again. I couldn't comprehend why I'd left in the first place.

After two weeks, I'd have given anything to get back on that bus.

It was barely a month after the Warped Tour. Planes flew into buildings. I don't need to tell you any more about this.

The night of September 11, 2001, I awkwardly tried to comfort Dana with so much macho History Channel bullshit. I told her that Pearl Harbor was actually worse because it destroyed our entire Pacific fleet and the Japanese could've walked right into California if they had wanted.

"Yeah, but Roosevelt was president back then," she said. She had a point.

Dana somehow got to sleep but I couldn't. The cable movie channels hadn't altered their previously programmed schedules to consider the terror attack. Appropriately, several of them were showing black and white horror movies. One channel had a movie where an army of invisible aliens brings the dead back to life so the reanimated corpses can crash planes, blow up bridges and burn down buildings in order to bring human civilization to its knees. On any other day, so much stock footage of fires and capsizing ships interspersed with extras stumbling around in pancake makeup would have been laughable. After that they showed *Night of the Living Dead*. It was really striking how much of that movie is made up of desperate people watching TV newscasts. I guess that's what you do when the world is falling apart.

Homomania was planned as our triumphant return to the Fillmore following Warped. It took place just over a month after 9/11 on October 16, 2001. During those days when American flags still hung from every front porch and street corner even in socialist San Francisco, the gallows humor that was ISW's stock in trade became problematic. In the end, we didn't hit the satiric highs of *The Onion*'s first post-9/11 paper with its headlines that blared, "Holy Fucking Shit: Attack on America" and "Hijackers Surprised to Find Selves in Hell." But we also resisted the urge to stoop to the crude Arab bashing skits that some of the wrestlers were calling for. We stuck to our original plan and presented our best matches from Warped that hadn't been seen in San Francisco. Homomania was our best show ever.

Señor Bueno arm-wrestled the Devil Chicken and Macho Sasquatcho took on the Ladies' Man. Super Pulga fought the Oi Boy instead of Frankie Dee, but the match was essentially the same except that the Mexican Viking ran in at a key moment to stop the neo-Nazi from flagrantly cheating with a dreaded foreign object. During the 69 Degrees match, El Gran Fangorio pushed Dancin' Joey off the top of the ring post. Joey plummeted ass-first onto a tiny Asian woman who didn't get out of the way. Surprisingly, no one was badly hurt. Even more surprisingly, no lawsuits were filed. The show also had the added bonus of the Poontangler pawing at El Homo Loco in an evening gown match.

Homomania was the show that Craig and I had known we could pull off ever since we'd seized the creative reigns of ISW a few years earlier. It didn't have any hired-on luchadores or any blowhard indie workers throwing their weight around backstage with all of their

BS about "real pro wrestling." Homomania was just us. The indie workers that were brought in had all earned their spots by being on the bus during Warped. Ladies' Man, Frankie and Shane may have trained in different leagues, but they had all been there for ISW's two-month punk rock gauntlet. They were now part of our crew as much as the Devil Chicken or the Cruiser.

As the tortilla dust cleared, a bittersweet feeling came over me. ISW had accomplished everything that it had set out to do. "You know it can all end here," I told Craig as he gathered up his gear into a duffel bag. Craig gave me a half smile but didn't say anything. It probably should have ended there.

But it didn't.

From August 1999 through October 2001, ISW had toured North America and played the Fillmore more times than many chart-topping acts. We should have had deals on the table and a future filled with tours and television, but Homomania was the last time our tortilla-tossing madness filled the Fillmore's storied ballroom. Follow-up tours to Warped also never materialized. ISW had fallen from the upper rungs of the showbiz ladder for a variety of reasons.

The dim post-9/11 landscape, with its recession and tougher travel restrictions, was especially harsh on the live music industry. That live music industry was under the increasing control of Clear Channel, which owned the Fillmore and every other significant music venue in the country. The multimedia mammoth maintained a corporate structure that stamped out the spontaneity so necessary for fostering interesting music scenes. It's doubtful if the company's suits in San Antonio ever understood, or cared for, ISW's controlled anarchy.

There was also that unresolved issue of the tortillas and Audra's winning ways with the Fillmore brass that led to the impasse. We could scapegoat the Fillmore's security dicks and their endless litany of rules ("Don't stand here, don't stand there") that fueled the flames of drunken discontent. They could blame our fans for showing up just to tear the place apart. Michael Bailey, the Fillmore's booker, told the *SF Weekly* in June 2002 that he was looking for a larger (and presumably less ornate) hall to host upcoming ISW shows. "It kind of has outgrown the venue," he said.

In the same article, Audra referred to Bailey's efforts as "a line of BS," and went on to accuse him of lying about any damage done by the tortillas. "They say there's been damage," she said, "but I've seen no proof. I've had to sign off [on the club's condition] after each show, and we've been okay."

That larger venue was never found.

The biggest cause of ISW's downfall may have stemmed from problems endemic to the pro wrestling industry as a whole. Wrestling was the big entertainment story of the late 1990s but was yesterday's news in 2001. By the time ISW shoved off for Warped, the violently innovative ECW had already collapsed under mountains of debt. World Championship Wrestling, a pillar of Ted Turner's broadcasting empire ever since he first bounced his Atlanta UHF station's signal off a satellite, was cancelled after the AOL/Time Warner merger. (ISW was actually the last promotion besides the WWE to mount a national tour, even though we went through the back door to do it.)

Vince McMahon gobbled up the remains of his former competitors at the ensuing sports entertainment fire sale. Wrestling effectively became a monopoly; Vince had finally outlasted and out-hustled his rivals. However, what should have been McMahon's greatest moment quickly gave way to lack of interest, lower ratings and shrinking attendance. The middle-aged rednecks that had always been there for WCW were tuning out WWE "attitude" and tuning in NASCAR. Teenage males, the WWE's most rabid fans, were more interested in playing the *Smackdown!* videogame than they were in attending live shows. As ISW's big-time counterpart became passé, interest in the quirky alternative that we presented petered out.

Audra had to shop around for a venue big enough for isw in an indifferent market that hadn't yet bounced back from the dot-com boom and bust, let alone the downturn that followed 9/11. In 2002, you could almost count the San Francisco clubs that booked punk and metal on one hand. A flap between Audra and the owners of the Covered Wagon caused her to pull Stinky's Peep Show from its longtime home, putting both of Audra's off-color enterprises on ice.

Stinky's occasionally reopened at nightclubs that were too big for the raunchy rock and roll burlesque show, but not big enough for isw. Where the Covered Wagon usually looked packed on Thursday nights, these larger rooms often appeared barren and empty. Stinky's semi-annual comebacks were always short-lived affairs. Where isw did nearly fifty dates in 2001, we only managed two shows in all of 2002. One was when a rich kid booked isw for his birthday party and rented out the old On Broadway, which was once a cornerstone of San Francisco's North Beach punk scene, now hired out for wedding receptions and private parties. The other was at a club so small that its doors had to be taken off the hinges to load in the ring.

Audra's future plans for isw amounted to little more than rumors. There were tours of Australia and Japan that never happened. Audra was briefly in negotiations for us to go on Ozzfest, but Vince McMahon cut a deal with Sharon Osbourne to send some of his wwe "superstars" out on the road with Sabbath and Slayer instead. isw was never a threat to the wwe, but Vince didn't get to where he was by leaving anything to chance. We put together a demo reel and tried to land a show on local tv, but even San Francisco station managers weren't ready to give El Homo Loco's dry humping antics a late night time slot.

As wrestling's overall fortunes worsened, it became hard not to contemplate that the scripted sport was headed for the same kind of pop cultural extinction that had already befallen roller derby and drive-in movies. And as the 21st century grew more grim, there lurked the possibility that even a seemingly unstoppable juggernaut like rock and roll might come to an end some day — not with the fury of Elvis' pelvis or a sneering Johnny Rotten, but with a corporate-sponsored whimper.

# 18

# MOVING IN WITH THE SASQUATCH

## (SLIGHT RETURN)

WRESTLERS GO CRAZY.

I know. I've said that already.

For some of us, the craziness passed. Craig pursued animation and I kept writing. When the wrestling show started to fade, we went back to doing what we'd always wanted to do. For us, wrestling was a detour. For others, it was a dead end.

In December 2002, Dana and I moved from our little house in Oceanview and into a spacious Victorian flat in Hunters Point. While Oceanview wasn't exactly SF's classiest locale, Hunters Point was universally agreed upon by city dwellers as the worst neighborhood in all of San Francisco. The district consisted of several square miles of urban blight and abandoned shipyards sitting on acres of toxic waste. At the neighborhood's southernmost tip lies Candlestick Park, the former home of the Giants and current home of the 49ers. The urban legends of my youth told of the baseball fans who took a wrong turn leaving the ballpark and were never heard from again.

Dana and I were looking for cheap rents and the next big thing. When I first moved to the city, the Mission District was a crime-ridden, death trap of a neighborhood, but today it's yuppie heaven with a tapas joint on every piss-stained corner. Friends of mine who signed their leases back when people were getting stabbed in front of the Taqueria San Jose are now paying $900 a month for rent-controlled three bedroom Victorian flats that would go for $2,500 on the current market.

We were going to dig in and wait for the gentrification even though we were all set to piss and moan about it when it finally happened. We had precedent on our side, but nobody was going to gentrify the HP anytime soon. After barely a month of living there, the windows to our cars were broken on a weekly basis and the batteries to my van were lifted just as often. A uniformed cop was gunned down with an AK-47 only blocks from our flat and some transportation workers laying tracks for a new rail line were sniped at as if they were in the Sunni Triangle.

While we had to get the hell out of Hunters Point, Tom Corgan had one roommate who hadn't paid rent in months and another who was bailing on him. He was going to have two rooms available and hadn't yet mastered the art of posting ads on Craigslist. We'd really be doing him a favor if we moved in with him. One room could be our bedroom and the other could be my office. The timing was just too good. It was too easy. We moved in with Tom Corgan. We hadn't even unpacked when things started to go wrong. Tom was always the last one to go to sleep and the first one to wake up in the morning. The cases of beer that he consumed daily were starting to give him wet brain or even worse. His skin began to take on a yellowish shade of pale. He was between jobs and collecting unemployment checks so he was home all the time. At night Tom had a crusty collection of losers and drinking buddies over to watch SportsCenter on his satellite TV and smoke his weed. Some of them were teenaged kids and some were aging burnouts with mullets. The party seemed to be comprised of whomever Tom could get to stop by.

On top of that, Tom was no longer sure if he was going to throw out the one deadbeat roommate that was still there after all. He liked the kid. The kid drank with him and was there to watch every boxing and wrestling pay-per-view that Tom's hacked cable box could give them. Pay-per-views were very, very important to Tom. He never missed one as long as it involved men beating the crap out of each other. He always made sure that everyone he knew was there to view the bloody spectacle with him.

This presented a big problem. Not only could Dana and I not unpack the copious amounts of crap that we had accumulated after four years of living together, but I also wouldn't have a place to set up my computer and write. At that time in early 2003, I was on a deadline to ghost write the autobiography of legendary Hollywood stuntman, judo champ and Los Angeles pro wrestler "Judo" Gene LeBell. He was the guy who taught Bruce Lee and Chuck Norris how to break arms and he was in thousands of movies and TV shows. It was a job that I had lucked into but it didn't pay me any advance or cover my expenses. It was still a really big break for me though and I had lost enough time on it during the retreat from Hunter's Point. A deadline was still a deadline and mine was coming up at the end of May.

When we agreed to move in with Tom, I believed that I'd have a room where I could set up shop, but now it looked like I might have to try to finish my book in a crowded kitchen or living room with the shouts of Vince McMahon's staged slugfests blaring from Tom's many televisions.

"Tom, we wouldn't have moved in here if we couldn't have the two rooms," I said after he had told me that he was considering letting the other roommate stay. "We're going to pay for them."

Tom looked at me blankly and said, "Alright." Who could tell what he was thinking or what he had promised his other room-mate? I was on a deadline. I had to write and it was impossible to get any work done at Tom's.

What I did next only poured gasoline on the fire. I moved my computer and tape recorder over to the other side of the Bay to my mom's house in Menlo Park. She was at work all day long and wouldn't get in my way at night nearly as much as Tom and his wrestling-watching cronies did. The scary thing about this was that it left Dana alone at Tom's on the nights that I worked late at my mother's, but Dana and Tom had been friends for years. Things should have worked out for a while.

However, after six days of living at Tom's place, Dana and I had already begun coming up with phased evacuation strategies. We looked at some high-rise apartments in downtown Oakland. But we didn't want to leave Tom high and dry, so we agreed we wouldn't leave until we had helped him find some more compatible boarders.

During the days that I was away working on the book, Tom only got stranger. He started bothering Dana when she was in the bathroom getting ready for work in the morning. He knocked on the door and asked her what she was doing in there. I later had to explain to him, "Yes, women really do take a longer time in the bathroom just like on TV." Dana had to ask him to keep it down a few times on work nights, requesting that he try not to have people over past eleven or midnight on weeknights. The tension was only mounting.

One afternoon, when I was leaving for my mother's house he stopped me and asked if I was going to be around to watch *Smackdown!* later that night.

"No," I explained, "I really have to get cracking on this book. My deadline's coming up pretty quick. I will be around this weekend and we'll sort through all of these boxes and get everything squared away then."

He gave me the "say it ain't so, Joe" look of a disappointed kid. He looked like he needed to tell me something, but for some reason he chose not to.

I was in Menlo Park working on the book when I got the phone call. Dana was sobbing hysterically. "Tom just threw me out," she cried.

"What?" I asked. I was stunned.

"He threw me out," she said choking back tears. "He said I had to leave, that I had to get out and he attacked me! He tried to grab me! He chased me down the hall!"

"What the fuck?" I said. I couldn't believe it. We had paid a deposit. Dana was the only one in the whole fucking house who was holding down a real job for Christ's sake. We were all friends. You don't just toss your rent paying friends out of the house with nothing more than a two-minute warning — or go around attacking girls. Even for Tom it just didn't make sense. Had he really slipped that far?

My heart rate quickened. I could hear banging, pounding and yelling in the background. I couldn't make out everything that she was saying with all of the noise. Driving to Oakland would take nearly an hour. There was nothing I could do. I felt powerless as I clutched the phone.

"Put him on the phone," I demanded. "Put him on the goddamned phone!" All I could do was talk.

I could hear her start to hand him the phone. "He wants to talk to you," she said in the distance.

"No, I don't want to talk to him right now," he argued through the white noise.

"Just talk to him," she sobbed. My heart was breaking. I was breaking out into a cold sweat only able to passively listen to what was happening.

He finally took the phone from her and said, "She has to go, Bob. She has to go. I have had it. You can stay, but she has to go!"

"What the fuck!" I yelled into the mouthpiece. "We were fucking friends! You don't throw out my fucking girlfriend and expect me to stay in your shitty house! You're the big tough wrestler! The big tough judo man and you attack girls! You sick son of a bitch! Dana and I are a package deal. Where she goes I fucking go. If you were half a man, if you were an adult, you would already fucking know that!"

I wasn't letting him explain himself. I wasn't letting him get a word in edgewise. I wasn't in the mood.

"You really need some fucking help, Tom," I continued. "You have a problem. You need to check into a fucking program somewhere!"

He lost it after that last remark. "Don't call me crazy," he shrieked. "Don't call me crazy!" He repeated that over and over again until his ranting became utterly unintelligible and animalistic. He sounded more like a howling beast than a human being. I could picture him all red-faced with veins popping out of his temples and spittle flying from his mouth in every direction.

"Give me back the phone, Tom," I heard Dana say in the background. "Give me back my phone!"

"Give her back the fucking phone!" I yelled. "God, give her back the fucking phone!" Then the phone went dead. I was scared. In his mental state, he was capable of anything. I needed to get the Oakland PD on the phone. I needed to call the police in a different county and hope to high holy fuck that they arrived on time. Do you just call 911 for that or do they route you to a local operator who can't do jack shit for you? Would it be different if I called from a cellphone? Technology questions crowded my mind right when I needed things to be very simple.

I was fumbling for a phone book when the phone rang again. It was Dana. She was in the car and she was driving to meet me. She was still hysterical but she was safe. "When he chased me down the hall, he stomped after me like Stone Cold," she recalled. "And then he waved his arms at me and flexed like Hogan does on TV before he tried to grab me."

Wrestlers use wildly caricatural motions in their form of theatre. While this looks goofy as all hell on TV, the stagecraft is developed so that the audience in the back of the arena can feel the full emotional impact of what is going on in the ring. The only audience at Corgan's house the night that he chased Dana consisted of Corgan, Dana, the kid who wasn't paying rent and the kid's mom who was visiting from Mexico. The kid and his mother locked themselves in a bedroom through the whole thing and weren't able to see Tom's well-honed theatrics, except when the mom quickly poked her head out the door and beckoned Dana to take shelter with them.

After Hunter's Point and moving in with the Sasquatch we were going to have to move into my mother's house. We hadn't even lived at Tom's for a whole two weeks.

Was Bill Clinton ever our president? Did those eight years even happen? It was as if some sick bastard had turned back the clock to 1990 on me. Someone named George Bush was president again and we were about to go to war with Iraq. I was back at my mom's house and living with my girlfriend in the same room that I had grown up in. A San Francisco Giants poster bearing the autographs of Bill North and Vida Blue was still stuck to the wall by an unmatching assortment of thumbtacks. Boxes of comic books were still stacked in the closet corner where I had left them.

Two weeks after moving into my mother's house, the Sasquatch left a very unapologetic apology on Dana's cellphone voice mail. "I'm sorry that things had to happen the way they did, Bob," he said, managing not to take any responsibility for threatening to give my girlfriend a swinging neck breaker. It was as if the whole thing was some kind of unavoidable natural disaster, or maybe he fancied himself akin to that tiger that mauled half of Siegfried and Roy. He went on to reiterate that I was welcome to stay at his place, but that Dana wasn't. He somehow thought that this should make everything okay. It did more to creep me out than anything else. I quickly deleted the message, never wanting to hear it again. He may have still feared that I would find a way to pull some strings and get him ejected from the wrestling show. But there was no apology that he could give that I could accept — not even if he had mustered a sincere one.

I kind of grew to like the solitude of the suburbs though. Menlo Park was only thirty-five miles away from San Francisco, but it might as well have been on a different planet. I threw myself into working on the "Judo" Gene book. My days were spent furiously cobbling chapters together from hours of tape-recorded transcripts. At night, I gobbled down chocolate buttermilk bars at the 24-hour Chuck's Donuts and chased them down with watery coffee that had been sitting on the warmer for far too long. I pecked away on my second-hand laptop until the batteries went dead and then drove aimlessly through the strip mall lined boulevards and sequestered cul-de-sacs of my old hometown waiting for the Yuban high to wear off.

Months passed and the wrestling show was the last thing that I needed to deal with. It was March or maybe April when Audra finally caught up with me.

"Dante, where the hell have you been?" she asked with her gravelly voice right when I picked up the phone.

"Well, we moved in with the Sasquatch, he threw Dana out, it got pretty nasty and now we're living at my mom's house," I answered calmly.

"Oh my God," she said with concern. "What happened?"

"I don't know," I replied. "We weren't even there two weeks before Corgan flipped out on Dana. It was pretty bad."

Audra's concern quickly melted away as she realized the consequences of what had happened. "I don't need to go through this bullshit with you again, Dante," she said in a growing fit of anger referring to the feud with Chango Loco.

"Look, Audra," I said, trying not to be combative. "You don't have to worry about me freaking out on you like Chango. I'll just leave. It's okay. You can keep Tom. It's the decision that I would make."

I could have done what Tom must have feared and tried to hit Audra with some half-baked demands, but the punk rock wrestling show was never going to be fun for me again. I couldn't have Dana backstage helping a luchadore lace up his mask with Tom skulking around. It wasn't like I could shoot the bull with Tom on the phone and work out the bugs of a whole slew of wrestling matches again either. There was no "either he goes or I go" moment. Audra could keep the Sasquatch and his dragon moonsaults. The 1990s needed to die. I was done.

"We've got a show at the Avalon Ballroom on April 12," she growled, "and I don't need this fucking headache right now!"

She still thought that she could bang Tom's and my heads together and that everything would be okay, but the Sasquatch incident wasn't going to blow over any time soon.

"This isn't about you," I said. "I've got to get my life back together. I've got to find a way to move out of my mom's house and get the book done. There are more important things to me right now than the wrestling show."

"What the hell is that supposed to mean?" she said after taking a deep breath.

I paused for a second to collect my thoughts. I don't know why, but I still had myself walking on a tightrope trying to be political. "It means that you should probably do this next show without me and let's talk about this at some other time."

I braced for her reply but I was first met with a click, then silence and then a dial tone. She had hung up the phone on me. She must have been on her mobile or a cordless phone because I didn't hear that distinctive sound of the receiver slamming down onto molded plastic, but I still remembered that clang as if I had.

A whole host of people got to Audra before she could call me back to curse me out. Even U.S. Steele put in a good word or two on my behalf. "He's writing a book," he told her. "He's been through a lot of shit with the Sasquatch. Give him a break."

Audra phoned back a few days later. This time she was sweeter than pie buried beneath mounds of whipped cream and topped with generous doses of chocolate syrup. This meant that she needed me for something more than another local show in a nightclub that had been closed for decades. Audra had pulled every string and called in every favor that she could to book us on a European tour. In doing so, she had picked the worst possible time to get the show back on the road.

The tour was called Deconstruction. It was a scaled-down Euro version of Warped with all of the same sights, sounds and corporate shilling, but served in more modest Old World portions. There'd be skaters in the half-pipe and happy punk onstage. NOFX was the headliner and an Austrian energy drink made from synthetic bovine testosterone sponsored the show. We were leaving on May 26 and coming back on June 10. It was only ten dates spread out over two weeks, but if it had been any longer, nobody would have gone.

Deconstruction was the European tour that nobody wanted. The Iraq War had started. On May 1, Bush declared that "all major combat operations had ended" from the deck of that aircraft carrier. The war went on anyway despite the president's, Cheney's and Rumsfeld's claims to the contrary. The economy still sucked. Wrestlers had trouble getting the time off work and were afraid of losing their jobs when they got back. Because of the war, the thought of jihadists blowing up our plane crossed everyone's mind.

Audra begged, pleaded and made promises to keep her biggest claim to cool from becoming nothing more than the drunken memories of aging party girls who'd hung up their binge drinking and bar-hopping for tattooed motherhood in the 'burbs. She relentlessly worked the phones bearing both carrots and sticks until each wrestler caved in one by one. Audra was fighting Father Time in a last-ditch effort to stave off that new bumper crop of Gen Y hipsters who bought their clothes at truck stops but still managed to look ultra effeminate and wanted to infuse everything with emo's bastard little brother, screamo. As the European tour neared, Audra became almost Ahab-like in her determination to jump-start isw.

My grudge against the Sasquatch cast an ominous pall over the entire trip. I had to finish my book and move out of my mom's house. I had to get my life back together before Dana got sick of it all and left my ass. I had every reason not to go and had even told Audra no a few times, but that only made her turn up the heat. She promised that Corgan would ride on a different bus. She kept calling and I kept answering. In the end, my resolve was weak. I'd spent too many years putting everything I had into isw. I didn't want to be the one to break up the band. Audra kept up the pressure and I gave in to indecision, and fame sucking nostalgia — just like everyone else.

It was only a week before I took off for Europe. Only a week until I'd have to look at Tom Corgan every day. I hated his living guts. I didn't even want to run into him in a bar let alone share buses and planes with him. But I didn't think about that much. I didn't have time to. I had to finish the book.

I would've liked to have spent some time with Dana before facing who knows what in Europe, but I didn't have time for her either. Deconstruction forced me to turn in the book a week early. With my expedited deadline looming, I had to spend every waking minute of my last week at home fastidiously smoothing out chapters and tying up loose ends in my prose. When I wasn't furiously typing on my PC, I was on the phone with Gene going over the revisions that I'd just faxed him. The revisions begat more revisions. It was LeBell's life story. He wasn't going to be rushed just because I was.

I had the manuscript finished by Saturday, May 24 with every chapter approved by Gene, but there were all kinds of last minute details to take care of. I had to format a piece that Chuck Norris had submitted for one foreword and I had to take dictation from "Rowdy" Roddy Piper for a second foreword. Gene wanted one foreword to reflect martial arts and the other to focus on wrestling.

Piper called me at 2 P.M. on Sunday afternoon. I was leaving for a wrestling tour the next day and I was talking to one of the most popular pro wrestlers of all time. Hogan may have been a bigger star but the Hulkster would have been nothing without Piper playing the foil. LeBell had given Piper his start in pro wrestling and had even awarded "Rowdy" Roddy with a black belt in grappling. As a heel in the wrestling ring, Piper was always snide and arrogant. When talking about Gene, he was reverent and sincere.

After recording his reminiscence, I had to take a few minutes to shoot the bull with him. He had a chapter of his autobiography called "The Sickness" about the messed up mental state that most pro wrestlers find themselves in. I knew a few Incredibly Strange Wrestlers who had the sickness. I had even lived with one.

"I've got to get this book to the publisher tonight," I said, "and then I'm leaving for Europe for a wrestling tour tomorrow."

Piper paused for a second. "That's rough, brother," the Rowdy One said with a mellower version of the same voice that I had once heard berating Jimmy "Superfly" Snuka, "that's real rough."

# 19

# AMSTERDAMAGE

THERE WAS A TRANSIT STRIKE in France. There was always a transit strike in France. We had been marooned in the Charles de Gaulle airport for nearly seven hours. Wrestlers sprawled out on uncomfortable concrete benches or sat on the floor while Audra stood at a grossly understaffed ticket counter in a frantic yet plodding effort to put all of us onto one of the few German flights that were cleared for takeoff. Shane and Manny looked increasingly forlorn as they passed the time by taking long drags off a steady supply of Camel Wides. The gendarmes kept coming by and making them put out their smokes.

"I will not warn you again," the French airport cop said while pointing to a sign above a perfectly maintained ashtray that read "NE FUMEZ PAS," which meant "No Smoking."

"They've got a fucking 'no smoking' sign right above an ashtray," Shane groused, "That's like putting a 'No shitting' sign above the toilet!"

I watched Tom Corgan as he enthusiastically recalled wrestling matches that he'd seen on television as if he'd been there. The mood of most of the wrestlers was dour but Corgan was finally back in the only element he understood. I thought of burying my big knuckle into his temple with all my weight behind it. I wanted that sick sense of satisfaction that comes with making a man's head snap back just a little farther than it was meant to and then watching him collapse into an unconscious heap. Then I thought about Dana back home and how I'd allowed myself to be talked into touring with a show that no longer mattered. My heart sank into my shoes.

I didn't really have that many choices on how to handle the situation. I had to work with Tom every day. If I scowled at him or gave him the silent treatment for the whole trip, I was going to make everyone else more miserable than they were already. Craig, Manny, Mextacy and U.S. Steele were still my friends even if Tom wasn't.

I looked at Corgan. I walked up to him. He was standing next to a very long staircase. It would have been so satisfying to push him down it.

"Hi, Tom," I said as if nothing had happened. There was a pause, but then I broke the ice a little further by telling Tom about talking to Piper the day before. I went on about working with LeBell and spun the little bits of gossip that I'd picked up about Andre the Giant and Mando Guerrero. I gave Tom the shoot interview material, the behind the scenes poop, and the stories that weren't making it into the book — the stuff that he lived for. I didn't talk about Dana. I didn't talk about the incident. I just blathered about stupid pro wrestling bullshit.

Corgan ate it all up with a spoon. He didn't mention Dana or the incident either. He didn't offer an apology. I was glad. That meant that I didn't have to accept one. Without telling him or anyone else, I had called a ceasefire. This temporary truce would last until we were done with Europe. After we got back, I fully intended to resume the icy hostilities.

Audra finally finagled some flights to Hanover. From there we could hopefully get booked on another puddle jumper to Vienna but everything wasn't in the bag yet.

We had to haul ass across the vast expanse of the Parisian airport to make it to our plane in time. Audra, Van Dyne and I ran across the tarmac as fast as our chubby little legs would carry us. We made it with barely a minute to spare before takeoff.

After we touched down in Hanover, we had to hustle again to catch our connecting flight to Austria. The small jet plane was filled with German businessmen wearing suits with slightly odd color combinations and overly wide lapels. I had gained at least another thirty pounds while working on the LeBell book and stood several inches taller than most Europeans. I was wearing a loud xxxL Hawaiian shirt and had let my hair grow well past my shoulders. As I entered the plane, the Teutonic travelers poked their heads out from behind their seats and started pointing at me, chatting wildly in German. They seemed happy to see me. I was a lard laden American colossus. I was a freak. It was as if King Kong had just boarded their flight.

We made it to Vienna in one piece. Surprisingly, only Shane's luggage ended up in Budapest. This forced him to borrow a mismatched ensemble of gear just to wrestle one match during our first show. He was already in a bad mood before we left San Francisco. This little indignity sent him on an irreversible downward spiral.

Shane's wife and kids back in Meadow Vista, California, didn't want him to go on the trip. Like the rest of us, he went anyway. Shane popped an ungodly amount of pills just to cope with the flight to France. He quickly crashed out with his face leaning on the flat panel video screen that was imbedded into the back of the seat in front of him. Its flickering menu gave Shane the choice of watching *Daredevil* with Ben Affleck, an old *Streets of San Francisco* episode or a European weather report. I reached over and turned Shane's set off for him. It woke him up. He turned to me and said, "I didn't know what that wassssss," and slipped back into his comatose state. Shane was that brute that we all feared when we first broke into ISW. Now he was just somebody's dad.

The ring that Audra had secured for the tour arrived in Vienna without any turnbuckle pads. Shane, Manny, U.S. Steele and I found these wacky pillows at an Austrian fabric store that resembled fruit with smiley faces. There was a happy pineapple, a grinning pear, a laughing apple and an overjoyed orange. We walked up to the checkout counter with twelve of those ridiculously cheery pillows. The two blonde teen girls laughed at us while we made our purchase. Those cushions became our turnbuckle pads for the entire tour.

The Europeans also didn't understand the concept of cheap, shitty folding tables that shatter upon minimal impact. When some stagehands brought us a Euro folding table, it was constructed with better craftsmanship than most Americans' dining room furniture. The tabletop was made from half-foot thick Congolese mahogany with legs cast from tempered steel instead of thin aluminum. It was a card table meant to last 1,000 years. We were still going to do the Chicken vs. Bueno arm-wrestling match. We hadn't had any new ideas in almost two years. There was no way that even our most rotund wrestlers were going to be able to break those tables in half. We thought of scoring them, but nobody had a Skilsaw. For the Vienna show, I scrounged up a pile of scrap wood and had some roadies nail together a makeshift table out of that. We hoped that we'd be able to find the familiar, cruddy tables that we so desperately needed in other cities, but we weren't so lucky. We wanted Wal-Mart but were confronted with quality merchandise made by people who paid union dues.

Despite being haggard from the hassle of getting there, Vienna was our best show on the Deconstruction tour. There was a second or two where we all thought that ISW could work again, but that was just the cruel Gods of grappling messing with our minds.

Dancin' Joey doubled as the death rocker wrestler Oh My Goth. A much-improved Mextacy was back and his spaced out character really connected with the fans. We had originally planned not to do the Oi Boy in the German speaking countries. For starters, it was in horrendously bad taste, plus Nazi displays or exhibitions of any kind are illegal in Germany. But with Shane only able to work one match, we chanced unleashing our skinhead in Austria. No cops caught wind of it. Nothing seemed to come of it.

In order to shamelessly cater to our European audiences' anti-American sentiments, every show ended with U.S. Steele losing to either El Homo Loco or Macho Sasquatcho. In Vienna, it was El Homo Loco's turn to beat the star spangled super patriot. After Homo pinned Steele's shoulders to the mat, the crowd erupted with an intensity that we had never heard before. The Austrian punk kids kept chanting, "*Homo! Homo! Homo!*" This went on for several minutes. Homo Loco came out and did a couple of curtain calls. Then they started working the name "El Homo Loco" into their soccer hooligan songs. It continued for another few minutes until they tired of El Homo Loco. Several punks started chanting for the Oi Boy. Soon, more than half the crowd joined in. There was something utterly unnerving about hundreds of teenagers wanting our neo-Nazi to do an encore in Hitler's hometown.

Two days later we were surrounded by 5,000 angry kids at an ice hockey arena in the suburbs of Zurich. None of those kids wanted us there. They hated America and they hated pro wrestling even more. As the set went on, we started to hate them back. Everyone thinks that the Swiss are so nice and neutral, but that just gives them carte blanche to be the worst shits in all Europe. Fuck the Swiss and their chocolates, cuckoo clocks, Nazi gold and army knives.

The trouble started before we'd even got there. The Swiss national wrestling team tried to pull some strings with the venue to get us booted off the show because our fake wrestling wasn't as real as their

Olympic wrestling. They were unsuccessful but Audra wanted to respond with a terrible skit. She wanted this bald, modern primitive guy with hoops through his ears and a spike through his nose to play the head of the Swiss Olympic committee and announce that ISW had been banned from their country.

"That's a terrible idea," I said, challenging Audra while we waited in the wings to go on for our second set. We had bombed during our first set. The Swiss punks weren't booing the individual wrestlers. They were booing ISW.

"That skit will only work if those kids actually want to see us. I'll tell you right now, those kids are gonna cheer like fuck when this guy announces that we aren't going on!"

"Fucking fine," Audra said and put her hand in front of my face.

"Because fucking Dante's such a fucking baby, we aren't gonna do the skit," she announced in a feeble attempt to make the wrestlers mad at me for stopping a skit that they didn't want to do. The wrestlers unanimously let out sighs of relief. It was ugly in that arena. The less time spent out there, the better.

Shane finally had his Gran Fangorio garb back. During his match, some freaky looking dudes with long stringy hair broke through the barricades. Gran Fangorio got out of the ring, punched one of them in the face and shoved them back into the crowd. We didn't have Gabriel working security on this trip and we really needed him. Instead, we had an overly cautious bouncer from the Fillmore named Eli who really had his hands full keeping those shits from storming the ring. The whole audience was against us and the ring was set up right in the middle of the main floor. We had no clear path back to the locker room without having to plow through hundreds of hate-filled people to get there. I wished that I had a Winchester repeating rifle as I continued to announce wrestling moves before a crowd that clearly couldn't make out a word I was saying.

Finally, it was time for the final bout. El Homo Loco was in the ring against U.S. Steele. They locked up and exchanged holds as hails of wadded up paper and even hard boiled eggs rained down on the ring. The match went on for a few more minutes, but then Steele went from a sickly shade of green to white as a ghost. He gave Homo the secret signal to end the match early. I thought that somebody had tagged him with a piece of metal or broken glass. It was worse than that: the Swiss were literally shitting and barfing in paper cups and then hurling those cups into the ring. A cup full of vomit had hit Steele in the face and some of its contents had worked its way into his mouth. Lumps of feces had left little brown stains all over our mat.

After the set, I waited on the side of the main stage for NOFX to go on. When Fat Mike started singing, all of those shit tossing Swiss teens massed around the stage. I pulled out the pair of dirty underwear that I'd worn for two days of touring in an overcrowded double-decker bus. I waved the sweaty and stinky cotton briefs over my head like David about to slay Goliath and hurled man panties big enough for my fat ass into the heart of the crowd. I probably netted three or four Swiss punks that way. The fuckers.

On the eve of the tour, Audra had picked up the sick habit of referring to herself as "Mama."

"If Mama ain't happy, then nobody's happy," she said over and over again. She had said it in the meeting a week before we shoved off. She said it in SFO and in Charles de Gaulle. She said it in Austria, Switzerland and Germany.

Thanks to the Sasquatch, I was living with my mom at the time. When other wrestlers started referring to Audra as Mama, the Oedipal connotations of her new nickname made me shudder from an involuntary gag reflex.

The stress of cozying up to Tom and working with an increasingly unglued Audra had started to manifest itself with a slew of psychological side effects. I suffered from panic attacks and hyperventilated every night as I struggled to catch some sleep in a claustrophobic berth that wasn't designed to accommodate a man of my height and girth. I'd never had a panic attack before — even through all of the shit with the Sasquatch or Chango or while my car burst into flames on I-5. To cope, I started sneaking shots of booze in the daytime, guzzling beer at night and smoking every ounce of Amsterdam hash that I could lay my hands on. Alka-Seltzer was my only sober beverage.

Contrary to Audra's earlier promises, the Sasquatch didn't ride on a separate bus but instead slept only a few bunks down from me. Sometimes I heard Corgan's alcoholic wheeze as the bus made its way to the next venue. I thought of crawling over to his bed and shoving a pillow over his face to smother the life out of him. Half conscious dreams of murder often shocked me awake just as I felt myself drifting off into a deep sleep.

At this Podunk lakeside resort in Germany, Audra finally succumbed to the bad wrestling craziness that had already consumed the likes of Chango and the Sasquatch. During isw's first set, a couple of creepy German kids started yelling for the Oi Boy. They must have heard about our neo-Nazi from some verboten Internet chat room for closeted Hitler Youth. These kids' enthusiasm for one of our characters made something snap in Audra.

"We're not doing Macho Sasquatcho versus Gran Fangorio in the second set," she commanded as we made our way back to the bus, "It's going to be the Oi Boy against Fangorio and Oi Boy's going over!"

Audra wanted to rearrange our show on the fly all just to please some little Aryan psych cases who fantasized about gassing Jews just like dear old grandpa used to do. And she was willing to risk landing Corgan's ass in the can in the process.

Shane stalked off and seemed more homesick than ever after hearing this edict. "I didn't know what to do, Dante," he later confided, "Fangorio's always been the heel. Against the Oi Boy, I'd have to change gears and work as a face. It just didn't make sense."

Nothing made sense. I wasn't even sure if Audra was planning on portraying the Oi Boy as the villain in the match. In ISW, I'd always been one to push the boundaries of bad taste with creations like the Oi Boy and Uncle N.A.M.B.L.A., but there was an enormity of history coming down on us at that moment in Germany. Everyone felt it but our promoter.

It was an hour until the second set. Corgan came up to me with a worried look in his eyes. "Bob, I really don't want to do this," he said.

It was more than just doing time in a foreign jail that was getting to Tom. He wasn't always the wrestling obsessed nutcase that he had worked so hard to become. He had earned a degree from some swank private college back East. During one of his more lucid moments, he understood the implications of what Audra was asking him to do and it just wasn't fun anymore. We may as well have been trying to put on a stage production of *Hogan's Heroes* in Tel Aviv.

"Yeah, Tom, you're right," I said, letting out a deep breath. "We're gonna have to tell her that we can't do it. We'll just have to tell her."

I had already locked horns with Audra once on this trip. I didn't look forward to doing it again. Under any other circumstances, I would have loved to send Corgan's ass to jail, but in Europe, ISW was saddled with a skeleton crew that made our Warped roster seem extravagant. We didn't have Libido Gigante, Frankie Dee or the Ladies' Man. We carried three less wrestlers on Deconstruction than we had in 2001. We needed Corgan to work two matches a day. The other guys couldn't afford to lose him. What's more, on so many levels Corgan was right about not playing the Nazi. I couldn't stand back and let it happen.

Audra was in the dining room. Corgan and I sucked it up and went over to talk to her. I hated him but we had to present a united front on this. Audra was chatting with some dudes I didn't recognize. We paced around by the catering tray and waited for her to finish. She never did. She just kept on gabbing. It was thirty minutes until showtime. I thought that I had caught her eye from across the room, but I couldn't tell if she was just blowing me off or if she hadn't seen me trying to get her attention.

We were down to twenty minutes before the second set. Audra was still gabbing away. "Shit, Tom," I said, "the show's gonna start soon. We don't have any choice. We just have to go up there."

We marched up to her table. Tom was right behind me. We stood there for a couple of moments, but Audra didn't acknowledge our presence. Finally, I butted in.

"Audra, we just can't do the Oi Boy today," I said looking down at her. "It isn't right. It could put Tom in jail. We're going to go ahead and do the Sasquatch match as originally planned."

We walked away and left her sitting at her table. As we left the dining room, I said, "Under no circumstances, Tom, are you to bring out your skinhead drag. Just don't bring it to the ring, okay." Corgan nodded in agreement and we braced ourselves for the oncoming shit storm.

We waited over by the buses. The wrestlers who knew what Tom and I had just done milled about nervously. Eli rounded everyone up and told us that there was a mandatory meeting on the bus in five minutes.

Wrestlers crowded into the aisles and the cramped bench seats on the bus. An eerie silence settled across the vehicle. Audra walked onto the bus. She had Eli shut the door behind her. We all knew what was coming, but we couldn't predict its magnitude.

*"Nobody tells me what to do! Nobody contradicts me! Nobody!"* Audra screamed while she stomped her feet in place like a child throwing a tantrum.

I'd seen Audra yell before. I'd seen her haul off and punch guys, but this was the worst. She gasped for air in between every sentence so she could scream louder than she'd ever screamed before. Her words became garbled with her fury.

"Do you fucking idiots know who I was talking to out there?!" Do you?! That was the head of the fucking tour! I was trying to arrange for a nice trip to Amsterdam for you, but these two idiots went and fucked that up!"

Audra was playing her old game of divide and conquer. She was attempting to set the other wrestlers against me just like she had tried to do in Switzerland. I didn't know if everybody would be able to see through this ploy of hers. Getting ripped on the streets of Amsterdam was the only reason that most of us had agreed to go on this tour of the damned. The whole trip would have been a total wash if she'd yanked that from us.

Audra continued with her rant: "Everybody wants to go to fucking Europe! That's all I hear from you! And now I give it to you and how do you repay me!?! You bitch behind my back! You all think you can run things better than *meeee!*"

Four years earlier, everyone had wanted to go to Europe. Four years earlier, everyone lived and breathed ISW. By 2003, most of us had moved on. Audra hadn't. That's when the bad wrestling craziness can get to you — when there's less wrestling. That's when wrestlers would be found dead from ODs in their hotel rooms. That's when wrestlers went berserk. Audra hadn't wrestled in years, but her whole identity was wrapped up in being the tough bitch promoter of ISW, and ISW had fallen apart two years earlier. Audra had deluded herself into believing that she was doing us some big favor by taking us on that tour, when in reality we were the ones doing her the favor by going. We were the ones risking our jobs and losing money to go over there for nothing more than auld lang syne — one last hurrah. Audra, filled with demagoguery and paranoia, was like a scorned cult leader. It wouldn't have surprised me if she had called for us to commit a "revolutionary act of suicide" and blamed ISW's fall from the Fillmore on a CIA plot.

Audra's harangue continued for several more minutes and then she grew quieter as if all the air had been let out of her. "If you want to leave this fucking tour, you can leave right fucking now!" she huffed and surveyed the room while she nervously waited to see if she had any takers.

God, I wanted to leave, but I didn't have the $2,000 or $3,000 that it would take to book a flight back to San Francisco. If she had been this bad on Warped, there would've been a mass exodus of wrestlers heading for the nearest Greyhound station. Getting home wasn't so simple when you were across the Atlantic.

We all just nodded and one by one we silently agreed to do what she said for the rest of the tour. There were only five shows left. I just wanted to get through this thing as painlessly as possible and get home.

We were late for our set time. Wrestlers hurried up to the second storey of our tour bus to get their gear and ran over to the ring. I briskly walked off the bus and didn't say a word to anybody. Corgan fished out his Sasquatch suit and headed for the changing tent. He didn't bring his boots and braces. Macho Sasquatcho entered the ring against Fangorio instead of the Oi Boy that afternoon.

After the show, I headed in the opposite direction from everyone else. I just wanted to be alone, but Corgan caught up with me.

"Hey thanks, Bob, for going to the mat for me like that," Corgan said as he trotted up alongside of me.

"It was the right thing to do," I said without breaking my stride.

Heading nowhere in particular, I stopped to finish the conversation. I had been walking across a roughly manicured grassy field. Young Germans sunned themselves while listening to headphones and several others started sloppy games of soccer. About 100 yards in the distance, Corgan and I spotted a punk rocker with a mohawk beating on a German Shepherd. The guy picked up the pooch, slammed it down hard on the ground and started kicking it. Europeans can be so much more civilized than Americans in so many ways, but nobody seemed to notice this guy beating his dog. He was surrounded by several teenage girls. None of them batted an eyelash while the dog yelped in pain. If he had tried that at an American resort, every girl there would have screamed. It was like those vacationing Germans were pod people.

"Hey, let's go kick that son of a bitch's ass," Corgan said.

I looked at Tom and nodded. Somebody had to do something, but then we saw a cluster of German cops walking towards him.

"Okay, the cops are here," Tom said, "we'll let them handle this."

The German cops were so meek. They stood around the guy and politely asked him to stop while he continued kicking the dog as if they weren't there. Finally he stopped. The cops didn't cuff him. They didn't cite him. They did nothing. Tom and I found ourselves wanting to go and beat the shit out of the guy again, but the *polizei* were still in eyeshot of us.

"Tom, I'm with you on this," I said, "but I just stuck my neck out to keep your ass out of jail. We just can't go and do this now."

The bitching-out on the bus and the dog beating left me closing ranks with Corgan. It was a bonding moment that revolted me when I had a chance to reflect on it later, but camaraderie was easy on the bus — too easy.

The Brits really wanted to talk about the war. (Maybe everyone else did too, but we couldn't understand them.) We played the massive Donington metal fest on June 1, 2003. Our ring was set up next to this Judge Dredd thrill ride that looked like it had been endangering the lives of U.K. carnival goers since the early '80s. Metallica was playing on a massive main stage about a mile away. I could hear the strains of "No Remorse" and "Harvester of Sorrow." Damn them. They were actually playing songs that I wanted to hear and I was stuck announcing a stupid wrestling show.

Like I'd done for the entire tour, I used the U.S. Steele match to make some barbed comments about the war. Unlike everywhere else, these people understood me. "If U.S. Steele looks a little tired today," I announced, "it's because he just can't stop Tony Blair from polishing his ass every time he comes here." The crowd of about 400 cockney blowhards booed that line with venom that I'd never quite heard before. They were pissed and I don't mean drunk.

As I was leaving the wrestling ring to get some beer backstage, this ten-year-old gave me a piece of his mind. "You said that U.S. Steele is out of control," he said sounding like a waif right out of *Oliver Twist*, only more politically astute. "It's all America that's out of control."

I told the kid that he was right, but went on to argue that England had enabled the supposedly preemptive war. "Every time that Bush ran into trouble selling this war," I said, "Tony Blair was right over there on American TV making everything sound so smart."

I was standing there in a leopard print kimono, right next to a wrestling ring and a Ferris wheel, having a more intelligent conversation with a ten-year-old than I could probably find on most American college campuses. "Look, kid," I said while I walked away, "I'm against the war. You're against the war. Okay?" There was really nothing else I could add.

We had a day off in London. I wanted to be by myself while I scouted around a sprawling city that I'd never seen before, but Tom Corgan caught up with me just like he had in Germany. He chased me down an overly wide drag as little cars drove past us on the wrong side of the road. I was too tired to tell him to get lost. It turned out that he had gotten into a slapping match with Manny on the bus the night before. The altercation was over nothing that made any sense and Tom became even more of a pariah for having instigated it. I had somehow slept through the whole thing and knew nothing about it that morning. My only thoughts were of trying to wake up over some bangers and mash.

The bus was parked in a dirt lot without any amenities. I was filthy and needed a shower. Corgan and I ran into some other wrestlers. Everyone else needed a shower too. We agreed to go in on the cheapest room we could find, which still set us back what amounted to over half a day's pay apiece even with five guys going in on it. The tumbling dollar and the strong Euro and pound were killing us on the exchange rates. We made that room our London base of operations.

I broke away from Corgan and wandered around the city with Craig and Mextacy. We marveled at ancient stone churches that were down the street from McDonald's franchises and mall stores. I looked for shoes for Dana but didn't dare chance those freaky U.K. sizes. The bookstores were so much better than in America. People seemed to read over there. We kept running into other wrestlers. A big gang had gathered into our tiny hotel room. We drank beer and gawked at the women who passed by our window like a bunch of uncouth jerks. "London belongs to black girls," Craig observed as a tall, slender dark beauty with boobs to die for walked past our room.

I could drink nearly a twelve-pack of watered-down American suds before I became falling down drunk, but it only took three or four of those strong British brews to get me plastered. At London's northerly latitude dusk didn't come until well after 9 P.M. The gate to the yard where the bus was parked was going to be locked promptly at ten. Around 8 P.M., wrestlers started heading back to the parking lot. The bus, with its low ceilings and tiny bunks, was making me claustrophobic and giving me back pain. Our crazy German bus driver also never emptied the bus' septic tank so the toilet was always filled nearly to the brim with a brownish, yellow chowder of wrestler piss. I wasn't going back to the bus. I held onto the hope that I'd be the last man outside the gate at ten and end up with that nice hotel room all to myself. Unfortunately, Tom had the same idea.

Ten o'clock rolled around. It had just started to get dark by then. It was too late for me to get back to the bus and my obese ass wasn't going to climb any 18-foot high fence that was built like a fortress wall. It was down to Tom and me. I headed down the street to a yuppie pub with Corgan in tow. How did I let this happen? I could blame the booze, but there was a part of me that wanted it to be 1999 all over again when we were all still in the last throes of our twenties with ISW still on the rise.

At least there was the pub. I figured that I could kill a few more hours there bullshitting with drunk Brit professionals about the war and how fucked up the United States had become. If I stayed until last call, I thought, I'd only have to spend a couple of hours in that hotel room with Corgan before they unlocked the gates to the parking lot.

At 10:45 a large, black bouncer with a crisp cockney accent announced last call. The bars in Britain closed at 11 P.M. At that moment, London became as rinky-dink as Salt Lake City. No wonder the Brits glued their arses to the pub stool as soon as they got off work at five. They'd probably curb the country's rampant alcoholism if they just kept the bars open for a few more hours over there.

Tom kept trying to pick a fight with that gargantuan bouncer but the African-Englishman effortlessly used his oversized mitts to politely guide Corgan out the door. I finished up my last bourbon and lemonade (they didn't have 7 Up in bars over there) and met Corgan staggering around the front of the building.

Back in the hotel room, Corgan popped open another Stella Artois. We still had nearly a case of them getting warm on a nightstand. I sat on the bed and surfed around some bad British television. All of our worst TV is just a rip-off of their dumb shows. We swiped it, but they originated it. It only took a couple of minutes to pass out.

I woke up about two hours later. Corgan wasn't on the chair or on the floor. He had passed out right next to me. I sat up and had the shakes. It was like waking up next to a partially decomposed corpse that was being gnawed on by mangy rats. I staggered to the toilet and dry heaved for a couple of minutes, but even with all the booze, I couldn't bring myself to barf.

It was only 2 A.M., still hours before I could get back on the bus. I sat on a white, leatherette chair and stared at Corgan while he slept. I thought about Dana crying on the phone on that terrible night when he went nuts and threw us out. I thought about him stomping after her and screaming at her. The homicidal urges came flooding back. I wanted to jump on Tom, sit on his chest and jam a pillow over his face. It would have felt so good to murder him.

Another half hour went by. Corgan still slept. I wondered if I could get away with it. His body was covered in bruises just like on the Warped Tour. Would that make an accurate autopsy impossible? I quietly speculated on the state of crime scene investigations in the U.K. I wondered if there was a way to make a man asphyxiate on his own vomit. No one would question a drunk like Corgan choking to death from blowing chunks. Could I induce such a thing by using some kind of olfactory agent?

I sat there for another hour while Corgan tossed and turned, not knowing that every labored breath was so close to being his last. I wished that we were in Paris instead. I had dark fantasies of a dashing French defense attorney getting the murder case against me thrown out by showing an octogenarian judge and jury (who'd all lived through the Nazi occupation) some video footage of Corgan goose stepping around the ring in his Oi Boy outfit.

I thought about how happy it would make Dana feel if I had killed Tom Corgan. Then I thought about how sad she'd be if I were locked up in some Euro prison cell for the rest of my life. I glared at Corgan for another few minutes while I fought back some tears. I had to get the hell out of that hotel room.

I walked around the desolate streets of London while the first rays of dawn peeked out over the city's tall buildings. It was 5 A.M. on a Tuesday morning. I walked to a Starbucks that was a few blocks away, thinking that it might be open. It wasn't. There was a Burger King around the corner. That wasn't open either. I walked down an empty boulevard and looked for an all night diner where

I could read the *Times* and eat some greasy eggs and canned beans. I couldn't find one. None of the fast food joints had their hours posted on their storefront windows. I went back to the Starbucks and back to the Burger King. They were both still closed even after 6 A.M. Didn't the English suits need their coffee and Croissan'Wiches as they staggered off to work after an early night of drinking? What was wrong with that country?

Exhausted, I sat down on a bench. Occasionally, a strangely shaped English cab drove by. It was like I'd taken any dignity I had left and flushed it down that fetid toilet on the bus. Why the fuck was I there? Was it for little sandwiches with the best prosciutto I'd ever eaten? To stand around in a karate suit so some Swiss brats could hurl shit at me? Was it for a minute of face time on a concert DVD that was only being released in Australia?

I passed by the Burger King at 8 A.M. as I made my way back to the bus. It still wasn't open.

Just as soon as the bus had parked in Amsterdam, everyone headed for the red-light district with a sense of urgency and purpose. Audra hadn't made good on her threat to keep us from that worldwide capital of legalized debauchery. She had gotten sick of us and the feeling was mutual. On our few days off, Audra thankfully rode with NOFX or rented a swank hotel room, leaving us to our own devices. With few friends among the rank and file, Paul usually hung out with Audra during the downtime. As the tour lurched forward Van Dyne and Audra had formed a kind of bourgeois bond.

We walked along cobblestone streets. Hookers with impatient looks on their faces were displayed behind large, plate glass windows illuminated with the pinkish glow of red neon. There were stubby African women, emaciated Ukrainians, red-headed Czechs and blonde Nordic beauties. Some whores were plain or homely. Others were drop dead fine. But none was very appealing. The sex trade in Amsterdam was as seductive as a badly kept zoo.

We crossed tiny canals over short bridges that made the city resemble a section of Disneyland if not for everything's obvious antiquity. Hard faced Moroccans hungrily scanned everyone who walked by, looking for easy prey. "Let's try to stick together tonight," I said, pointing them out to Craig. "Those guys are looking for someone to roll."

We piled into the first hash bar that we came to and everyone bought bricks of hash and individually wrapped joints by the fistful. We sat outside at café style tables and openly smoked mechanically rolled joints made from a mixture of Thai weed and Turkish tobacco. "If smoking pot was always this civilized, I'd do it all the time," I remarked.

An oversized clock in a large tower that resembled Big Ben started sounding out the eleventh hour.

"Festival! Festival!" I said, compulsively quoting an old *Star Trek* episode where a whole planet of teetotalers goes bananas at the stroke of six and everyone starts groping and punching each other.

Shane nearly fell out of his chair laughing. "Dante, dude," he said, trying to catch his breath. "My geek days are behind me. Please, don't remind me of *Star Trek*. Not while I'm here."

We smoked more grass, drank more beer and inescapably got hungry. Mextacy and Manny headed off by themselves, Corgan disappeared for the night and the rest of us found this gyro place. After we finished our kabob platters, I noticed that the cook had locked us in until we'd paid our bill.

We hit the streets to look for another hash bar that was still open. Manny and Mextacy ran past us chasing after a pair of Moroccan street kids. They had taken Manny for 20 Euros in a dope deal gone bad. Here we were in a city filled with legalized narcotics and Manny went and stupidly tried to score on the street.

We all chased after Manny through narrow streets and alleys. Shane went on Atkins before the tour and was the only one of us over thirty who had actually lost weight since Warped. He was way ahead of us. Steele and this sound guy named Ted were in the middle and Craig and I chugged along in the rear. We turned a hairpin corner and almost ran into each other like the Keystone Cops.

Shane had one of the Moroccan kids pinned to a brick wall. "Give him back his fucking money," Shane yelled. The Moroccan tried to get away, but Shane shoved him back against the wall and got in the kid's face. Shane towered over him and still outweighed him by a good 80 pounds even after his success with fad diets.

In broken English the Moroccan tried to deny he had taken the money. Shane slapped him for his trouble. "You're fucking lying," Shane said. Shane had grown nearly suicidal with his homesickness. During his matches, he performed riskier and riskier moves in the hopes that he would get injured and be sent home early. Now he was unloading all of his frustrations on that stupid thief.

More Moroccans started emerging out of the darkness and it became a tense standoff. I looked at Amsterdam's short, spindly street trash and realized that we were in Europe and that nobody had guns. I had lived in the worst part of San Francisco where cops were gunned down on the streets. The small menacing guy who, back home, was probably packing was, in Europe, less than intimidating. These kids weren't going to bust a cap in my ass. I was older and fatter but so much bigger than they were. I was ready for a fight.

We were about to throw down when this middle-aged West African stepped out of the shadows and told the kid to give Manny his money back. The man was obviously the boss of that street corner. An open brawl between Moroccan thieves and freakishly large Americans who resembled a berserker horde was going to be bad for whatever business was still illicit in that liberal city.

The Moroccan tried to tell the African boss that he didn't have the money. The criminal patriarch shot the street hustler a cold look that let everyone there know that he wasn't a guy you could fuck with and live to tell about it. The Moroccan pulled Manny's 20-Euro bill out of his pocket and handed it to Shane. The tension had dissipated and our frenzy for fighting was gone. There was nothing left to do but go back to the bus and sleep off the adrenaline.

The attendance for the Deconstruction Tour was down that year: American entertainment was taking a hit from Bush's unpopular war. The mood on the bus had only grown more mutinous since Germany as some of the wrestlers and ring crew guys figured out that Audra was botching the exchange rate and shorting us by as much as 20 Euros a day. I didn't care if I made it home without a dime; I just wanted to go home. The wind was out of my sails and I was just marking my time. I wasn't going to tangle with Audra again unless I really had to.

We played more backwater burgs that nobody had ever heard of. In Clermont-Ferrant, France, Paul Van Dyne broke his arm going through one of those slapdash tables that we'd made for the Devil Chicken–arm wrestling match. When a wrestler gets injured in the ring, he's usually treated with awe and respect. With Van Dyne, the wrestlers still remembered his comments from the Warped Tour about having "better things to do than wrestle two matches a day," so everyone mostly just snickered at him. Van Dyne was taken to a French hospital in an ambulance where they bandaged up his busted arm, gave him a pile of painkillers and let him take home his X-rays all for only 25 Euros. In the United States, the ambulance ride alone would have set him back 600 bucks.

The tour ended on a dusty field in Bologna, Italy. I'd barely started to announce the set when the ancient PA that we were using shorted out with a puff of smoke. Audra convinced me to come on that tour because she needed me to announce, but nobody on the continent understood a word that I was saying. Now they couldn't even hear me. The ring was lopsided and the Italians started kicking up dirt and throwing tiny pebbles at us. We cut the set short and hightailed it back to the bus. That was the ignominious end to my seven years of strange wrestling. For some of us, it was the end of the line, but not quite the end of the story.

We were on the bus again headed back for Vienna. I was so shit-faced that I couldn't even understand what I was trying to say. There was a tour wrap party held at a bare bones dance club that was downhill from Deconstruction's last gig. I had slammed down a rapid succession of shots of Drambuie and Red Label with the kilt-wearing singer of this Scottish punk band called the Real McKenzies. We broke out into a chorus of "Flower of Scotland" where he slurred the words and I mumbled out the melody. There was almost another near brawl with Moroccans that I seem to remember and somebody called the *polizia* on Corgan after he started jumping through tables in the dance hall. They had the flimsy tables that we had so desperately needed all along and twisted Tom couldn't resist breaking them. Corgan ran back to the bus and passed out leaving the Deconstruction Tour to pick up the tab for the broken furniture.

Back on the bus, the Drambuie started attacking my stomach, trying to force its way out. I ran to the can to hurl. I pulled up the toilet seat. The bus driver still hadn't emptied out the septic tank. The pisser was still filled to the brim. Every bump in the road threatened to splash fermented urine on me. That toilet was too disgusting to even barf in. I went back to my bunk and slept it off. Manny wasn't so lucky. He poked his head out of the bus' ceiling vent and puked on the roof while gusts of wind blew his barf back in his face.

We had another day off in Vienna and we flew out the next day. Most of us wanted to just go home with what little money we had left, but at least we had rooms at this funky, aging hotel. Somehow, I lucked out and had a small one all to myself.

Walking around Vienna, I looked at ancient buildings — spared by the Allied bombing of the previous century — that were interspersed with new construction that could have been in San Diego or Tempe. I found a phone card and called Dana. Our one-eyed cat had run away. Great.

Tom Corgan was never the clotheshorse. He walked around the old European capital in his Oi Boy drag without thinking about any consequences. Late that night, he and Mextacy had gone to get something from the hotel's desk clerk. A 400-pound Englishman, a longtime resident of the hotel, saw Corgan looking like a skinhead and immediately attacked him.

The guy shoved Corgan against the wall. Corgan tried to use his collar to get him in a Gracie Jiu-Jitsu cross choke. The walrus-like Brit was having none of that. He bit down hard on Corgan's forearm, drawing blood and taking out chunks of flesh. Corgan tried to hit him. The Brit headbutted Corgan hard and opened up another gash across his forehead. All of Corgan's attempts at grappling failed. The Brit used his ponderous weight to shove Corgan down to the floor and grabbed a dining room chair. This wasn't a flimsy American chair bought at Wal-Mart. This was one of those European chairs made from ample amounts of solid oak.

Just as the Brit was about to bring the heavy chair down on Corgan, Mextacy jumped on the Brit's back. Mextacy slapped the chokehold on him that Corgan hadn't been able to. The Brit stumbled back with Mextacy hanging onto the hold. They fell backwards. Both men went through a French door. Mextacy kept the chokehold even after the heavy Englishman landed on him in a pile of broken glass. The desk clerk finally arrived and called for an ambulance. Mextacy released the choke and crawled out from under the Brit who lay there like a beached whale, unable to move. "I'm dyin', I'm dyin'," he moaned.

The ambulance took Corgan to a nearby hospital. The concierge got the Brit back to his room. Corgan had to have several stitches in his arm and forehead. Mextacy, a man who had never considered himself a badass and never even wanted to be one, had saved Corgan's bacon.

There was maybe a time that I should have fought Corgan. There was a night that I could have killed him. I turned the other cheek just to get my stuff out of his house. I looked the other way for bullshit business reasons and palled around with him just to get through the wrestling tour. I felt bad about that. My pent-up hostilities made me think that I should have socked him in the face or sent him to the hospital. However, like Chango Loco before him, Tom Corgan lived for violence and that violence had a way of finding him. In the end, the street kicked those guys' asses so that I didn't have to. Karmic comeuppance doesn't come often enough, but it has always worked for me.

I was in the Vienna airport. The air among the wrestling crew was like that of a somber wake and everybody kept to themselves. I was sitting across from Tom Corgan and Paul Van Dyne. They had hated each other for the last three years of the wrestling show but they'd ended up sitting side by side. I looked over at them. Corgan sat hunched over with his hand on his face and several stitches across his forehead. Van Dyne sat up uncomfortably with his arm in a sling. I focused my disposable camera on them and snapped its last picture, knowing that I'd never have to see them again.

# 20

# EPILOGUE

THE SCENE IS OVER. The scene is always over, yet it keeps going. Clubs started opening again here and there. The Tenderloin is referred to as the "Trendyloin" in certain shameless SF society mags. There's the Red Devil Lounge and the Hemlock on Polk Street There are also terrible yuppie bars with monosyllabic names like "Lush." The transvestite hookers are still there but they are fewer and farther between.

There still isn't a rock club on Haight Street. A Whole Foods overpriced organic grocery store for rich people is being built across the street from where the Nightbreak used to be. The Department of Public Works fines bands and clubs $1,000 a pop if one of their fliers ends up on the wrong street pole. The city claims it costs that much to rip the taped up bills off certain picturesque poles that mostly look no different from any other poles. Bass players and drummers (who make their cut of eighty bucks a gig if they've had a really good night) are supposed to be able to tell the difference. A lot of bands have started promoting themselves on Rupert Murdoch's MySpace instead. There's something wrong with that but I'm not sure what.

After a long dormancy, the Count Dante Internet Wars have heated up again. This time the recipient of badly spelled and threatening e-mails is a Chicago filmmaker named Floyd Webb. Floyd met the genuine Count back in the 1960s and started putting together a documentary about him a couple of years ago. It wasn't long after putting up a website for his project before the Aguiars of Fall River, Massachusetts, resurfaced with all of their ownership claims of everything Dante. After the documentarian's attempts at rational negotiations failed, the neo-BDFS filed a copyright infringement lawsuit against Webb with a local court in Bristol County, Massachusetts. The suit also names Ashida Kim and the proprietor of Bad Ass Fight Wear for some reason. The complaint as filed contains a stunning amount of unnecessary apostrophes. BDFS Supreme Grand Master William V. Aguiar III (son of the now deceased Bill Aguiar who gave me trouble back in 1999) is acting as his own attorney in this case. Floyd is represented by the Fair Use Project for Documentary Film at Stanford University.

Back in SF, Audra still had the wrestling bug. She couldn't let go. After Europe, ISW did a couple of shows before going into unintentional dry-dock for nearly three years. Their October 24, 2004, show stayed listed on their website in near perpetuity as 2005 and 2006 rolled on. The ISW website's message board had the occasional posting asking if the promotion was still running. Nobody ever bothered to reply. A bunch of kids in Montana who caught ISW on the 2001 Warped Tour named their ska punk band El Pollo Diablo. They e-mailed Audra about permissions. They never heard back from anyone. They've played the Warped Tour's smaller stages a few times. It's strange to think that the Devil Chicken is still doing Warped.

But Audra did manage to stay busy during this hiatus. She produced a low-budget iSW feature film called *El Presidente* along with some South City production house. She e-mailed me in late 2003 about writing a screenplay for it. I ignored the e-mail. People who don't take no for an answer just stop getting answers eventually. The last thing I wanted in life was to haggle points with Audra over a project that wasn't going to make a dime. She called me again about emceeing a show in January 2004. I left a message on her machine saying, "iSW just isn't fun for me anymore." I wished her the best of luck. She replaced me with Blag Dahlia from the Dwarves who had bigger punk appeal but probably didn't book matches, write press releases or lose temp jobs because he had to spend a half hour on the phone with U.S. Steele.

The plot of *El Presidente* concerns a hotly contested political race between El Homo Loco and the Oi Boy. The election farce was shot in late 2004 and it became dated before it was even completed. Still, Audra has finagled the movie into small-time film festivals. The trailer turns up on YouTube and MySpace and really isn't all that bad in an umpteenth generation rip-off of John Waters kind of a way. Paul Van Dyne plays the Snack Master. Allan Bolte lends some credibility as a newscaster. There are some drag queens and gutter sluts whom I don't recognize. Everyone's a little too old to be in student films (or films that look like student films) and they've all put on weight with the exception of El Homo Loco, who's actually in better shape than when he was wrestling regularly.

An L.A. promotion called Lucha Va Voom stepped in to fill California's masked wrestling void during the iSW hiatus. Their shows combine lucha libre and postmodern burlesque revival into a slicker amalgam of both Stinky's and iSW. They spring for way better luchadores than Audra ever did, but then they have nebbish, white comedians like Patton Oswalt crack wise over their acrobatic artistry. On their site, they have a QuickTime movie of their Fox News story. It looks a lot like our Fox News story from seven years earlier. They sell out grand, old ballrooms and famous people come to their shows. That may be about all that these things add up to.

While Lucha Va Voom may have stolen ISW's hipster media spotlight, Audra got the show back on the road with some bookings at summer music festivals in Baltimore and Washington State in the summer of 2007. The shows were headlined by acts like Björk, Modest Mouse and the Police. You know, when I joined ISW I never saw us sharing a stage with Sting.

On August 12, 2007, ISW finally returned to the city with a show at the DNA Lounge just down the block from the former site of the Transmission Theatre. The DNA made streaming video of the show available on their web page. Through Real Media Player, I got to be an actual fly on the wall and view my old troupe from a rotation of three different webcam angles. The hall was about half full. I'd never seen a crowd so anemic for a show in our SF stomping grounds before. Audra had never posted an update detailing the event on ISW's website. Fans who wanted to go probably clicked on the site, didn't see anything about it, assumed it wasn't happening and stayed home. Despite her resilience, the lessons of new media still come hard to Audra.

The final set of wrestling was maybe the worst that I'd ever seen and I've even programmed some pretty regrettable shows when you look at Europe and some of those Warped Tour stops. This time Audra provided the color commentary alongside a disinterested Allan Bolte. She spent most of the night desperately trying to cue the audience in on the angles that they had concocted.

Despite being the star of the ISW movie that Audra's still rolling out, El Homo Loco was no longer with the promotion. I don't know why. On that Sunday night in August, wrestlers who could work a decent match looked confused in the ring. As a riff on the *Pirates of the Caribbean* movies, there was a bad parrot skit that would have made Tony Danza's favorite scriptwriter shudder. The main event was an unending Chris Benoit joke that pitted Chris "Benoit Balls" against El Gran Fangorio for ISW's only title. The bout ended with

Benoit Balls killing baby Rasputin, strangling Suzy Ming and then hanging himself. Some black guy who looked nothing like Barry Bonds did a run-in as the Giants' homerun king.

There's a fine line between bad taste that works and bad taste that doesn't. I've crossed it the wrong way myself more than once, but ISW's newer creative team isn't even aware that this line exists.

My band still plays. We put out another record. Classic Marvel Comics artist Steve Leialoha did the cover. We open for this band called ArnoCorps a lot now. Because of them, we've played packed shows at the Red Devil and the Bottom of the Hill that draw rowdy dudes and computer nerds in their early twenties from San Jose and the East Bay. To them, seeing Count Dante open for ArnoCorps is their night of catching strange bands in the city just like when I used to drive up to see MIRV and Idiot Flesh at the Paradise Lounge. The scene is having its teeth kicked out of it by greedy bureaucrats, but it still isn't over. It's just somebody else's scene now.

Sometimes ArnoCorps' singer Holzfeuer calls me to talk about pro wrestling.

"Count," he says, "it's time to bring it back. We can get a ring. We can put on a wrestling show." Then he starts sounding like Schwarzenegger from *Predator* and grunts, "Come on! I am here! What are you waiting for?!"

Every time I caution him that he doesn't know what he's getting himself into, that he really doesn't want to put up with wrestling and wrestlers. That his fantasies of the squared circle should remain just that — fantasies. But each time he mentions starting a new wrestling show, I can't help but run logistics in my head. I start thinking about calling up wrestlers and scaring up a ring and a venue. Every time, Count Dante is just a little bit closer to getting back in the business.

# ACKNOWLEDGEMENTS

WRITING A BOOK is a solitary exercise, but when it's all done and the final word of that pretty damned close to final draft of your manuscript is typed, there are a lot of people along the way who helped bring that book into being. Like any author, I had an invaluable group of friends who helped me realize the book that you now hold in your hands.

First, I'd like to thank my editor, Michael Holmes, and everybody at ECW Press for believing in a weird wrestling book laced with cultural commentary and socioeconomic overtones.

An extra special thank-you goes to Roger Franklin for making so many wonderful photographs available and taking a few Sunday afternoons to painstakingly go through and scan them. This book would not have half of its appeal without the inclusion of Rog's fabulous photography.

And then there are the readers. Some of them read entire chapters; others just received bits and pieces hurriedly sent via instant messenger in the middle of the night. Without their encouragement and advice, I could have never finished *Beer, Blood & Cornmeal.* Chief among these is Robert Barnett for patiently proofreading the entire manuscript and subsequent rewrites. I could not have gotten this book ready for submission to publishers without him. Patrick Burger read every chapter as soon as I finished it, as well as a few alternate takes. Brandi Valenza and Adam Cantwell both read and spot edited what were probably an embarrassing amount of disjointed paragraphs sent through AOL IM (the indecisive author's new best friend). Now they can both finally read the complete story.

Further kudos go to literary (as well as literate) bartender Alan Black for psychically believing in my writing ability way before I had actually written anything. He's a great judge of talent on a barstool that guy. Also to Patricia Wakida for her expert assistance with query letters, marketing reports, book proposals and the other assorted nuts and bolts of getting published. Without her enthusiasm for books and authors, more than a few Bay Area writers would have failed to make it into print. And lastly to "Judo" Gene LeBell (www.genelebell.com) for allowing me the honor of co-authoring his autobiography, *The Godfather of Grappling.* Without being able to help him tell his story, I could have never told my own.

# SELECTED
# BIBLIOGRAPHY

Hanson, Shane. "[ISW] results (4-28-97)." *Rec.sport.pro-wrestling* 4 May 1997.

Humpreys, Quannah. "Faces of Death." *Punk Planet* Jan/Feb. 1998: 110.

Jacobson, Sarah. "Incredibly Strange Wrestling: Punk Rock in the Ring." *Gettingit.com* 26 Jul. 1999: <http://gettingit.com/article/543>.

Mayhew, Don. "Strange Crew Flying Tortillas and Satire Make Warped Tour Wrestling Unique." *Fresno Bee* 21 Jun. 2001: E1.

Powers, Ann. "ROCK REVIEW; Punk, Served More Often Sweet Than Raw." *New York Times* 7 Aug. 2001: Section E; Column 1.

Smith, Tootie. "Professional Wrestling Stimulus Plan Flys [sic] through the Oregon House General Government Committee." *Press Release* 1 Apr. 2003.

Strachota, Dan. "The Wrath and the Calm, El Pollo Diablo's Righteous Klucking; Wussom*Pow!'s Fruitful Gestation." *SF Weekly* 19 Jun. 2002.

Swartz, Jon. "Behind Fun Facade, Professional Wrestling Sees 65 Deaths in 7 Years." *USA Today* 12 Mar. 2004: 1C.

Tillman, Sean. "Blood, Sweat and Tears: On the Road with 1SW." *Punk Planet* Jan/Feb. 1998: 112-115.

Whiteside, Johnny. "Count Dante & the Black Dragon Fighting Society at the Garage." *LA Weekly* 7-13 Jul. 2000: 137.